ILLINOIS/INDIANA
TRAVEL ✦ SMART®

A GUIDE THAT GUIDES

WHY VISIT ILLINOIS AND I~~N~~

PLANNING YOUR TRIP
How Much Will It Cost? 9 • Climate 11 • ~~Whi~~
12 • Camping, Lodging, and Dining 14 • Recommended Reading ~~1~~
Suggested Listening 16 • Suggested Viewing 16

GARDEN OF THE GODS
WILDERNESS
SHAWNEE *National Forest*

SEP 1 5 2000			
MAY 19 2004			
May 34 2007			

Demco, Inc. 38-293

John Muir Publications
Santa Fe, New Mexico

Acknowledgments

Researching and writing a travel book is a time-consuming process, and we could not have completed the task without the love, time, and support of our spouses, Gwen Wilson and Chris Kaler; or our children's grandparents, Brad and Zelma Neal. Thanks also to our children, Zoë and Emily Kaler and Miles Wilson. Others who have earned our gratitude include: Patrick Kaler, Kay Abbadi, Brad Neal Jr., Larry and Alaina Kanfer, Holly Raver, Sharon Kenny, Dave Burns, Glenn and Peg Hansen, Pam Winsor, Pam Hohn, Roz Lewis, and Sonna and Tom Iorio.

Special thanks to Marybeth Griffin and Mari Szatkowski for having faith in our ability to complete this project—and for laughing at our jokes.

John Muir Publications, P.O. Box 613, Santa Fe, New Mexico 87504

Printed in the United States of America
First edition. First printing June 1999.

ISSN: 1520-9113
ISBN: 1-56261-473-8

Editors: Marybeth Griffin, Chris Hayhurst
Graphics Editor: Laura Perfetti
Production: Marie J.T. Vigil
Design: Marie J.T. Vigil
Cover Design: Janine Lehmann, Marie J.T. Vigil
Map Style Development: American Maps—Jemez Springs, NM USA
Map Style Illustrator: Scott Lockheed, Carta Graphics
Printer: Publishers Press
Front Cover Photos: *small*—© Christian Heeb/Gnass Photo Images (Chicago Theater in Downtown, Chicago, IL)
large—© Dennis MacDonald/Photo Network (Billie Creek Village, Rockville in Park County, IN)
Back Cover Photo: © Howard A. Leistner (Kayaks on Wabash River in Posey County, IN)

Distributed to the book trade by
Publishers Group West
Berkeley, California

ILLINOIS/INDIANA TRAVEL·SMART: A GUIDE THAT GUIDES

Most guidebooks are basically directories, providing information but very little help in making choices—you have to guess how to make the most of your time and money. *Illinois/Indiana Travel•Smart* is different: By highlighting the very best of both states and offering various time-saving features, it acts like a personal tour guide rather than a directory.

TAKE THE STRESS OUT OF TRAVEL

Sometimes traveling causes more stress than it relieves. Sorting through information, figuring out the best routes, determining what to see and where to eat and stay, scheduling each day in order to get the most out of your time—all of this can make a vacation feel daunting rather than fun. Relax. This book has done a lot of the legwork for you. Use it to help you plan a trip that suits *you*—whatever your time frame, budget, and interests.

SEE THE BEST OF ILLINOIS AND INDIANA

Authors Robin Neal Kaler and Eric Todd Wilson have hand-picked every listing in this book, and they give you an insider's perspective on what makes each one worthwhile. So while you will find many of the big tourist attractions listed here, you'll also find lots of smaller, lesser known treasures, such as the World's Largest Catsup Bottle in Collinsville, Illinois, or the beautiful covered bridges sprinkled throughout the two states. And each sight is described to let you know what's most—and sometimes least—interesting about it. If a certain place is too popular to ignore but not especially appealing, they'll tell you so.

In selecting the restaurants and accommodations for this book, the authors sought out unusual spots with local flavor. While in some areas of each state chains are unavoidable, wherever possible this book directs you to one-of-a-kind places.

We also know that you want a range of options: One day you may crave the international cuisine of Chicago's finest restaurants, while the next day you would be just as happy (as would your wallet) with a deep-dish pizza pie. Most of the restaurants and accommodations listed here are moderately priced, but where the destination merits it the authors also include budget and splurge options.

CREATE THE TRIP YOU WANT

Everyone has different travel styles. Some people like spontaneous weekend jaunts, while others plan longer, more leisurely trips. You may want to cover as much ground as possible, no matter how much time you have. Or maybe you prefer to focus your trip on one part of the state or on some special interest, such as history, nature, or art. This book takes these differences into account.

Though the individual chapters stand on their own, they are organized in a geographically logical sequence, so that you could conceivably fly into Chicago, drive chapter by chapter to each destination in the book, and end up close to where you started. Of course, you don't have to follow that sequence, but it's there if you want a complete picture of the state.

Each destination chapter offers ways of prioritizing when time is limited: In the Perfect Day section, the authors suggest what to do if you have only one day to spend in the area. Also, every sightseeing highlight is rated, from one to four stars: ★★★★—or "must see"—sights first, followed by ★★★ sights, then ★★ sights, and finally ★—or "see if you have spare time"—sights. At the end of each sight listing is a time recommendation in parentheses. User-friendly maps help you locate the sights, food, and lodging of your choice.

And if you're in it for the ride, so to speak, you'll want to check out the scenic routes described at the end of several chapters. They describe some of the prettiest ways in the state to get from here to there.

In addition to these special features, the appendix has other useful travel tools:

- The Planning Map and Mileage Chart help you determine your own route and calculate travel time.
- The Special Interest Tours show you how to design your trip around any of six favorite interests.
- The Calendar of Events provides an at-a-glance view of when and where major events occur throughout the state.
- The Resources tell you where to go for more information about national and state parks, individual cities and counties, local bed-and-breakfasts, and more.

HAPPY TRAVELS

With this book in hand, you have many travel tools at your fingertips. Use them to make the most of your trip. And have a great time!

WHY VISIT ILLINOIS AND INDIANA?

If you ask people outside the Midwest about Illinois and Indiana, you're likely to get a one-word response—corn. But if you ask those of us who live here, we'll tell you the story of a much more complex and beautiful country. We'll share the wonder of discovering a lonely barn silhouetted in a farm field at dawn or the majesty of standing at the top of one of the world's tallest buildings as the city lights begin to fight away the evening's darkness. Illinois and Indiana have sandy beaches, major metropolitan centers, beautiful river drives, major sports teams, wooded hills, fantastic shopping, and even a piece of the great Mississippi River. History buffs can trace the paths of several American Indian nations or follow the circuit that Abraham Lincoln rode years before he made his mark as the nation's Great Emancipator. Automobile buffs will love the historical sites and museums in Indiana, and underground railroad sites in Illinois will help bring to life a tragic part of American history.

The region's diversity also extends to lodging, food, and entertainment. You can bunk in isolated cabins, historical bed-and-breakfast inns, or quiet lodges. But if that's not your style, you might enjoy being pampered in some of the world's finest hotels, spas, and resorts. You can dine one night family style in a cozy mom-and-pop restaurant in Indiana's Amish country, and the next day enjoy Chicago's famous deep-dish pizza or a gourmet meal at a five-star bistro. Visit Illinois and Indiana and fall in love with the beauty, history, and grace of America's heartland.

LAY OF THE LAND

A discussion of the topography of Illinois and Indiana must begin with the glaciers. With the exception of the northwest corner of Illinois, the last glaciers covered the northern half of Illinois and much of northern Indiana. As you drive from north to south it's remarkable how distinct the line is between the flatland that was "shaved off" by glaciers, and the hills left standing when the glaciers retreated.

Illinois and Indiana are known primarily for their prairies. Aside from being a curse to those who have to cross the states in cars (although, to be fair, crossing these two states is in no way comparable to the monotony of driving across Kansas or the Dakotas), the prairies of Illinois and Indiana have served well the people who live here. This is some of the most fertile farmland in the world, and it provides an important component of both states' economies. It can also be strikingly beautiful. To our eyes, the black dirt is awesome, since we know what its nutrients produce.

Larry Kanfer, a well-known prairie photographer, says the beauty of this flat prairie is as far as the eye can see. Look at the barn or the silo on the horizon and wonder at its apparent isolation. See the homestead miles away, and realize that's the closest neighbor. Or notice the storm clouds gathering, still hours from dumping their deluge here, and watch them march steadily across the sky.

We hope you appreciate the prairie for its unique beauty, but we also hope to dispel the common misconception that Illinois and Indiana have nothing more to offer than unending prairie. If you drive along the major rivers (Mississippi, Illinois, Wabash, Ohio) you'll also find beautiful hills and valleys. In the south, both states become more hilly, covered in thick forests, ready for the outdoor enthusiast and nature lover. The northwest corner of Illinois, untouched by the glaciers, contains the jutting rocks, limestone bluffs, and deep ravines that will remind you of northern Minnesota. The beaches of Lake Michigan will introduce you to the windswept sand dunes and their strange variety of knotted plants and screaming gulls.

There is something for everyone here. Decide what you want in a vacation spot. We may not have oceans or arctic tundra, but just about anything else you choose can be found in Illinois and Indiana.

FLORA AND FAUNA

Bird-watchers will enjoy the woodlands of the south for its indigo buntings, orioles, and woodpeckers (among many other species). But every traveler will have the chance to see red-winged blackbirds keeping watch over ground nests, and perched on fence posts along interstates or smaller roads. Both states named the cardinal their state bird, probably because of its abundance and, of course, the male's brilliant plumage. But when you spot the bright red male, keep watching for his mate. She's not as eye catching, but she is a beautiful bird. The bald eagle, an American symbol once nearly extinct, is making a terrific recovery, and can be seen along the rivers of Illinois and Indiana. The Mississippi River along Illinois' western border has become an outstanding place to spot them.

Both states also share huge populations (in fact, overpopulations in some places) of white-tailed deer. Hunting of deer has always been popular, and remains essential in the effort to control their populations. Even urban dwellers will occasionally

Travelers in rural areas of Illinois and Indiana are well advised to get the inexpensive "deer whistles" that stick to the front bumper of vehicles.

see deer in the neighborhood. That may be charming at times, but deer present a very real danger to travelers when the animals bound out of ditches and collide with vehicles. Unfortunately, the density of their populations force some out of the woodlands, and that often requires crossing roads.

Raccoons, opossums, and squirrels are plentiful in rural areas. In the cities they've been forced to adapt, but have not been pushed out completely. Backyard compost bins are a good place for opossums to find a late-night snack, and raccoons are dexterous enough, and bold enough, to eat out of loose-lidded garbage cans any time of day.

The prairie lands offer other wildlife, including endangered species like the prairie chicken (it's unlikely you'll see them as they are very shy) and several species of frogs and turtles. The forests and wetlands provide protection for innumerable water fowl, wild turkeys, beavers, and, rarely, mink. Several species once nearly extinct have come back in abundance thanks to strong conservation and management programs and the dedication of both states in preserving natural habitats. As residents, we enjoy these areas immensely, and know you will too.

As mentioned earlier, greenery, if not scenery, is plentiful. During the winter, though, central Illinois and Indiana can lack color beyond the browns of crop residue and the white snow that covers it. The acres of short prairie trees that once covered the area can be sorely missed at those times. But if you'll travel to the southern reaches, you'll find abundant and varied woods. A large majority of the woods are privately owned, but even in state parks you'll find sycamore, walnut, hickory, many types of oak and maple, ash, and sassafras. We use the redbud extensively in our landscaping, and children in rural areas still search for mulberries, cherries, and other fruit trees along roadsides.

Many people use the state parks to harvest fallen persimmons. When ripe, the fruit is yellow or orange, and must be used when mushy. Taste one, and collect them if you like, but we give them a big "YUCK!"

HISTORY

Illinois and Indiana share much of their history, including thousands of years of Indian habitation. Tribes that predate Jesus Christ left burial mounds. Several of these sites in Indiana and Illinois remind us that man learned to make pottery and weapons on these lands. The Indian tribes moved from hunting and gathering to an agrarian life more similar to our own. Indiana is believed to have been largely uninhabited for a time in the 16th and 17th centuries (no one knows why the former population left), but several tribes returned to the fertile soils of modern day Indiana in the mid 1600s. The Kickapoo and Wei came from Illinois; the Miami came down from Wisconsin and were soon followed by the Potawatomi.

Illinois takes its name from the Illiniwek confederation of Indian tribes that inhabited all of what is now Illinois, and some of the neighboring states. They had to be well organized to keep so many groups banded together, and fend off encroachment by neighboring tribes. An important date for both states, 1673 is generally considered the dividing line between historic and prehistoric times. That's the year Father Jacques Marquette and Louis Joliet crossed both states and recorded their first meeting with the Indians who lived here.

Over the next decade the French explored the new land which was considered part of their Louisiana Territory. The French built forts in the late 17th and early 18th centuries; for example, Fort de Chartres was built in 1720. This fort's thick stone walls still stand near Prairie Du Rocher, Illinois, enclosing nearly four acres and act as a reminder of the time when folks in Illinois spoke French. The French became friends of the Indians during their tenure by trading modern goods for furs, but they never inhabited the region in sufficient numbers to hold it against British expansionists.

The British seized Fort de Chartres and most of Illinois and Indiana as a result of the French and Indian War in 1763, but many of the natives remained allied with the French. An Ottawa chief named Pontiac particularly hated the British encroachment, and led an awful war to push the white man back. It was unsuccessful, but certainly made Britain aware of the price that would have to be paid for its expansion.

Indiana became the 19th state in 1816; Illinois became the 21st in 1818. Indians struggled to maintain their control of lands, but were systematically removed, or forced to occupy smaller and smaller parcels, until they finally were pushed too far. Various Indian groups banded together to fight the Black Hawk War of 1832. Their defeat virtually removed any Native American presence in the state of Illinois, although people continued to memorialize the tribes who once lived here by naming places after them. Virtually all of the Indian names mentioned above have been attached to places, and there are hundreds more. The University of Illinois uses "Fighting Illini" as the name of its sports teams, despite the fact that some Native Americans say they are insulted by the "Chief Illiniwek" mascot—and most evidence shows the Illiniwek (meaning "the perfect and accomplished men") were among the most gentle Natives.

Abraham Lincoln "fought" in the Black Hawk War, but later joked that the only combat he saw involved the bloodsucking mosquitoes. Indeed, Lincoln is another big part of our shared history. He spent 14 boyhood years in southern Indiana before moving with his family to central Illinois, striking out on his own to New Salem. For several years he rode the judicial circuit in central Illinois as an attorney. And eventually he made his way to the state capital as a member of the Illinois House of Representatives.

In the Civil War, both states found themselves aligned with the North, but not without intense internal struggle. The southern reaches of both states are geographically similar to the bordering state of Kentucky and there were many who said the states had more to gain by aligning with the southern states. Both Illinois and Indiana saw bloody battles and many families lost fathers, husbands, and brothers. But both states avoided the magnitude of damage seen in the south and east.

In more modern history, Illinois and Indiana have seen their agrarian population reduced, and their cities grow. Chicago and Indianapolis have flourished as centers for commerce and culture. Chicago has its own rich history in the stockyards and the mobsters, power politics and powerful political protests (most notably the 1968 Democratic National Convention that gave the city a black eye that lasted years).

CULTURES

The French and British made their mark on this region, and their ancestors remain. But continual immigration brought virtually every nationality to the midwest. One has only to look at the neighborhoods of Chicago to know that waves of immigrants brought some of their homeland here. They often remained as a group in Irish, German, Polish, Ukrainian, Chinese, and Mexican sections of the city. But by mixing their cultures with those of the established residents, they created a unique atmosphere. Indianapolis, and to a greater degree, Chicago became destinations for a generation of African Americans leaving the south, who were sure that the factory jobs of the north would be an improvement over the cotton fields and levee camps of the south.

Much of Illinois and Indiana remains the epitome of "Americana," small-town life where not much out of the ordinary happens, people are friendly, and everyone is pretty doggone sure of what is right or wrong. Many areas of northern and western Indiana and east-central Illinois are dominated by the Amish and Mennonite people who came from Germany after being persecuted for their faith. Today they still cling to traditional ways, leaving the rush to modern advances to the rest of the world.

We can't leave the discussion about culture without mentioning basketball. Indiana is big-time basketball country, as the movie Hoosiers and Bobby Knight have taught us all. But Illinois loves its basketball, too, and that's the source of some heavy—but generally friendly—competition between the neighbors.

THE ARTS

You might think that the cities of Chicago and Indianapolis have a monopoly on the arts in Illinois and Indiana, but if your definition of art includes handmade Amish quilts and furniture, or country music played at county fairs, that's certainly not the case. True enough, Chicago and Indianapolis have outstanding art museums—featuring works by the masters of all time—and the most important traveling exhibits in the world usually stop here too. You can spend days in the galleries in both cities checking out the modern and the traditional, as well as the local and the exotic.

The shows are top-notch Broadway material, shown in theaters that are, in themselves, artistically noteworthy. Both cities feature world-class symphonies, and routinely attract the top contemporary, rock, country, jazz, and blues bands, among others. If you enjoy music, theater, dance, or art, you'll want to check the schedules of the venues in Chicago and Indianapolis while planning your visit here. Chances are you won't even have to adjust your schedule at all to fit in a performance or exhibition of your favorite work. Make sure to include a few of the smaller venues on your list of places to see, as most of the hottest performers today began their careers with stops at some of these venues. Just make sure to get autographs from the best performers you see. You might be able to sell them one day to finance another vacation!

And look for art throughout the two states. Chicago may have its Picasso, but you'll also find sculptures from Europe and Asia along wooded paths in Monticello, Illinois' Allerton Park. Indianapolis has its Midsummer Fest (misnamed, as it starts just days after summer has officially begun), but you can also have a great time at the Orange County Pumpkin Festival in southern Indiana.

Some of the biggest events have become nationally famous, like Chicago's annual summer Blues Festival (this is the greatest town in the world for blues—sorry, Memphis) or the Parke County Covered Bridge Festival, held each October when the trees in western Indiana wear their fanciest colors. But some of the smallest events, shared with people who love their town and the festivals they've grown up with, may be the most memorable.

Nearly every town you come to in Illinois and Indiana will have its own fest. It may be celebrating food: bagel festivals, sweet corn festivals, strawberry celebrations, and maple syrup days. It may be celebrating the Irish, German, or American Indian ancestry of the area. Whatever the reason we find for a festival, we do it right—with local artists' work displayed and available for sale, music that aims directly at your feet (even if they are both "lefties"), and fun by the ton.

CUISINE

What'll ya have? Fast or fancy? Good for you, or just plain good? Special creations by the world's most talented chefs, or everyday cooking by people who are still making grandma's secret family recipes?

Illinois and Indiana can dish up all of that and everything in between. Start with a Chicago hot dog. Make sure it's on a poppy-seed bun with big chunks of cucumbers and tomatoes. Don't leave the big city without one of its famous pizzas. And dress up for several courses at Charlie Trotter's, or sit high above the world on the 95th floor of the John Hancock building for the Signature Room's fine cuisine.

Then move on to the fantastic variety of offerings awaiting you in Illinois and Indiana. Beef plays a major part in our economy, and our diet. You'll find some of the finest steaks in the world on our tables, fresh and thick. This is the land where deep freezers on the back porch hold half a cow, and where barbecue can be found sweet or spicy, hot or mild, but can always be found. We raise pigs, chickens, and the vegetables we serve beside them. The bounty of these two states feeds the world, and these people work hard to provide it. When they sit down to eat, they sit down to a feast. So what if we can't catch the finest seafood?—We fly it in!

Don't miss the cooking of the Amish people. Everything is honest, from the fresh baked bread to the meats with gravy and hand-mashed potatoes. The green beans are straight from the garden, and there's no margarine—only butter, please. Top that off with a big piece of pie filled with fruit that was on the vine or in the tree just yesterday.

The people of the world have settled in these states, and they brought their special ingredients, cooking styles, and wonderful spices with them. Have an

Italian beef at the Italian Fest in Indianapolis, then cool off with a cannoli. Have a pork roast dinner in a German restaurant and savor the special sweet sauerkraut that always comes with it. Chinese, Middle Eastern, Mexican, French, and much more. If you expect to taste it all, you'd better extend your stay!

OUTDOOR ACTIVITIES

Once you arrive at your chosen destination you'll want to get out and enjoy it, and outdoor activities are never very far away. Even in Chicago and Indianapolis you'll find extraordinary bike and jogging paths, greenways that wind their way through the excitement of the Indy, or the tremendous bike path that traces the Lake Michigan shore bordering Chicago. (Going to a baseball game and going out to the beer garden are also considered outdoor activities in Chicago.) Many of our cities grew up around rivers, and nearly all have improved their riverfront areas to provide relaxing or invigorating walkways and bikeways.

If you want to get outside and stay outside a while, the general rule is to head south. Both states offer loads of excellent camping, hiking, fishing, and hunting in their southern woods and hills. One particular area to highlight is covered in Chapter 11, Bloomington, Indiana. The camping and water recreation opportunities surrounding this central Indiana town will keep the outdoor enthusiast very busy.

Golf is everywhere, from Michael Jordan's mighty pro-shop in Aurora, to the fine courses offered in many of our state parks. No matter what part of these states you visit, pack the clubs.

PLANNING YOUR TRIP

Before you set out on your trip, you'll need to do some planning. Use this chapter in conjunction with the tools in the appendix to answer some basic questions. First of all, when are you going? You may already have specific dates in mind; if not, various factors will probably influence your timing. Either way, you'll want to know about local events, the weather, and other seasonal considerations. The When to Go section of this chapter discusses all of that, the calendar in the appendix provides a view of major area events.

How much should you expect to spend on your trip? This chapter addresses various regional factors you'll want to consider in estimating your travel expenses. How will you get around? Check out the section on local transportation. If you decide to travel by car, the planning map and mileage chart in the appendix can help you figure out exact routes and driving times. The chapter concludes with some reading recommendations, both fiction and nonfiction, to give you various perspectives on the region. If you want specific information about individual cities or counties, use the Resources in the appendix.

HOW MUCH WILL IT COST?

One of the best things about vacationing in the Midwest is the price. Everything from gas and groceries to amusement park rides and souvenirs is priced by people who understand budgets. Many attractions, parks, and museums are free, and so is the scenery. While Illinois and Indiana offer plenty of fun memories at affordable prices, visitors can also choose luxurious accommodations, five-star dining, and front-row seats at some of the hottest shows on stage. In general, expect to pay more when you're staying in Chicago or Indianapolis. However, with a little bit of planning, you can explore either city with nothing more than a tank of gas, a basket of sandwiches, and your Travel•Smart guide.

Your largest expense anywhere in the region will usually be for sleeping accommodations. If you enjoy sleeping under the stars you can find camp-sites for as little as $5. They top out at about $25 for some of the fancier facilities. Bed-and-breakfasts typically charge anywhere from $70 to $80 for a room with a shared bath and $70 to $100 for a room with a bit more pri-vacy. Many require a two-night minimum stay, and some even require a three-night minimum stay, especially during special events. Chain hotels fre-quently offer special rates; for more information on them, call 800/555-1212.

Both Illinois and Indiana offer countless privately-owned hotels, motels, lodges, and inns—as well as state-owned facilities—that provide their guests comfort, quality, and hospitality at a reasonable price. Count on spending from $40 to $250 a night, and make sure to book your room as early as pos-sible if you're planning to attend a festival or special event. Otherwise, you may find yourself staying up to 100 miles away from the fun.

When you're in Illinois and Indiana you're never very far from wonderful food at a reasonable price. Diners, family restaurants, and theme-based offer-ings will satisfy even the hungriest traveler for between $5 and $10 for break-fast or lunch, and $5 to $15 for dinner. For an evening to remember, though, you may want to try one of the finer restaurants in Chicago or Indianapolis—but be prepared to pay between $50 and $100 per person.

Attractions in the major cities tend to cost more than in the smaller com-munities, but each one in this book is well worth the price of admission. Children and senior citizens usually get a break, but adult fares can be steep. Be prepared to pay as much as $10 per person—substantially more for big amuse-ment parks. State parks and recreation areas usually charge a small fee per vehi-cle. Many historic sites and museums are free, but theme parks, golf courses, and nightlife can wipe out those savings. In Chicago and Indianapolis, budget at least $15 a day just to park your car.

The best trip-planning advice for Illinois and Indiana is to divide your time between the "must see" sites, even though they charge admission, and the nat-ural (and free!) beauty of the land. This region isn't the most exotic part of the country, but it is a great value and just plain old fun.

THUNDERSTORM WARNING

If you hear that a thunderstorm is rolling in, ask the locals where they go to storm-watch. The rolling hills of northern and southern Illinois and Indiana, as well as the wide-open plains of the central parts of the region, offer many spectacular places to watch storms percolate and swoop in. Just make sure to stay in your vehicle and be ready to head for cover before the storm actually hits. Never try to watch a storm when a tornado watch or warning is in effect. The best viewing for these deadly storms is the day after—on the news. Instead, make sure to listen to the staff of the site you're visiting and head immediately for the designated safety area—usually a basement or windowless room.

CLIMATE

There's an old saying in the Midwest that "if you don't like the weather, stick around a few minutes, it'll change." Most parts of this region are known for windy and rainy springs, hot and humid summers, beautifully crisp and sunny falls, and frequently snowy, icy, cold winters. Tornado season runs from early spring right into summer. If you visit in that time frame, listen to or watch the local weather forecast each evening. Even if you're planning a get-close-to-nature kind of vacation here, it's always wise to have a few indoor sites on your itinerary. That way you won't be stuck in your hotel room—or worse yet, your soaking wet tent—with nothing to do during a rainstorm.

If you're visiting in the winter, be sure to check road conditions frequently. Winter driving requires a bit more caution than normal driving conditions do, and it's always a good idea to pack an emergency kit including blankets, food, candles, matches, bottled water, mittens, hats, scarves, and boots. If you find yourself stuck in the snow, crack your window a couple of inches and run your car's engine just a few minutes every hour.

In the grand scheme of things, tornadoes and blizzards are fairly rare occurrences, but when they happen, a little common sense can mean the difference between life and death. Most of the 365 days you could choose for your visit will be pleasant, and the only weather inconvenience you'll experience is having to tie your jacket around your waist when the morning chill is dissipated by the noonday sun.

The mileage chart located in the appendix shows the wide range of weather conditions you'll find in Illinois and Indiana. All figures were supplied by the Midwestern Climate Center.

WHEN TO GO

Unless you're headed to the ski slopes of southern Indiana or a professional basketball game or off-Broadway show in the big cities, you might not think of visiting Illinois or Indiana in the winter. But there are many things to do, especially in December: winter carnivals, cross-country skiing, festivals of holiday lights, and, of course, holiday shopping. Downtown Chicago is one of the best places in the world to find that perfect gift, and several of the big department stores have internationally famous window displays for the holidays. A word of caution, though: With several feet of snow each year plus wind chills that drop well below zero, you could experience occasional flight delays and road closures.

The rest of the year offers visitors a wide array of flora and fauna, as well as a diverse calendar of events. Most summer pastimes don't get into full swing until the traditional start of the season. So, by the time you pull out your white shoes for that Memorial Day weekend barbecue, your hosts in Illinois and Indiana will have the welcome mat out for you! Festivals celebrate an eclectic array of foods, including sweet corn, popcorn, apples, bagels, maple syrup, hot dogs, marshmallows, and pumpkins.

From early June through mid-September, you can expect warm, fairly humid weather. During hot spells, night doesn't bring much relief, so make sure to stay near the Midwestern summer essentials: air conditioning and water. Summer vacations here present enough activities to wear out even the most adventurous families, and fall color tours provide one of the most inspiring experiences in the region. But the magic of spring is always a special time of celebration for folks who have survived another winter. If you visit in early May, you probably won't find water in your hotel's outdoor pool, but you can expect to meet some of the happiest people anywhere.

TRANSPORTATION

O'Hare Airport in Chicago is the busiest airport in the world, but if you're willing to give up the ability to catch a flight to just about anywhere, the smaller Midway Airport is another option. Indianapolis International Airport is one of the most convenient airports anywhere. Most mid-sized communities in both states have their own airports, and a few even offer jet service.

Amtrak has several routes in both states; most are used by business travelers and college students commuting home for the weekend. Still, they offer a scenic, affordable alternative way to see the region.

Most vacationers will find that the best way to travel is by car. Indiana's highway system is—for the most part—arranged like the spokes of a wheel with Indianapolis as the hub. Interstates 74, 70, 65, and 69 all pass through the capital city. I-465 around Indianapolis has confused many an out-of-town driver, with most making their third pass by the same billboards before figuring out the road forms a complete loop. The main exception to the wheel analogy is I-64, which runs east-west across the southern edge of the state. In Illinois you can count on the interstates to connect larger cities to Chicago as well as two or three other major communities. Interstate 57 leads from Chicago to the southern tip of Illinois, and I-55 goes from the Windy City to St. Louis.

TIME ZONES

When traveling from Illinois to Indiana and back, remember the two states are in different time zones (Illinois: central, Indiana: eastern). The exception is the Indiana counties of Gibson, Jasper, Lake, LaPorte, Newton, Porter, Posey, Spencer, Starke, Vanderburgh, and Warrick, which are all in the central time zone. To further confuse you, only five counties in the state (Clark, Dearborn, Floyd, Harrison, and Ohio) observe Daylight Saving Time. If you're scheduling flights into or out of the state, or attending events on your first day in Indiana, the best advice is to double-check the time ... and time *zone*!

Remember when you were a kid and your dad used to say that half the fun of vacation was getting there? It may not have seemed like that sitting in the back–back seat of the family station wagon, watching the whole trip in reverse, but now that you're behind the wheel, it's a whole new ball game. Some of the most beautiful scenery in the region is just a two-lane road away. One of the best is tracing the original Route 66, which has excellent signage and tons of history.

Bicyclists have rediscovered the region's back roads, and they say it's an invigorating way to fully experience the views. But if you aren't in training, you may want to limit that method of transportation to leisurely evening rides to take advantage of cool country breezes or early morning treks to watch the sun rise over the prairie. For bicycle tours, Indiana offers the Hoosier Bikeway System (the State Park office stocks guidebooks with suggested routes); and in Illinois, the Department of Transportation offers bicycle maps, 217/782-0834.

CAMPING, LODGING, AND DINING

Throughout this book we share with you some of our favorite places to eat and sleep in Illinois and Indiana. Some are quite affordable, others will empty even the thickest of wallets. All are worth a visit. To get the full dining experience, we recommend snacking between meals!

Dinner plates here tend to be large and heaping. Lunch portions aren't much smaller. While you can find a light breakfast (if you're willing to go to the very back, bottom section of the menu), most good restaurants pride themselves in entrées hefty enough to satisfy a lumberjack. Biscuits and gravy are common, as well as pigs-in-a-poke and "numbered" specials with various combinations of eggs, bacon, sausage, hash browns, toast, and pancakes.

For some of the best food around, spend at least a night in one of the many bed-and-breakfasts in the region. Comfortable, elegant, historic, and unique are all options for bed-and-breakfast stays. Other lodging choices include motels, hotels, inns, cabins, lodges, and resorts. Accommodations of all prices and levels of luxuriousness are available. Always ask about special rates.

If you're interested in finding whether your favorite national chain has a facility in the community you're going to visit, call their toll-free number for details; information on independent facilities—and a few of the most outstanding chain offerings in some areas—is in the lodging section of each chapter.

State parks offer some wonderful camping experiences, but many privately owned facilities are also worth exploring. Campsites range from primitive to quite civilized, and prices usually serve as a good judge of where they fall in that spectrum. The camping season is a bit longer in the southern third of the region, but late-fall visits (after the harvest) in the central and northern thirds can provide some excellent wildlife and night sky viewing.

RECOMMENDED READING

There's just about no better way to enhance the vacation experience than by immersing yourself in the region's history, lifestyles, and politics before your trip. We recommend selecting at least one nonfiction and one fiction book from the list following. A Web search of the region, including the keyword of your own hobby or interest, can be a quick way to personalize your trip with some stops at places that might not be in the guide.

Museum of Science and Industry, Chicago (Abrams, 1997), by Jay Pridmore chronicles the exhibits of the museum and is the next best thing to actually going there. If you're taking your daughters to the museum, they'll be enchanted by its fairy dollhouse no matter what, but they'll appreciate it even more if you can track down a copy of *The Dollhouse of Colleen Moore* (Museum of Science and Industry, 1949) to read before you go.

A visit to Chicago is a great time to experience your own family's heritage. *A Review of Ethnic Chicago* (Passport Books, 1997), by Richard Lindberg, before your trip will help you locate the sites, shops, and even media to introduce to just about any culture or people on the globe.

Don Davenport traces Abraham Lincoln's life in Kentucky, Indiana, and Illinois in his book *In Lincoln's Footsteps* (Prairie Oak Press, 1991). This is the type of book that will help you sound like a genius historian when your family actually visits the places Mr. Davenport describes. *Lincoln* (Ballantine Books, 1984), by Gore Vidal, offers a brilliantly told story of the 16th president's final years. While this historical novel takes a bit of license with minor details, it stays absolutely true to the important facts and historical record of Lincoln's personality. *Ulysses S. Grant: Essays and Documents* (Southern Illinois University Press, 1981) contains contributions from several authors who examine the life of this native son of Illinois. This is a good read before visiting the Galena, Illinois, area. If you enjoy reading histories and you'd like to know more about the native people of Indiana, you'll like *The Miami Indians of Indiana: A Persistent People, 1654–1994* (Indiana Historical Society, 1996).

For kids, *Abe Lincoln: The Young Years* (Troll Associates, 1982) explains how events in Honest Abe's youth influenced him as he became a national leader. Children will enjoy reading just about any book about Johnny Appleseed, who planted the ancestors of many trees you will find when you visit apple orchards in Illinois and Indiana. *The Life and Times of the Apple* (Orchard Books, 1992), by Charles Micucci, also provides a thorough overview of this popular regional fruit.

Slats Grobnik and Some Other Friends (Dutton, 1973): This book (or another of the witty collections of newspaper columns) by Mike Royko is required reading for anyone who wants to be able to speak fluent "Chicago-ese" to the locals. *Ernie's America: the Best of Ernie Pyle's 1930's Travel Dispatches*, by Ernie Pyle (Random House, 1989), is a collection of newspaper columns written during the Great Depression from all across the nation, including several from his home state of Indiana.

Hiking and Biking the Fox River Valley (Roots & Wings, 1997), by Jim Hochgesang, guides nature lovers over the 275 miles of trails and bike paths in 36 forest preserves in northeastern Illinois. And if you're planning to drive the

Great River Road, you'll enjoy it more after reading Mark Twain's *Life on the Mississippi* (Oxford University Press, 1997). *The Traveler's Guide to Native America: The Great Lakes Region* (NorthWard Press, 1992), by Hayward Allen, details not only current museum displays, memorials, and festivals of Native American people, but also puts those things into context through an empathetic—and balanced—history of the region. Everything you always wanted to know about Indiana—and then some—is in Fred Cavinder's *The Indiana Book of Records, Firsts, and Fascinating Facts* (Indiana University Press, 1985).

State Parks of the Midwest (Cordillera Press, 1993), by Vici DeHaan, includes detailed information for virtually every state-run park facility in Illinois and Indiana. *On Second Glance* (U of I Press, 1992), *Postcards from the Prairie* (Larry Kanfer Gallery, 1996) and *Prairiescapes* (U of I Press, 1987), all by Larry Kanfer, show you the region at its best—through graceful, captivating photographs.

Finally, *The Complete Poems of Carl Sandburg* (Harcourt Brace, 1970) and *The Best Loved Poems and Ballads of James Whitcomb Riley* (Blue Ribbon, 1934) prove that Midwesterners (Sandburg was from Illinois, Riley from Indiana) can express themselves with as much color and imagery as the world's greatest writers.

SUGGESTED LISTENING

If you're going to be in Chicago, you have to know a little about blues. While you're at the library selecting a few of the books mentioned above, pick out a couple of these CDs: *Chicken, Gravy, and Biscuits*, by Lil' Ed and the Blues Imperials, *Queen of the Blues* by Koko Taylor, or anything (and everything!) by Buddy Guy.

If you're visiting Indiana you'll enjoy the music of two of the state's most musically gifted sons: John Cougar Mellencamp (*Scarecrow*) and Hoagy Carmichael (*The Song is . . . Hoagy Carmichael*).

SUGGESTED VIEWING

It's nothing like L.A., but Chicago has certainly managed to serve as the setting for plenty of movies. If you want to see where you'll be visiting, watch *The Blues Brothers*, *The Fugitive*, *Ferris Bueller's Day Off*, and *My Best Friend's Wedding*. These movies feature a wide array of Chicago landmarks.

To get a look at the people and scenery of Indiana, try *Hoosiers*, *Breaking Away*, and *Rebel Without a Cause*. *A League of Their Own* is worth renting before a visit to southern Indiana, where most of it was filmed.

1
CHICAGO

What can you say about Chicago that hasn't already been said? Even people from other countries know about Chicago's gangster connection. And if you follow politics at all, you know Chicago has a reputation for high voter turnout—thanks to the old "vote early, vote often" attitude, as well as those conscientious folks who cast ballots from beyond the grave. We've all heard how in 1871, Mrs. O'Leary's cow kicked over a lantern igniting the great Chicago fire. And every self-respecting *Saturday Night Live* fan can do a halfway decent "cheesebugga" or "Da Bears" routine. Movie buffs can tell you about Harrison Ford searching throughout the city to find "the real killer" as Tommy Lee Jones closes in on him in *The Fugitive*.

Without any prompting, you can probably come up with several nicknames for Chicago: "Windy City," "City with the Big Shoulders," "Chi (pronounced 'shy') Town," or "Second City." You get the idea. And who didn't watch Geraldo that night he opened Al Capone's safe on national television to find it filled with . . . nothing? Perhaps we all know so much about Chicago because it's a big city filled with a lot of little guys—who are just like us. Mike Royko was the kind of man who might have been sitting next to you in the local tavern when he wasn't busy writing columns for the *Chicago Tribune*. And although Michael Jordans aren't a dime a dozen, even he was cut from his high school basketball team. As the song goes—sort of—Chicago is our kind of town, and we think that after you give it a try, it'll be your kind, too.

DOWNTOWN CHICAGO

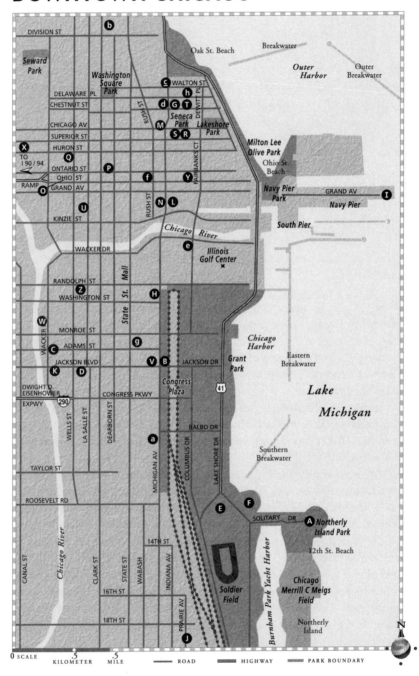

A PERFECT DAY IN CHICAGO

Go for a jog along the lakefront, grab breakfast at Ann Sathers, and head for Shedd Aquarium. Make sure to stop at the temporary exhibit and the dolphin demonstration. Then go shopping on Michigan Avenue, and don't forget to check out the Tribune Tower. For lunch, eat at Ed Debevic's. Then, if it's summer, take in a baseball game in the afternoon, go to the Chicago Chop House for dinner, and stroll Navy Pier in the evening. If it's winter, spend the afternoon at the Museum of Science and Industry and hit a Bulls or Blackhawks game after dinner.

GETTING AROUND CHICAGO

Part of the fun of visiting Chicago is figuring out how to get where you want to go. Expect to get lost at least once (it is a big city), but if you keep a map handy, you'll get back on track pretty quickly. Tourist sites tend to be clustered together, so driving across town and then walking from site to site works well for most folks. If you want to avoid the hassle of finding a parking place, cabs are a great option. Most drivers will point out attractions along your route, and we like to ask them about their most famous passengers; we've found they usually have at least one "brush with celebrity" story they like to share.

SIGHTS

- **A** Adler Planetarium
- **B** Art Institute of Chicago
- **C** Chicago Board of Trade
- **D** Federal Reserve Bank
- **E** Field Museum
- **F** John G. Shedd Aquarium/ Oceanarium
- **G** John Hancock Center Observatory
- **H** Museum of Broadcast Communications
- **I** Navy Pier
- **J** Prairie Avenue Historic District
- **K** Sears Tower

SIGHTS (continued)

- **L** Tribune Tower
- **M** Water Tower Welcome Center

FOOD

- **N** Billy Goat Tavern
- **O** Carson's
- **P** Chicago Chop House
- **Q** Ed Debevic's
- **R** Eli's the Place for Steak
- **S** Gino's East
- **T** Grappa
- **U** Michael Jordan's
- **V** Rhapsody
- **W** Rivers
- **X** Scoozi!
- **Y** Spruce

LODGING

- **Z** Allegro Hotel Chicago
- **a** Blackstone Hotel
- **b** Claridge Hotel
- **c** Drake Hotel
- **d** Four Seasons Hotel Chicago
- **e** Hyatt Regency Chicago
- **f** Lenox Suites
- **g** Palmer House Hilton
- **h** Regal Knickerbocker Hotel

If taxis are out of your price range, we recommend using one of the city's many forms of public transportation. The Chicago Transit Authority (CTA), is not only convenient, but is also reasonably priced. The cost per ride, on either the bus or train, is $1.50. If you aren't staying downtown, the subway system (known as The El) can be a great way to get into and out of the city. It's also great for going from downtown to a Cubs or Sox game. There are five major train lines that are identified by color. Buses run regularly throughout the morning and afternoon, but their frequency begins to slow down toward evening. CTA transit cards are available at a number of locations, including Jewel supermarkets and currency exchange houses. The Metra commuter trains are yet another option. These buses are especially fun for kids, since they're double-deckered and quite roomy, but their prices are a bit higher than the CTA's. Their main office in Chicago is located at 547 West Jackson Boulevard; call 312/322-6777 for more information.

SIGHTSEEING HIGHLIGHTS

★★★★ **ADLER PLANETARIUM**
1300 S. Lake Shore Dr., Chicago, 312/922-STAR
There's nothing like a planetarium to bring out the astronaut in you. At Adler you'll be able to travel the galaxy without ever having to conquer the fine art of using a bathroom in zero gravity. Space exploration is just one facet of this museum. You can also learn about astronomy, telescopes, and even how to navigate using the stars. The **Sky Theater** has a variety of shows throughout the year that are as educational as they are fun.

> *Details: Mon–Thu 9–5, Fri 9–9, Sat–Sun 9–6; $3 adults, $2 seniors and children ages 4–17, under 4 free (separate charge for the Sky Show), free admission Tue; wheelchair accessible. (2 hours)*

★★★★ **ART INSTITUTE OF CHICAGO**
Michigan Ave. at Adams St., Chicago, 312/443-3600
The two lions who stand permanent guard in front of this building provide a hint at the grace, beauty, and strength of the works that are housed inside. The Art Institute is one of the best art museums in the world, and offers a comprehensive look at just about every genre and medium known to man. A real crowd pleaser is the collection of French Impressionist masterpieces, but the exhibits of African, ancient American, and Asian art are popular, too. The nicest thing about this

gallery is that you don't have to be an art snob to appreciate the works. You might not understand every piece you see, but even folks whose taste run toward the velvet *Dogs Playing Poker*, will find something that touches them.

Details: Mon and Wed–Fri 10:30–4:30, Tue 10:30–8, Sat 10–5, Sun noon–5; suggested donation: $8 adults, $5 seniors and children ages 6–14, ages 5 and under free, additional charge for special exhibits, free admission; wheelchair accessible. (3 hours)

Check ahead to see what temporary exhibit will be on display at the Art Institute during your visit to Chicago. You'll need to do this as far in advance of your trip as possible, though, because these shows usually sell out quickly.

★★★★ **CHICAGO BOARD OF TRADE**
141 W. Jackson Blvd., Chicago, 312/435-3500

Yes, in real life action on the floor of the Board of Trade (or as they call it, CBOT) is just as crazy as it looks on television. When you first see it, it'll remind you more of the food fight in *Animal House* than of professionals creating a market for commodities. But by the time you complete the half-hour tour, you'll be able to view the trading with a more discriminating eye. You'll understand how to identify the traders' corporate affiliation, what in the world they mean when they yell and use those wild hand gestures, and which trading pit is which. You'll also get to see some historical artifacts, including the original CBOT bell (used to signal the opening of trading) and the old grain probes they used to use to make sure sellers weren't hiding crummy grain under a thin layer of the good stuff.

Details: Mon–Fri 9:15 a.m.–12:30 p.m.; free; wheelchair accessible. (1 hour)

★★★★ **FEDERAL RESERVE BANK**
230 S. LaSalle, Chicago, 312/322-5322

The tourist attraction even Scrooge McDuck could enjoy—one of the most popular displays here is the million dollar stack made entirely of $1 bills. They have everything from fake money to antique currency at the Federal Reserve. When I visited this place with my high school economics class, there was even a room filled with workers flipping through stacks of bills, efficiently—and amazingly quickly—detecting counterfeits (many of them could tell by the feel of it). These days machines do that work, but it's still fascinating to see. The bank for banks is the grown-up equivalent of touring a candy factory, and it's a great diversion from more traditional attractions. Make sure to stop in the bookstore/gift shop after your tour.

Details: *Mon–Fri 8–5, individual tours Tue 1 p.m.; adults only (17 and older or senior in high school); free; wheelchair accessible. (1 hour)*

★★★★ FIELD MUSEUM
Roosevelt Rd. at Lake Shore Dr., Chicago, 312/922-9410

The greeter in the great hall of the Field Museum is an enormous brachiosaurus dinosaur skeleton who looks like he could take on Godzilla with one arm tied behind his back. As soon as you drag your kids away from it, head straight for the special exhibits. Lines can be long in this area, so you'll want to go while you're still fresh. After you finish here, you can head upstairs to learn about rocks, plants, and people. And don't miss the rest of the dinosaur exhibit, including the working prep lab. Watch scientists remove the crud from Sue—a *Tyrannosaurus rex* discovered a few years ago in South Dakota—and get the skeleton ready for permanent display. On the main floor you can see a wide array of displays featuring animals in their natural habitats, plus some interactive offerings, and the exhibit on ancient Egypt that will take you to the ground floor, which also has a display of sea mammals.

Details: *Web site: www.fmnh.org; daily 9–5; $7 adults; $4 seniors, students with identification, and children ages 3–17; ages 2 and under free; free admission Wed; wheelchair accessible. (2 hours)*

★★★★ JOHN G. SHEDD AQUARIUM/OCEANARIUM
1200 S. Lake Shore Dr., Chicago, 312/939-2438

Arguably the most popular attraction in the city, the Shedd Aquarium has the largest indoor aquarium in the world, and it's filled with some of the most colorful and interestingly shaped sea creatures you've ever seen. You wouldn't want to have to pay the bill for the glass cleaner at this place, but you will want to press your nose against the glass for the sensation of being underwater yourself. The countless smaller tanks and displays throughout this living museum offer glimpses into the lives of everything from sea turtles to penguins. The oceanarium is configured so that it appears to flow seemlessly into Lake Michigan, which is really several hundred feet away. The dolphins—with their trainers—offer demonstrations that explain why they sometimes jump out of the water and what they mean when they do that dolphin moon-walk thing. This is one of the most relaxing, fascinating places in Chicago, and the temporary exhibits (featuring animals such as frogs and seahorses) will give you plenty of reasons for return visits. For music lovers there's the Thursday night Jazzin' at the Shedd party during the tourist season.

Details: Mon–Wed and Fri 9–5, Sat–Sun 9–6, Thu 9–10; $11 adults, $9 seniors and children ages 3–11, ages 2 and under free, free admission (to aquarium only) Thu; wheelchair accessible. (2 hours)

★★★★ JOHN HANCOCK CENTER OBSERVATORY
875 N. Michigan Ave., Chicago, 888/875-8439

One of the best views of the city is at the observatory on the 94th floor of the Hancock building. The outdoor walkway open all year, and the high-tech telescopes talk to you in four different languages. As you scan the city, describe what you're seeing.

Enjoy seeing the city, the lake, and trying to see if you can tell where Indiana, Michigan, and Wisconsin begin. After you finish searching for the pool on the roof of your hotel, there's also the *Windows on Chicago* exhibit featuring virtual tours of several Chicago attractions. Another option for great views from the Hancock is at the Signature Room restaurant on the 95th floor and ordering dinner or drinks.

Details: Daily 9 a.m.–midnight; $7 adults, $5 seniors and children ages 6–16, 5 and under free; additional charge for Soundscopes; wheelchair accessible. (45 minutes)

★★★★ LINCOLN PARK ZOO
2200 N. Cannon Dr., Chicago, 312/742-2000

A true urban jungle, the Lincoln Park Zoo is home to everything from guinea pigs and polar bears to lowland gorillas and flamingos. LPZ is the oldest zoo in the country, and still one of the most important. It manages to help save endangered species, teach people about animals, and offer folks a place to relax and enjoy their fellow creatures. Kids really enjoy renting the tiger-shaped Zoo Keys that "unlock" audio files stored throughout the grounds. They also have a blast at the Farm-in-the-Zoo, where they can milk cows, churn butter, and play "games" their grandparents considered chores.

Details: Web site: www.lpzoo.com; daily 9–5; free; wheelchair accessible. (2 hours)

★★★★ MUSEUM OF BROADCAST COMMUNICATIONS
Chicago Cultural Center, Michigan Ave. at Washington St. Chicago, 312/629-6000

You could spend all day at this museum with its archive of about 70,000 old—and new—television shows, radio programs, and commercials. Try your hand at anchoring the news on their real TV news set (you can even buy a VHS copy of your work), listen to your favorite commercials and play-by-plays, and sit in the studio audience of a real radio program to see the ins and outs of putting together a radio show.

Details: Mon–Sat 10–4:30, Sun noon–5, call in advance for a guided tour; free; wheelchair accessible. (1 hour)

★★★★ MUSEUM OF SCIENCE AND INDUSTRY
5700 S. Lake Shore Dr., 773/684-1414

This is the kind of place where grown-ups can recapture the childhood joy of discovery, the adventure of scientific achievement, and the possibilities of their own minds. Although the most popular exhibits have been around for many years, they continue to amaze and excite thousands of new visitors every year. Things have changed a lot since the days of the touch tone versus rotary dial phone display, where you and a friend could race each other to see who could dial a number the fastest. But the absolute must-see exhibits are still the same: the coal mine, the German submarine, and the fairy dollhouse. One of the best new exhibits is the restored Burlington *Pioneer Zephyr*, the train that made people forget about the Depression for 13 hours—the time it took to travel from Denver to Chicago—on May 26, 1934. The *Zephyr* exhibit includes fantastic animatronic and audiovisual enhancements.

Details: Memorial Day–Labor Day daily 9:30–5:30; Labor Day–Memorial Day Mon–Fri 9:30–4, Sat, Sun, and holidays 9:30–5:30; $7 adults, $6 seniors, $3.50 children ages 3–11, ages 2 and under free, additional charge for Omnimax Theater; wheelchair accessible. (3 hours)

★★★★ NAVY PIER
600 E. Grand Ave., Chicago, 800/595-PIER

The Pier opened in 1916 as a working pier. Since then it's been home to many things, including a military training center, an emergency hospital, freight and passenger shipping facilities, and even a branch campus of the University of Illinois. But after $150 million in renovation work, the Pier has come full circle and is once again one of the hottest places in Chicago. There's an enormous Ferris wheel, an old-fashioned merry-go-round, a children's museum, an IMAX theater, a beautiful botanical garden, a 1,500-seat performance stage that always has something going on, lots of shops and restaurants, and plenty of room to walk, ride bikes, or in-line skate. Don't try to take Navy Pier in too quickly, though. It's the type of place you have to absorb—a unique blend of aromas, languages, and colors that makes people-watching a legitimate pastime.

Details: *Web site: www.navypier.com; Ferris wheel, merry-go-round, shops and food vendors: Sun–Thu 10–10, Fri–Sat 10 a.m.–midnight; free with some charges for individual attractions; wheelchair accessible. (2 hours)*

★★★★ **THE OPRAH WINFREY SHOW TAPING**
Chicago, 312/633-1000

If you have some time to plan your visit to Chicago, see if you can get tickets to watch a taping of *The Oprah Winfrey Show*. It's not easy. This attraction is so popular, it's next to impossible to get in, but if you do, you're in for a real treat. She's the queen of television talk shows for a reason—she's the best. And it's a blast to watch her in action. You might even get to ask her a question.

Details: *Web site: www.oprahshow.com. Free, but tickets are in extremely high demand. If you are planning to be in Chicago and you want to attend this show's taping, get your request in several months in advance, and don't hesitate to use any connections you have with family or friends. (2 hours)*

★★★★ **SEARS TOWER**
233 S. Wacker, Chicago, 312/875-9696

Other buildings may scrape the sky, but this one pokes a hole right through it. And while folks in other parts of the world claim to have the tallest building in their city, people from Chicago *know* it's right here. The interior of this so-called "vertical village" is as big as 78 football fields. It's so big it has its own zip code! On a windy Chicago day the building sways as much as a foot. Believe it or not, that's done on purpose—so the structure won't break apart.

Details: *Mar–Sep daily 9 a.m.–11 p.m., Oct–Feb daily 9 a.m.–10 p.m.; $8 adults, $6 seniors, $5 children ages 5–12, 4 and under free, $20 family (2 adults and up to 3 children); wheelchair accessible. (45 minutes)*

★★★★ TRIBUNE TOWER
435 N. Michigan Ave., Chicago

One of the easiest sites to miss in Chicago is the Tribune building. Sitting just north of the Chicago River on Michigan Avenue, it houses offices of the *Chicago Tribune*, as well as the studios for WGN Radio. One of the studios is at street level, so passersby can watch and hear some of the programming live (including the popular *Kathy and Judy Show*). But the must see at this place is the exterior of the building itself. Its facade is inlaid with fragments of some of the most famous structures around the world. You can find a piece of the Taj Mahal, the White House, the Kremlin, the Great Wall of China, the Cathedral at Notre Dame, and a bunch more as you walk around the building. A nice bonus is there's never a line, and there are so many different fragments that you can spend a few minutes here every time you walk by, and you'll always find something new.

A caution, though—bone up on your geography before you go. Our four-year-old daughter asked us where a couple of the represented buildings actually were, and she got the same blank look we gave our fourth-grade teachers when they asked tough questions.

Details: *Best viewing is in the day, but many areas are well lit; free; wheelchair accessible. (1/2 hour—at a time)*

★★★★ UNIVERSITY OF CHICAGO
5801 S. Ellis Ave. (Hyde Park), Chicago, 773/702-8374

This prestigious university's historic campus (with everything from Frank Lloyd Wright's Robie House to Rockefeller Memorial Chapel) is a popular setting for movies (*When Harry Met Sally* and *The Fugitive*). If you take a walking tour on campus, chances are you'll bump into a Nobel Prize winner or two; this place has as much brainpower as a small country.

Details: *Tours offered 10 a.m. Sat starting at Idanoyes Hall (1212 E. 59th St.); free; wheelchair accessible. (1 hour)*

★★★★ WATER TOWER WELCOME CENTER
811 N. Michigan Ave., Chicago, 312/744-2400

When they finally put out the great Chicago fire, one of the few buildings still standing was the Water Tower. Today this historic building is a great place to get your bearings to tackle the sights and sounds of the rest of the city. The Welcome Center offers displays on the history of

Chicago, as well as oodles of maps and brochures about sights throughout the area.

Details: *Mon–Sat 10–6, Sun 11–5; free; wheelchair accessible.* (½ hour)

★★★ PRAIRIE AVENUE HISTORIC DISTRICT
1800 S. Prairie Ave., Chicago, 773/326-1480

What did Chicago look like when it was still a relatively small town? A visit to Prairie Avenue Historic District will give you an idea. The Clarke House, which is open for tours, is recognized as the oldest structure in the city. The couple who built it had the vision to recognize that this frontier town would be around long enough to make the investment worthwhile. After you tour Clarke House, make sure to visit the Glessner House, too. Its architect was way ahead of his time and incorporated design techniques you probably have in your own house today. A walk around the neighborhood will allow you to see the former homes of Chicago's most famous (and wealthiest) residents.

Details: *Wed–Sun noon–4; $8 adults, $6 seniors and students, pre-schoolers free; Clarke House is wheelchair accessible. (2 hours)*

★★ MUSEUM OF HOLOGRAPHY/CHICAGO
1134 W. Washington Blvd., Chicago, 312/226-1007

What it lacks in square footage, this museum makes up in coolness. There are just a couple hundred or so works, but they're all laser-generated 3-D holograms, sort of like the ones on your credit cards, but much more realistic. Exhibits, which include moving people as well as scientific and technical holographic applications, change frequently. Popular displays include: Michael Jordan passing a basketball; a human heart; and the head of a *Tyrannosaurus rex*. These optical illusions are created by lasers that bend and focus light in a way that photographic film cannot. The gift shop here is small, but we dare you to leave without buying something.

Details: *Wed–Sun 12:30–5; $2.50 adults, under age 6 free. Exterior not wheelchair accessible, so call ahead for accommodations. (1 hour)*

SPORTS

Chicago's **Wrigley Field** is the quintessential baseball park. The grass is real, the scoreboard is manual, and ivy covers the outfield wall. The **Chicago Cubs**

WRIGLEY FIELD

Carolyn Crimi

haven't won the World Series in a while (OK, almost a century), but you wouldn't know it by the passion of the people who come here to follow them. Call 773/404-CUBS for ticket and tour information. The **Chicago White Sox** play at **Comisky Park**. The post–home run fireworks here are some of the best anywhere, and several times a season they offer great post-game concerts. Check the parking lot to find the old Comisky's home plate.

The House That Michael Built (a.k.a. the **United Center**) is a wonderful place to see the six-time NBA-champion **Chicago Bulls** (there's nothing like the team-introduction hoopla), the **Chicago Blackhawks** NHL team (their intro isn't bad either, and the laser show looks neat on the ice), and all sorts of special events. Call 312/455-4500 for details.

A classic football stadium, **Soldier Field** is home of the **Chicago Bears**. It's usually pretty cold during games, thanks to the lake effect and frequent seasonal precipitation, but it is definitely an experience you won't forget. The ticket office is at 312/747-1285.

When the Bulls win the championship, **Grant Park** is where the town comes to celebrate. It's also home to Taste of Chicago and countless other festivals throughout the year. The Buckingham Fountain (of *Married with Children* fame) is in this park, as is a statue of Lincoln. (So where's the statue of Grant? In Lincoln Park, of course.) In the winter, you can even go smelt fishing at Lincoln Park. Just cut a hole in the ice and watch the fish find you.

ORGANIZED TOURS

The Chicago Architecture Foundation offers several ways to see the city (by foot, bus, and boat), but the best part of **Chicago Architecture Tours**, 312/922-TOUR, is learning the stories behind the buildings that make this one of the nicest skylines in the nation.

Ducks all around the world probably take for granted the sensation of walking on dry land and then splashing into the water. For people, however, it's quite a thrill, and it's one you'll experience if you take a tour with **Chicago Duck Tours**. For reservations, call the Quack Shack at 312/461-1133.

Chicago Neighborhood Tours, 312/742-1190, will take you to see, smell, touch, hear, and—best of all—taste Chinatown, Little Italy, Greektown, Pilsen's Little Village (which is home to more people of Mexican descent than Bohemians these days), Ravenswood, and more.

Hop aboard old-fashioned trolleys—complete with lots of brass and wood detailing inside—and see the sights of Chicago with **Chicago Trolley Company**, 312/663-0260.

Mercury, Chicago's Skyline Cruiseline, 312/332-1353, tours start on the Chicago River and head through the locks onto the lake, where you'll get a good view of several important buildings. You'll also learn some great Chicago trivia, including why the Civic Opera House is shaped like a giant chair with its back to the city. Sorry, we're not telling.

You'll see the **Noble Horse Carriage Rides** all over the downtown area. These tours are most fun in late spring and early summer or in the Christmas season (when you can snuggle under a thick blanket and enjoy becoming a part of the city's decorations). For information call 312/266-7878.

One of the fastest ways to see the city is with **Seadog Cruises**, 312/822-7200. It's not as comprehensive as some of the slower tours, but it sure is a rush! Buildings that blur by include the planetarium, Soldier Field, and the lighthouse.

With **Ticker Tape Tours**, 312/644-9001, you can visit the city's financial exchanges and watch fortunes being won and lost as your guide explains such mysteries as futures contracts and stock options. This tour includes visits to the Mercantile Exchange, the Board of Trade, and the Chicago Board Options Exchange.

Chicago is well known for its historic connections to the gangster world, and the **Untouchables Tour** takes you (in a black bus complete with bullet holes) to a dozen or so of the places the bad guys worked, played, and met with untimely deaths. Call 773/881-1195 for information.

Loop Train Tours, 312/744-2400, let you ride the train for a fast-moving look at the sights throughout the Loop. Reservations aren't required, but if you're going to be here when there's a big event scheduled, call ahead to save your space.

SPECIAL EVENTS

The city dyes the river green on Saint Patrick's Day, sets off an arsenal of fire-works on the third of July (a day early so suburban folks can catch their own Independence Day celebrations), and funds the quarterly dividends for the local electric company with their massive holiday displays every Christmas. And when the federal calendar doesn't present a reason to celebrate, they come up with one of their own. Some of the biggest and best are the **Saint Patrick's Day Parade** (March 17th), the **Taste of Chicago** in Grant Park (late June–early July), and the **Chicago Jazz Festival** (late August–early September). The **Cinco de Mayo Festival** and a huge **Flower and Garden Show** take place every April. Also in May is the **Buckingham Fountain Lighting Ceremony**. In June the **Chicago Blues Fest**, **Chicago Gospel Music Festival**, the **Country Music Festival**, and the **"Celebrate on State Street" Festival** offer lots of great music and food.

Venetian Night is a long-standing celebration that includes an orchestra concert, a boat parade, and fireworks. The **Chicago Air and Water Show** and **Viva! Chicago Latin Music Festival** are in August; while in September it's the **Chicago Jazz Festival**, the **German-American Fest**, the **Mexican Independence Day Parade**, and the **Celtic Fest**. The city sponsors a wide array of special events to draw people downtown on Thursday nights, and the **Halloween** festivities are a real scream. In December **Skate on State** and the store window decorations with the **Magnificent Mile of Lights Festival** will get even the "bah-humbuggiest" folks into the holiday spirit.

If you want details on any event or festival in Chicago throughout the year, contact the Mayor's Office of Special Events at 312/744-3315.

SHOPPING

Whether you're a bargain hunter or someone who appreciates a good brand-name label, you'll find enough good buys to push the limits of even the most generous credit cards.

The **Magnificent Mile** (the blocks just north of the Chicago River on Michigan Avenue) is a shopping mecca for folks throughout the Midwest. **Water Tower Place**, 835 N. Michigan Ave., 312/440-3165, is the most famous group of stores. Its anchors are **Marshall Fields**, 312/781-4486, and **Lord & Taylor**, 312/787-7400.

On the other side of the street, the relatively new **Chicago Place** mall, 700 N. Michigan Ave., 312/266-7710, houses **Sak's Fifth Avenue**, 312/944-6500, and much more. **Bloomingdale's**, 312/440-4460, is in the vertical mall at (and called) **900 North Michigan Avenue**. While you're on Michigan, you'll probably notice the huge line out the door of **Garrett Popcorn Shop**, 670 N. Michigan Ave., 312/944-2630. If you want to taste why, budget 30 minutes or so for waiting to get to the counter.

There's great shopping on State Street, where the historic **Marshall Fields**, 111 N. State St., 312/781-4486, sits. Another popular State Street offering is the original **Carson Pirie Scott**, 1 State St., 312/641-7000. On Oak Street you'll find lots of upscale boutiques and art galleries. The **Merchandise Mart**, Orleans and Kinzie, 312/527-4141, is where store buyers go to choose the things you'll find on your local store shelves in the coming season. But there's plenty of retail shopping on the first two floors.

Neighborhoods throughout the city offer a diverse array of clothing, food, furniture, and collectibles. To find them, take a neighborhood tour before venturing out on your own. If you need groceries, **Treasure Island**, 75 W. Elm, 312/440-1144, is a fun place to shop. If you're looking for a rare—or just really good—bottle of wine, go to **Sam's Liquors**, 1720 N. Mercey, 312/664-4394.

FITNESS AND RECREATION

Throughout the year the city hosts a variety of special sporting events—three-on-three basketball tournaments, triathlons, marathons, bicycle races, and the like. To receive a schedule and information on participating, call 312/744-3315. If you don't want to get quite that competitive, you can start your day with a **jog along the downtown beaches** or by using a one-day pass at any of the major **health clubs** (check with the front desk at your hotel for information).

At **Navy Pier** you can rent in-line skates, bicycles, or tandem bikes. Call 800/915-2453 for more information. You might want to plan your route to pass some of the city's bold outdoor artwork, including the **Picasso sculpture**, the **Miro sculpture**, and the **Chagall mosaic** (a route around the area bounded by South Clark Street, Jackson Boulevard, Dearborn Street, and Randolph Street will take you by all three).

The **Chicago Lakefront Bike Path** that runs from Bryn Mawr Avenue to 79th Street is great for exercise and is even a good place to cross-country ski when it's too crummy out to bike, jog, or skate.

If you prefer the lake to the city, several boat companies offer rides of varying lengths and speeds. Just walk the length of Navy Pier to see them all. One of the most unusual is the tall ship *Windy*, 312/595-5555. You can also board boats along the Chicago River for tours of the city (see Organized Tours). There's some fantastic fishing in Lake Michigan, so you might want to charter a boat. The **William W. Powers Conservation Area**, 12949 S. Ave. "O," 773/646-3270, has settings perfect for fishing and picnicking.

CHICAGO

To North Chicago, Waukegan

Lake
Michigan

Highland Park

Buffalo
Grove

Palatine

Northbrook
WILLOW RD

PALATINE RD

Arlington
Heights

Glenview

Skokie

Evanston

Des Plaines

DEVON AV

KENNEDY EXPY

Chicago
O'Hare
International
Airport

Bloomingdale

SCHICK RD **H**

Chicago

G
E
J
A

Lincoln Park

BELMONT AV

Glendale
Heights

FULLERTON AV

GRAND AV

NORTH AV

Elmhurst

Oak Park
WASHINTON BLVD

B

EISENHOWER EXPY

Wheaton

35TH ST

F

Oak
Brook **I**
OGDEN AV

Cicero

Comiskey
Park

STEVENSON EXPY

47TH ST

D
C

Downers
Grove

63RD ST

Naperville

Burbank

79TH ST

To
East
Chicago

95TH ST

Oak
Lawn

William W
Powers
Conservetion
Area
130TH ST

Bolingbrook

MC CARTHY RD

Orland
Park

Oak
Forest

159TH ST

K

Joliet

Tinley
Park

Chicago Heights

N

ROSELLE RD

ELGIN O'HARE EXPY

HARLEM AV

CICERO AV

WESTERN AV

ASHLAND AV

HALSTED ST

DAN RYAN EXPY

ML KING DR

MICHIGAN AV

LAKE SHORE DR

SHERIDAN RD

LINCOLN

Chicago River

Sanitary & Ship Canal

ARCHER AV

TRI-STATE TLWY.

WAUKEGAN R

TRI-STATE TLWY

Waukegan R

80TH AV

0 SCALE

10
KILOMETERS

10
MILES

—— ROAD

══ HIGHWAY

✕ PLACE OF INTEREST

FOOD

There are so many restaurants here, you could eat at a different place for breakfast, lunch, and dinner each day and still not hit them all in six or seven years. In addition to the dizzying number of choices here, you'll need to consider the cost. If you're not from a very large city, prices here seem high. But you're on vacation, so relax and enjoy yourself.

Start your culinary adventure by getting a table at **Ann Sather's**, 2665 N. Clark, 773/327-9522. They bill themselves as "Chicago's Swedish Diner." You can get Swedish pancakes with lingonberries, limpa bread (by the loaf), and the biggest, gooeyist cinnamon rolls you've ever sunk your teeth into. Lunch and dinner here are good, too. **Ed Debevic's**, 640 N. Wells St., 312/664-4993, has diner-style food and a wait staff with an attitude. It's all in fun, though, and the food is really cheap and really good. Classic Chicago-style pizza is waiting for you at **Gino's East**, 160 E. Superior, 312/943-1124 (plus five other locations throughout the Chicagoland area). OK, it's not exactly waiting for you. In fact, you'll have to wait an hour or so for it, but you can pass the time reading (or adding to) the graffiti scribbled all over the cave-like walls. The place John Belushi made famous when he did the "cheesebugga" sketch on *Saturday Night Live* is the **Billy Goat Tavern**, 430 N. Michigan Ave., 312/222-1525. And yes, they still yell "Cheesbugga, cheesebugga" after you order.

In Chicago there are plenty of places where you can get great steaks, chops, and ribs. On your way out of **Carson's**, 612 N. Wells St., 312/280-9200, Web site: www.ribs.com, you'll want to ask what brand of laundry detergent they use on the tablecloths, because it doesn't seem possible to keep them so white with such messy—but delicious—ribs being served every day. Eat at **Chicago Chop House**, 60 W. Ontario St., 800/229-2356, and discover why it's ranked as one of the best in the entire country. It's pricier than Carson's, but their steaks, prime rib, wine, and—well—everything else is magnificent. You've probably heard of Eli's cheesecake, but did you know they make a mean steak, too? At **Eli's the Place for Steak**, 215 E. Chicago

Ave., 312/642-1393, you'll want to top off a steak or their popular calf's liver with some of that famous cheesecake. It's rather expensive, but it's very good.

So maybe we can't all be like Mike, but we can sure eat like him. At **Michael Jordan's**, 500 N. LaSalle, 312/644-3865, you can get all the usual celebrity restaurant offerings, plus some stick-to-your-ribs macaroni and cheese or garlic mashed potatoes—all at reasonable prices.

You're sitting at an outdoor café in Amalfi, and you're savoring your last meal in Italy, because you know you'll never find food like this back home. But you can if you go to **Scoozi!**, 410 W. Huron St., 312/943-5900. Everything from the pizza and pasta to the seafood and the desserts in this upscale restaurant takes you back to Italy. Another good choice for elegant Italian dining is **Grappa**, 200 E. Chestnut St., 312/337-4500. The homemade pastas are served in generous portions, and the risottos are a real treat.

Food connoisseurs come to **Charlie Trotter's**, 816 W. Armitage Ave., 312/248-6228, from all around the world to taste the creations of chef and owner Charlie Trotter. The selections on this menu are a blend of flavors from around the world. **Spruce**, 238 E. Ontario, 312/642-3757, is very upscale and very good, with contemporary American cuisine. Another sure bet for great contemporary food in an elegant setting is **Rivers**, 30 S. Wacker Dr., 312/559-1515. At **Rhapsody**, 65 E. Adams, 312/786-9911, you can enjoy regional American food with a European flair. If you want to be a bit more adventurous in your search for excellent food, you'll find a fantastic selection in the city's ethnic neighborhoods.

LODGING

Some of the best views of the city and the lake are no further than your hotel room window. Hotels generally offer a variety of amenities, including pools, exercise facilities, concierge service, continental breakfasts, turn-down service, and more. Expect to pay more for each of those comforts, as well as for proximity to the Loop. When you're budgeting for your lodging, remember that you'll have to pay 14.9 percent in taxes on top of the nightly rate.

For a very special experience, you should book a room at the **Four Seasons Hotel Chicago**, 120 E. Delaware Pl., 800/332-3442. Hotel critics have given it their highest rating—five stars—and it lives up to the accolade. It offers luxurious accommodations and amenities that include an in-house masseuse. The **Drake Hotel**, 140 E. Walton Pl., 800/55-DRAKE, is another highly-rated hotel and the choice of many celebrities. The **Palmer House Hilton**, 17 E. Monroe St., 800/HILTONS, is a classic. This hotel is an affordable and convenient place to stay if you're in town for an event at Grant Park or on the lakefront. The **Blackstone Hotel**, 636 S. Michigan Ave., 800/622-6330, which offers nice views of Buckingham Fountain, is a bargain. Another historic setting is the **Regal Knickerbocker Hotel**, 163 E. Walton Pl., 800/621-8140, a mid-range facility just off Michigan Avenue. It's a good home base for a shopping vacation. American history buffs will enjoy checking out the Knickerbocker's secret doors that were installed back in Prohibition to help customers sneak out.

Surf Hotel, 555 W. Surf St., 800/SURF-108, is a charming, exquisitely detailed hotel that's close to lots of the city's best sights, but still far enough away to seem like a retreat. **Claridge Hotel**, 1244 N. Dearborn, 800/245-1258, is located in the Gold Coast area. It's reasonably priced and just a block from Rush Street. If you don't feel like that sort of nightlife, just watch an in-room movie. A really inexpensive place that's close to lots of nightlife is **City Suites Hotel**, 933 W. Belmont Ave., 800/CITY-108. In fact, many of the entertainers you'll go to see perform in the city stay here. It has a fun retro feel and spacious, hip rooms. **Lenox Suites**, 616 N. Rush St., 800/44-LENOX, is a great place for vacationers staying for a week or more. They have kitchenettes, so you can do your own cooking (saving wear and tear on your wallet and your waistline). A recently renovated downtown facility is **Allegro Hotel Chicago**, 171 W. Randolph, 312/236-0123. It has colorful and funky—but tastefully decorated—rooms, and a very friendly staff. It's a bit pricey, but you get what you pay for. One of the nicest chains in the city is the **Hyatt Regency Chicago**, 151 E. Wacker Dr., 800/233-1234. The lobby's wide open lounge is a great place to watch the bartenders work. For fun, try ordering some exotic liqueur and see how fast they can retrieve it from the many rows of bottles.

Two excellent resorts are close enough to Chicago for visitors, and they're priced right, too. **Indian Lakes Resort**, 250 W. Schick Rd., Bloomingdale, 630/529-0200, is just a few miles west of O'Hare Airport. It has two 18-hole golf courses, two pools, and much more. **Oak Brook Hills Hotel & Resort**, 3500 Midwest Rd., Oak Brook, 630/850-5500, Web site: www.oakbrookhills.com, is a four-star facility with a great golf course, pools, tennis, and more.

You can also find some wonderful bed-and-breakfast accommodations in Chicago. An easy way to get access to information on—and to make reservations for—lots of them is through **Bed & Breakfast Chicago**, 800/375-7084, Web site: www.bnbchicago.com. They are very popular, so you need to make reservations early. Most places have a two night minimum, and few accept smokers.

CAMPING

Chicago seems about as far from wilderness as you can get, but if camping is your bag, you can find a nearby place to stay. The **Windy City Beach and Camping Resort**, 18701 S. 80th Ave., Tinley Park, 708/720-0030, has a lake with a nice beach, and if you want to get a little deeper there's fishing and boating, too. On land there are horseshoe pits, a playground, and a game room. When you want to head into the city, just go one mile to the Metra station and you can be at the Loop after a pleasant 45-minute ride. Sites here cost $10 per adult, $18 per family (for a primitive spot), and $24.50 for an RV hook-up.

NIGHTLIFE

Even if we didn't offer you ideas for what to do at night, you'd probably know to ask around for the **Second City Comedy Club**, 1616 N. Wells, 312/337-3992. Just about everybody who's anybody in the world of stand-up has done a stint at Second City. It's an intimate setting in which to see the future stars of television and cinema.

Chicago is also a hot spot for blues, and there are several blues clubs you should visit. Try **Buddy Guy's Legends**, 754 S. Wabash Ave., 312/427-1190, Web site: www.buddyguy.com (yes, he does play at his namesake club occasionally); **Blue Chicago**, 736 N. Clark St., 312/642-6261; and **House of Blues**, 329 N. Dearborn St., 312/527-2583, a self-described "juke joint/opera house" where you can hear some fabulous music.

For jazz, **Dick's Last Resort**, 435 E. Illinois St., 312/836-7870, is a fun spot (enjoy crab legs, chicken, or ribs in a bucket while you listen). The **Rush Street** bars are legendary as the place to be if you're young and single (and they're fun for the rest of us, too). **The Drink**, 702 W. Fulton St., 312/733-7800, is one of the hippest places around these days; and **Polly Esther's**, 213 W. Institute Pl., 312/664-0777, is a great theme bar with a 70s feel.

A fairly new and very hot pastime in Chicago is **Whirlyball**, 1880 W. Fullerton, 800/894-4759. It's a team game that involves driving a bumper car while using a scoop to get a whiffle ball to hit a goal. It's a combination of demolition derby, soccer, lacrosse, hockey, basketball, and polo.

If you just want to keep moving, you can hop on the *Odyssey*, Navy Pier, 312/321-7620, Web site: www.odyssey-cruises.com, for an evening of fine dining, dancing, and views. For a less formal experience there's **Uglyduck Cruises**, Navy Pier, 312/663-0260, featuring a huge yellow boat with food, dancing, and what they like to call "a duck's-eye view" of the skyline. On land, the **Party Bus**, 312/266-7330, is a "nightclub on wheels" (an English double-decker bus) that takes passengers to a handful of hot nightspots throughout the city.

PERFORMING ARTS

For a more cultured night on the town, you can't beat the **Chicago Symphony Orchestra**, which performs at **Symphony Center**, 220 S. Michigan Ave., 312/294-3000. The acoustics are first-rate, the building is fit for royalty, and the music is simply the best. **Chicago Theatre**, 175 N. State St., 312/902-1500, is a restored movie temple that hosts the most popular Broadway productions. You'll also want to check the schedule of the popular **Goodman**, 200 S. Columbia Dr., 3122/443-3800. The **Civic Opera House**, 20 N. Wacker, 312/332-2244, is home of the **Lyric Opera of Chicago**, and world-class performances of the classics.

There are loads of stage shows happening in Chicago on any given night. ***Tony 'n' Tina's Wedding***, Piper's Alley, 230 W. North Ave., 312/664-8844, is a stage show without a stage. You're a guest at the service held in the "Chapel of Love;" then you join the couple for the reception, which includes an Italian food buffet, lots of toasting, dancing, and a few surprises. Another long-running show is ***Shear Madness***, Mayfair Theatre, Blackstone Hotel, 636 S. Michigan Ave., 312/786-9120, the popular mystery that audiences help solve.

Lake Michigan Circle Tour

The Lake Michigan Circle Tour is more than 1,000 miles through four states (Illinois, Indiana, Michigan, and Wisconsin). It runs—along or very near the coast of the largest of the Great Lakes. Geographic attractions along this route include beaches, sand dunes, forests, and some fantastic views of the water. You'll also pass plenty of man-made attractions: amusement parks, historic homes, museums, shopping, and more than 70 lighthouses, many of which are open for public tours. Finally, there are festivals along this route throughout the year.

Start your drive in Winthrop Harbor, Illinois, and head south. If you don't have time to make the whole tour, just use the Illinois section as your path to attractions in Lake County and Chicago. In Chicago the famous **Lake Shore Drive**. You'll see posh **Gold Coast** homes, beaches, and attractions such as **Lincoln Park Zoo**, **Navy Pier**, the **Field Museum**, **Adler Planetarium**, **Shedd Aquarium**, **Soldier Field**, and the **Museum of Science and Industry**. (See Sightseeing Highlights for more information on these attractions.)

2
LAKE COUNTY

This self-described "Great American County" does live up to the name. Lake County has everything from glacier-created natural landmarks and stomach-churning theme-park rides to historic sites and state-of-the-art technology displayed in its museums,

Thousands of years before the tourists arrived here, glaciers were busy sculpting the gorgeous terrain that would become one of the most popular outdoor recreation spots in the region. Long before European settlers found the area, though, several Native American tribes hunted, fished, and farmed the region—at least until they were forced to move west.

Lake County has played an important role in the nation's military history, serving as the site of a prisoner of war camp in the Civil War, as well as a training facility for the army in both World Wars.

These days the county is close enough to both Chicago and Milwaukee to have a very cosmopolitan feel, but its natural areas are so treasured and protected that being in them gives visitors plenty of space to fully enjoy the flora and fauna and the peace and quiet.

Lake County has a full schedule of annual events and festivals, including a stunning Orchard Blossom Walk, a huge water-ski show and tournament, Native American powwows, an antique car show, and festivals featuring apples and strawberries. There are also several antique and flea markets, farmers markets, and arts and crafts fairs.

LAKE COUNTY

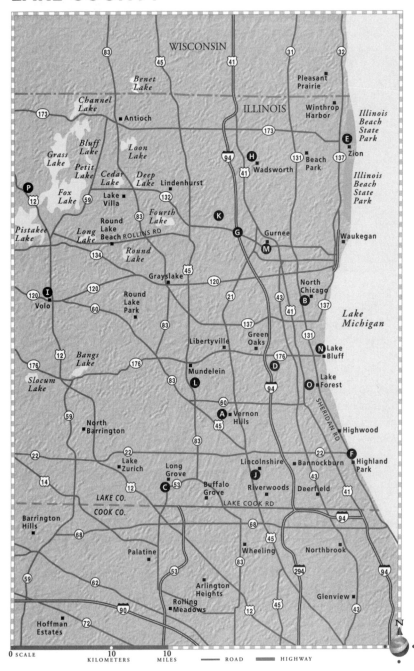

WISCONSIN

83

45

31

32

Benet
Lake

Pleasant
Prairie

Channel
Lake

173

Antioch

ILLINOIS

Winthrop
Harbor

Illinois
Beach
State
Park

173

94

E
Zion

131
137

Bluff
Lake

Grass
Lake

Loon
Lake

H

94

41
Wadsworth

131
Beach
Park

Illinois
Beach
State
Park

Petit
Lake

Cedar
Lake

Deep
Lake

Lindenhurst

Fox
Lake

59

Lake
Villa

132

Waukegan

Pistakee
Lake

P
12

Round
Lake
Beach

83

Fourth
Lake

K

ROLLINS RD

Long
Lake

G

Gurnee

Round
Lake

134

M

Grayslake

45

120

21

North
Chicago

Round
Lake
Park

120

I

120

Volo

60

43

B

41

137

Lake
Michigan

83

137

131

Bangs
Lake

Libertyville

Green
Oaks

N
Lake
Bluff

176

12

176

176

D

Slocum
Lake

83

Mundelein

O
Lake
Forest

L

94

60

59

North
Barrington

A

45

Vernon
Hills

SHERIDAN RD

Highwood

83

22

22

22

Lincolnshire

Bannockburn

F
Highland
Park

14

Lake
Zurich

Long
Grove

J
Riverwoods

43

Deerfield

41

12

C
53

Buffalo
Grove

Barrington
Hills

LAKE CO.
COOK CO.

LAKE COOK RD

68

68

45

94

59

Palatine

53

Wheeling

83

Northbrook

294

59

62

Arlington
Heights

12

45

94

Glenview

43

Hoffman
Estates

72

90

Rolling
Meadows

N

0 SCALE   10   10
              KILOMETERS   MILES   —— ROAD   ══ HIGHWAY

Shopping and sightseeing are popular among adults, but kids come here for one thing only: Six Flags Great America.

A PERFECT DAY IN LAKE COUNTY

The best time to visit Historic Long Grove Village is in the morning, as the shopkeepers are opening their doors and the town is beginning to come to life. Although the folks here are dressed in contemporary clothing, the early morning sun on the whitewashed buildings and the brightly-colored flower beds gives you the feeling of stepping back in time. Stay in town long enough to eat lunch at one of the specialty restaurants, then head to Gurnee Mills Mall. Stop by your room to drop off the bargains you've found, then head to Ravinia for a relaxing picnic under the stars while you lose yourself in some of the most beautiful music ever performed.

SIGHTSEEING HIGHLIGHTS

★★★★ GOELITZ CONFECTIONERY JELLY BELLY FACTORY
1539 Morrow Ave., North Chicago, 847/689-8950
What do Candy Corn and Jelly Belly™ jelly beans have in common? They're the two most famous products created by Gustav and Albert Goelitz and their family. Touring this candy factory is like getting a part

---

SIGHTS
- **A** Cuneo Museum and Gardens
- **B** Goelitz Confectionery™ Jelly Belly Factory
- **C** Historic Long Grove
- **D** Lamb's Farm
- **E** The Power House
- **F** Ravinia Festival
- **G** Six Flags Great America
- **H** Tempel Lipizzans
- **I** Volo Antique Auto Museum

FOOD
- **J** Flatlander's Restaurant and Brewery
- **D** Mickey Finn's Brewery
- **K** Planet Hollywood
- **L** Quig's Orchard
- **K** Rainforest Cafe
- **C** Seasons of Long Grove

LODGING
- **M** Adventure Inn Motel
- **N** By The Way Motel
- **O** Deer Path Inn
- **N** Great Lakes Motel
- **E** Illinois Beach Resort

LODGING (continued)
- **L** Round-Robin Guesthouse
- **N** Sunset Motel
- **M** Sweet Basil Hill Farm B&B

CAMPING
- **P** Chain O' Lakes State Park
- **E** Illinois Beach State Park

Note: Items with the same letter are located in the same area.

Make sure to buy some Belly Flops while you're here. These beans may not be up to the factory's high standards, but you sure wouldn't know it by the way they taste!

in Willy Wonka's operations. You get to see—and smell—the famous jelly beans being made, plus tour guides share a few trade secrets with you and explain how they come up with those wacky new flavors (blueberry, for example, was invented for a red, white, and blue mix to serve at Ronald Reagan's 1981 inauguration).

Details: *Mon–Fri 10–4:30; closed for tours on holidays, Apr 1, and the last week of June through the first week of July; free. (1 hour)*

★★★★ **THE POWER HOUSE**
100 Shiloh Blvd., Zion, 847/746-7080
Developed by utility giant Commonwealth Edison, this hands-on museum allows kids to have a great and safe time playing with electricity. Ideas and theories aren't displayed in dusty dioramas here. Instead, they're brought to life in a way that demonstrates the power, danger, and magic of energy. After learning how energy works, what it does, and what it can do, try your hand at creating an energy policy for the new millennium.

Details: *Mon–Sat 10–5; free; wheelchair accessible. (2 hours)*

★★★★ **RAVINIA FESTIVAL**
400 Iris Ln., Highland Park, 847/266-5100
A half million people flock to the grounds of this outdoor music festival each year . . . with good reason. Every night (and many days) from mid-June to early September the grounds at Ravinia come alive with delightful music by an eclectic mix of performers. A David Sanborn show one night might be followed by Willie Nelson the next and Poi Dog Pondering after that. The house special, though, is the world-famous Chicago Symphony Orchestra.

Jazz, classical, contemporary music, and ballet are sprinkled throughout the season's calendar, along with a variety of other styles. Special concerts for kids, as well as some two-for-one deals, are available, and you are welcome to bring your own lawn chairs and picnic baskets (if you forget, chairs are available for rent and there are three walk-up restaurants on site).

Details: *Web site: www.ravinia.org; most performances begin at 8 p.m., children's performances 11 a.m.; admission $15–$60. (3 hours)*

★★★★ SIX FLAGS GREAT AMERICA
Midway between Chicago and Milwaukee on I-94 at Rte. 132 (Grand Ave.), 847/249-INFO

It'll take your stomach at least a day to recover from the tossing, spinning, and dropping you'll subject it to at Six Flags Great America. This huge park is divided into seven areas, and it's a challenge to cover them all in one day. The roller coasters are the most popular attractions, with their speed, gravity-defying loops, and vertical drops. The park averages a new thrill ride every two to three years, and the new ones usually break records for height, speed, or use of new technology. Those who prefer a slightly less thrilling day will find plenty of the traditional amusement park attractions, including carousels, a scenic railway, water rides, bumper cars, Ferris wheels, and a special park for young children.

Head straight to the Country Fair section of the park first. It has some great rides and shorter lines. Also, park officials suggest eating lunch at 11 a.m. or 2 p.m. to avoid crowds.

There are plenty of places to eat—budget some money for these, because you are not allowed to bring your own food. A dress code prohibits bikini tops and shirts with offensive messages.

Details: *Web site: www.sixflags.com; early May–late Oct, varying hours; $34 adults, $29 children ages 4–10, $17 seniors, car parking $7; special park guidebook for guests with disabilities. (1–2 days)*

★★★ CUNEO MUSEUM AND GARDENS
1350 N. Milwaukee Ave., Vernon Hills, 847/362-3042

Thomas Edison's business partner, Samuel Insull, built this lavish estate on 75 acres back in 1914. Chicago businessman John Cuneo bought the place 23 years later. The design of the home is Venetian, and the builders were obviously told to spare no expense—the ceilings are frescoed, the 40-foot-high great hall is accented with arcaded balconies, and the walls of the indoor pool are travertine marble. The furnishings are equally spectacular, and a walk through the grounds will make you think you're Mary Lennox in *The Secret Garden*.

Details: *Feb–Dec Tue–Sun 10–5; $10 adults, $5 children 5–12, $9 seniors; bathrooms are not wheelchair accessible. (2 hours)*

★★★ HISTORIC LONG GROVE
847/634-0888

This village was founded in 1847 and has been restored to let visitors see what life here was like in those earlier days. To get the feel for the place, walk the brick paths that connect an old-fashioned covered bridge, church, country store, artisan shops, and much more, but also take a ride in a horse-drawn carriage. This is a wonderful place to eat; the Village Tavern is a must-see, and the Strawberry Festival, Apple Fest, and Countryside Christmas are great family outings.

Details: *Open year-round Mon–Sat 10–5, Sun 11–5; free. (4 hours)*

★★★ LAMB'S FARM
Rte. 176 (Rockland Rd.) at I-94, Libertyville, 847/362-4636

An extensive petting zoo highlights this attraction-filled farm-style workshop. Kids also love the train, pet shop, ice-cream parlor, and miniature golf course. Special entertainment includes crafts shows and waterskiing shows. Another wonderful dimension to Lamb's Farm is the friendly employees, many of whom are living with disabilities. The gift shop here offers yummy treats to take home.

Details: *Open year-round 9–6; free. (2 hours)*

★★★ THE VOLO ANTIQUE AUTO MUSEUM
27582 Volo Village Rd., Volo, 815/385-3644

The best way to describe this place is that it's the Pegasus (or should we say El Camino?) of exhibition galleries—half museum, half car dealer. Every car on display is also on sale. You'll find everything from the earliest luxury models to premium muscle cars of your youth. This multimillion dollar collection is a fun place to visit when you're in the neighborhood, since it averages about 40 new cars each month. An antique mall, gift shop, book shop, and restaurant are also in the complex.

Details: *Open year-round 10–5; $4.25 adults, $2 children ages 6–12, $3 seniors. (2 hours)*

★ TEMPEL LIPIZZANS
17000 Wadsworth Rd., Wadsworth, 847/623-7272

This is the only place in the United States where you can watch Lipizzan horses perform in the same manner as those at the world-famous Spanish Riding School in Vienna.

Details: *Schedule varies; $14 adults, $12 seniors, $5 children ages 4–14, under 4 free. (1½ hours)*

SHOPPING

Ask just about anyone who lives in the Chicago area where to find the best bargains, and chances are they'll tell you the **Gurnee Mills Mall**, 6170 W. Grand Ave., Gurnee, 847/263-7500 in Illinois, 800/YES-SHOP outside of the state. It offers some of the best shopping in the region, with more than a dozen major anchors, as well as scores of smaller boutique and specialty shops. A fairly new addition to the mall is **Outdoor World**, 847/856-1229—133,000 square feet of hunting, fishing, golfing, backpacking, and camping gear (including boats and RVs). There's even a three-story waterfall and an aquarium where you can test the tackle equipment.

The **downtown Libertyville** shops and the **shops at Long Grove** offer some wonderful hand-crafted items, antiques, collectibles, accessories, clothes, and jewelry, among other things. The **Lamb's Farm** gift shop, Libertyville, 847/362-4636, offers some fantastic edibles that help support the disabled men and women who live and work there.

In Lake Zurich, the **Country Sampler**, 847/726-2606, specializes in folk art, home accessories, and custom furniture.

FITNESS AND RECREATION

Lake County has certainly earned its name: Fitness and recreation in this neck of the woods usually involve water.

The **Chain O' Lakes State Park** three miles east of Spring Grove, 312/587-5512, gives campers access to some of the best fishing in Illinois. If fishing isn't your cup of tea, you can hike the park's trails or ride them on horseback. The **Dunes of Lake Michigan** in Zion, 312/662-4811, provide the backdrop for the beautiful stretch of beach known as Illinois Beach State Park. Fishing, swimming, hiking, and biking are popular here. If you aren't sure what the word bog means, The National Natural Landmark **Volo Bog**, in Ingleside, 815/344-1294, is a great living dictionary entry. The spongy sphagnum moss ground cover helps create unique combinations of plants that are constantly changing. The **Illinois Beach State Park** in Zion, 847/662-4811, presents miles of stunning views and Lake Michigan shoreline to swimmers and boaters. This is also a fantastic bird-watching spot.

Lake County also has several forest preserves, 847/367-6640, great for hiking and fishing in the summer and cross-country skiing in the winter. If you're interested in deep-water fishing you can charter a boat and head out onto Lake Michigan. The **North Point Charter Boat Association** can help you schedule outings. For information call 800/247-6727.

The golf courses in Lake County have plenty of water, making them an exciting challenge for even low-handicap golfers. **Kemper Lakes Golf Course**, 847/320-3450, in Long Grove is nationally acclaimed—and our favorite.

FOOD

Many national dining trends are big hits in Lake County, too. The Gurnee Mills Mall, 6170 W. Grand Ave., Gurnee, is home to both a **Planet Hollywood**, 847/856-1916, and a **Rainforest Cafe**, 847/855-7800. If you've never visited either of these theme dining experiences, Lake County is a great place to try them. At Planet Hollywood you'll find all kinds of movie memorabilia, including Arnold Schwarzenegger's costume from *The Terminator* and one of the Cindy Brady outfits from *The Very Brady Sequel*. At the Rainforest Cafe you'll enjoy all the sights and sounds of eating lunch in a real rain forest. For something a little different, try **Flatlander's Restaurant and Brewery**, 200 Village Green, Lincolnshire, 847/821-1234. It has reasonable prices and a big Sunday brunch with some great live entertainment. If you go to **Mickey Finn's Brewery**, 412 N. Milwaukee Ave., Libertyville, 847/362-6688, you'll want to try the famous nine-ounce "Mickey Burger" and one of the seasonal brews. The specialty at the **Seasons of Long Grove**, 314 Old McHenry Rd., 847/634-9150, is the unique "Mad Hatter" afternoon tea party. The Sunday "chocolate" brunch is just as sinful as it sounds, but well worth the calories. This restaurant hosts an eclectic mix of special events throughout the year, and the owners operate a cooking school across the street. **Quig's Orchard**, 847/566-4520, 300 S. Rte. 83 (a quarter mile west of Midlothian Rd.), Mundelein, started as an apple orchard more than 50 years ago. Today it includes a country store, greenhouse, bakery, gift shop, and Quig's, a breakfast-lunch restaurant (with dinner served Friday nights only). This place gets lots of repeat customers—who know a good meal when they taste one. The food is priced low, but the quality is high and the portions are generous.

LODGING

The bulk of rooms in the Lake County area are provided by the major chain hotels, but there are also a few great local options. The **Adventure Inn Motel**, Grand Ave., Gurnee, 800/373-5245, is actually four reasonably priced motels in one. It includes a variety of theme rooms—geared toward both families and couples, all with refrigerators, microwaves, and free HBO. The "Jail Motel" is a portion of the motel designed to look like something out of an old Western movie. The indoor pool and game room are next door.

The **Sweet Basil Hill Farm B&B**, 15937 W. Washington St., Gurnee, 847/244-3333, sits on several wooded acres and is nationally recognized as one of the most inviting, elegant retreats in the region. All baths are private.

Round-Robin Guesthouse, 231 E. Maple Ave. (Rte. 176), Mundelein, 708/566-7664, is another highly acclaimed bed-and-breakfast. It has a Victorian flavor, and parchment and quill are supplied in each room for letter writing (no Internet connections here!).

If you plan to spend much time at Illinois Beach State Park, the **Illinois Beach Resort**, 847/625-7300, is an excellent lodging choice. The rooms are elegant and spacious, and if your room doesn't have a view of Lake Michigan, that just means you're on the side with the brilliant sunsets. After a day of sightseeing, the whirlpool and the heated indoor pool are the best places to unwind.

Lake Bluff offers three small, inexpensive choices: **By The Way Motel**, 123 Skokie Hwy., 847/234-1789; **Great Lakes Motel**, Buckley Rd. and Rte. 41, 847/689-1520; and **Sunset Motel**, 511 Rockland Rd., 847/234-4669. The **Deer Path Inn**, 255 E. Illinois Rd., Lake Forest, 847/234-2280, boasts seven more rooms than those three motels combined, plus a restaurant.

CAMPING

Chain O' Lakes State Park, east of Spring Grove, 312/587-5512, has 191 campsites—ones with electric hook-ups and shower facilities nearby cost $11 a night, sites without electricity are $8. You can make reservations by calling 847/587-5512, but it will cost you an extra $5. Swimming is not allowed.

Illinois Beach State Park, in Zion, 847/662-4811, offers electricity and nearby showers for $11 and primitive sites for $8. Swimming is allowed. Both parks have wheelchair-accessible bathrooms.

PERFORMING ARTS

Ravinia Festival gets the nod again. It's romantic, fun, relaxing, and cultured. After the rest of your vacation is a fading memory, your night at Ravinia will still help you take a mental break from the pile of work on your desk.

Mariott's Lincolnshire Theatre, 10 Marriott Dr., Lincolnshire, 847/634-7030, offers a year-round schedule of popular musicals. The theater tends to cater to large groups, but small parties are welcome, too.

3
NORTHWEST ILLINOIS

The far northwest corner of Illinois has great shopping, priceless antiques, and loads of U.S. history, but the number one reason people say they come here is for the scenic beauty and topography. The area is about the only place in Illinois that doesn't show evidence of glacial activity. Instead, you'll find a breathtaking combination of sweeping valleys, rolling hills, majestic bluffs, and rugged cliffs. Long ago, glaciers, driving southward, mysteriously parted to spare this amazing scenery. Later, Native American tribes settled in this land they called "Sacred Ground." Then European miners began hauling away the region's valuable lead ore. Later, fleets of steamboats carried the goods that made this area a thriving center for commerce. During the Civil War, resident Ulysses S. Grant left Galena to serve as the military leader for Union troops.

Today the area has become a popular weekend and vacation getaway. The countryside, historic sites, restaurants, recreational activities, and shops all offer plenty to do. The people who live here take great pride in all they've done to restore their community to its glory days, and they love to entertain.

A PERFECT DAY IN NORTHWEST ILLINOIS

To enjoy Galena properly you must first put away your cell phone, turn off your beeper, and unplug your laptop. Then, take a leisurely stroll down Main Street. Visit the museums and shops, and have a casual lunch at any of the excellent restaurants listed in this chapter. In the afternoon, rent some bikes and tour the county's country roads. If you aren't too tired by nightfall, head to the Trolley Depot Theatre and catch a show.

SIGHTSEEING HIGHLIGHTS

★★★★ BELVEDERE MANSION
1008 Park Ave., Galena, 815/777-0747
What happened to those green drapes in *Gone With the Wind* that Scarlett O'Hara supposedly sewed into a dress? If you visit the Belvedere Mansion you'll find out. They grace some of the windows in this stately mansion. It's also home to several items once owned by Liberace, as well as some excellent examples of formal Victorian furnishings.
Details: Memorial Day–Oct Sun–Fri 11–4, Sat 11–5; $5 adults, $2 children ages 6–16, under age 6 free; wheelchair accessible. (½ hour)

★★★★ TROLLEY TOURS
314 S. Main St., Galena, 815/777-1248
A fun way to get the lay of the land in Galena is by using one of the town's two trolley tour services. They'll take you by all of the main attractions and help you get oriented for the rest of your visit.
Details: Brill's Trolley Tours, tours begin at 9 a.m. each day; last tour begins at 5:30 p.m. Galena Trolley Tours Depot, 314 S. Main St., tours offered on the hour beginning at 10 a.m.; also at 10:30 a.m., 12:30 p.m., and 2:30 p.m. Prices for tours vary. (1–2 hours)

★★★★ ULYSSES S. GRANT HOME STATE HISTORIC SITE
500 Bouthillier St., Galena, 815/777-3310
Although his famous tomb is nowhere near this historic site, you can feel the presence of the 18th president as soon as you step into his former home. After General Ulysses Grant accepted the surrender of the Confederacy, he headed home to Galena. When he arrived he was given this beautiful red-brick home. Tour guides here wear period clothes as they share stories of Grant, his family, and his house.
Details: Daily 9–5 except most major holidays; suggested donation $2 adults, $1 children; second floor of home is not wheelchair accessible. (½ hour)

★★★ DOWLING HOUSE
220 Diagonal St., Galena, 815/777-1250

If you're going to visit the Belvedere Mansion, a great way to round out the hour is by stopping in at the Dowling House. More than 150 years ago this became the first house ever built in Galena. The owners also operated a general store inside the house back then. Today you'll find an exquisite collection of pottery created by local artists.

Buy your tickets to Belvedere and Dowling together and save $2.50 per adult and $1 per child.

Details: *Memorial Day–Oct Sun–Fri 11–4, Sat 11–5; Apr, Nov, and Dec Fri–Sun, Jan–Mar weekends only; $3.50 adults, $1.50 children ages 6–16, under age 6 free; wheelchair accessible. (½ hour)*

★★★ GALENA CELLARS VINEYARD TASTING ROOM
4746 N. Ford Rd., Galena, 815/777-3330

If you enjoy wine, this is what you'd call a full-bodied wine experience. After touring the winery and bottling area (plus a great miniseminar on wine tasting), you can lounge on the wraparound deck that overlooks some gorgeous scenery. You'll also be invited to taste a few of the more than 20 varieties offered.

Details: *Tours Memorial Day–Oct daily 2 p.m.; $2.50 per person. Children are allowed on the tours, but will not be served wine. (1 hour)*

★★★ THE OLD MARKET HOUSE STATE HISTORIC SITE
Commerce St., Galena, 815/777-2570

When Galena was very young, this was the place to be. Today it's still a fun place to be and there's plenty to see, too. You can walk back in time and experience life as it was for the people who founded this community. If you hear about a special event in town, but you aren't sure where it is, this is the best place to start looking.

Details: *Thu–Mon 9–noon and 1–5, in winter closing is at 4 p.m.; suggested donation $2 adults, $1 children; wheelchair accessible. (1 hour)*

★★★ WARREN CHEESE PLANT
415 Jefferson St., Warren, 815/745-2627

If your kids are always asking how things are made, this is a fun place

GALENA

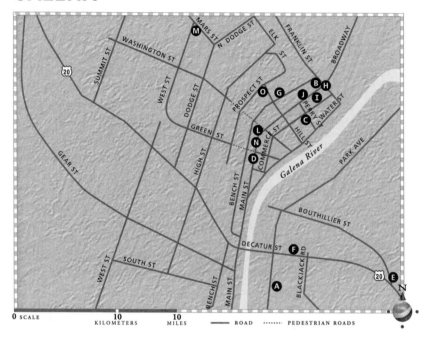

SIGHTS

- **A** Belvedere Mansion
- **B** Dowling House
- **C** The Old Market House State Historic Site
- **D** Trolley Tours
- **E** Ulysses S. Grant Home State Historic Site
- **F** Washburne House

FOOD

- **G** American Old Fashioned Ice Cream Parlor
- **D** Boone's Place
- **H** Bubba's Seafood, Pasta & Smokehouse
- **H** Café Italia
- **I** Eldorado Grill
- **J** Emmy Lou's Cafe
- **K** Grant's Place
- **J** Log Cabin
- **H** Twisted Taco Café
- **L** Vinny Vannucchi's

LODGING

- **M** Bielenda's Mars Avenue Guest House
- **N** DeSoto House Hotel
- **O** Felt Manor Guest House
- **E** Grant Hills Motel

Note: Items with the same letter are located in the same area.

to show them. You'll view the entire cheese-making process up close enough to finally figure out what Miss Muffet was eating in that poem. This is also the place that gave the world Apple Jack cheese—a blend of cheddar, Monterey Jack, and Swiss.

Details: Mon–Fri 8–4, Sat 8–12; free; wheelchair accessible. (1 hour)

★★ WASHBURNE HOUSE
908 Third St., Galena, 815/777-3310

In 1868, presidential candidates didn't have huge auditoriums where they could watch election returns on television with their supporters. Instead, most of them did what Ulysses Grant did—they got together with a few friends to wait for the news. When you step in the living room of Elihu B. Washburne's Greek Revival home, you'll be standing right where Grant was when he got the call to go to Washington.

Details: Fri–Sun 10–noon and 1–4; suggested donation $2 adults, $1 children (18 and under); first floor is wheelchair accessible. (½ hour)

★ SCALES MOUND
about 10 miles northeast of Galena

This entire town is listed as a National Register Historic District. It's also on the National Register of Historic Places. If you're heading through the area, make sure to drive through Scales Mound and enjoy its rich history. This community also contains the spot that's supposed to be the highest point in Illinois. It's on private property and is closed to the public without the owner's permission (call 815/845-2625 to request admission).

Details: (½ hour)

SPECIAL EVENTS

If you want to stay in shape while you're on vacation, you could join the competitors in the **Galena Triathlon and Duathlon** that's held in late May. The annual **June Tour of Historic Homes** doesn't move quite as quickly, but you'll get plenty of exercise walking through these beautiful homes and the **Galena/Jo Daviess County History Museum**. Everyone will enjoy the **Stagecoach Trail Festival** in late June. It includes demonstrations and activities that celebrate the area's history, with emphasis on Native Americans and Pioneers. The **Galena Arts Festival**, in mid-July, is a juried art show that features works by more than 100 artists. At **Civil War Weekend** in early August you can watch battles being fought, learn the Virginia reel, and hear an excellent Abe Lincoln clone deliver the famous Gettysburg Address.

SHOPPING

Any place with as much history as Galena is a gold mine of well-preserved, elegant antiques. A couple of places to look are: **Beneath the Dust Antiques and Refinishing**, 302 S. Main St., 815/777-3202, specializing in antique furniture and trunks; and **Colonial Antique Shop**, 1004 Park Ave., 815/777-0336, where you'll find an impressive selection of glass items and Haviland china. If you prefer one-stop shopping, try the **Galena Antique Mall**, 8201 Hwy. 20 E., 815/777-3440, with no fewer than 50 dealers selling an eclectic variety of items; or **Red's Antiques, Wholesale Barn and Flea Market**, 11658 Red Gates Rd.,

If you're an antique lover and you're planning a trip here, make sure to check the local paper, Galena Gazette, for any upcoming auctions.

815/777-9675, an enormous red barn filled with antiques and home to huge flea markets and auctions. The nearby towns of East Dubuque, Elizabeth, Hanover, Stockton, Warren, and Woodbine are worth exploring for antiques, too.

Galena is home to many talented artists. A sample of the diverse offerings of Galena galleries follows, but remember, this book isn't big enough to include more than a sampling of them. **American Eagle Galleries**, 114 S. Main St., 815/777-3504, offers bronze work, serigraphs, Civil War items, and much more. **Carl Johnson's Gallery**, 202 Main St., 815/777-1222, houses original watercolors of scenes near and far. Pottery is a big thing in Galena, and some of the coolest available is in **Galena Clay Works—Kent Henderson**, 704 Dewey Ave., 815/777-0364. **Denise Tollensdorf Art Glass Studio**, 9637 W. Buckhill Rd., 815/777-9157, has custom shades and leaded-glass windows in a rainbow of colors and a wide variety of styles.

FITNESS AND RECREATION

Apple River Canyon State Park, between Stockton and Warren, 815/745-3302, has some great hiking trails. If you'd prefer to ride, you can get a thorough workout biking the winding country roads of Galena. **Chestnut**

NORTHWEST ILLINOIS

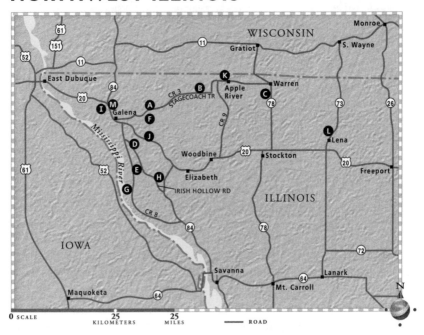

SIGHTS

- **Ⓐ** Galena Cellars Vineyard Tasting Room
- **Ⓑ** Scales Mound
- **Ⓒ** Warren Cheese Plant

FOOD

- **Ⓓ** Fried Green Tomatoes

LODGING

- **Ⓔ** Chestnut Mountain Resort
- **Ⓕ** Eagle Ridge Inn and Resort

LODGING (continued)

- **Ⓖ** Early American Settlement Log Cabin Lodging
- **Ⓗ** Inn at Irish Hollow
- **Ⓘ** Log Cabin Guest House
- **Ⓙ** Longhollow Point Inn

CAMPING

- **Ⓚ** Apple River Canyon State Park
- **Ⓛ** Lake Le-Aqua-Na State Park
- **Ⓜ** Palace Campground

Mountain Resort, 8700 W. Chestnut Rd., Galena, 800/397-1320, and **Galena Mountain Bike Rental**, 517 S. Main St., Galena, 815/777-3409, both offer mountain bike rentals by the hour or day.

Horseback riding is offered at **Shenandoah Riding Center**, The Galena Territory, 200 N. Brodrecht Rd., 815/777-2373, with one-hour guided rides.

Stagecoach rides are a favorite with kids. **Stagecoach Trails Livery**, 203 Hickory St., Apple River, 815/594-2423, even serves a chuck-wagon dinner. For a more modern diversion, the golf courses at **Eagle Ridge Inn**, the Galena Territory, Hwy. 20 E., Galena, 800/892-2269, are some of the best in the nation. For a less serious round on the links, **Li'l General Miniature Golf**, 11357 Rte. 20 W., Galena, 815/777-6911, is new, clean, and heavy on the obstacles.

Hunting, fishing, and eagle-watching are all popular here. The **Savanna District of the Upper Mississippi River National Wildlife and Fish Refuge**, 815/273-2732, is home to just about any indigenous animal you can name—and quite a few you probably can't. **Bald Eagle Bus Tours**, 815/594-2306, has a great record for making sure its customers see plenty of eagles going about their daily lives.

In winter you can ski, skate, sled, or snowmobile. **Chestnut Mountain Resort**, 8700 W. Chestnut Rd., Galena, 800/397-1320, offers great downhill and cross-country skiing for folks of all abilities. Eagle Ridge Inn, Hwy. 20 E., Galena, 800/892-2269, has miles and miles of well-groomed trails, plus a fantastic sledding hill and an ice rink. Several companies offer hayrack, sleigh, and bobsled rides. Call the **Galena—JoDaviess County Convention and Visitors Bureau** at 800/747-9377 for more information.

FOOD

If you get lost in Galena, just head to Main Street—at least that way you won't starve. This town—and the surrounding area—is filled with a variety of foods with one theme in common: They're all wonderful.

The **American Old Fashioned Ice Cream Parlor**, 102 N. Main St., Galena, 815/777-3121, is a 150-year-old soda fountain that is a perfect place to cool off while you're touring downtown. Another circa 1846 building hosts **Boone's Place** at 305 S. Main St. in Galena, 815/777-4488. It features excellent, inexpensive home-cooking for breakfast, lunch, or dinner. The French dip is a favorite of meat eaters, while vegetarians enjoy the stuffed potatoes. **Bubba's Seafood, Pasta & Smokehouse**, 300 N. Main St., Galena, 815/777-8030, will empty your wallet a little faster, but it's so good, you won't mind. The ribs are a hickory-smoked feast! **Café Italia** and **Twisted Taco Café** at 301 N. Main St. in Galena, 815/777-0033, are two restaurants in one. That means plenty of choices, ranging from Italian and American to Mexican—all at reasonable prices. At the **Eldorado Grill**, 219 N. Main St., Galena, 815/777-1224, the gourmet meals are complimented with some to-die-for sauces and an extensive wine list. It's a little pricey, but very chic. Everyone loves breakfast at **Emmy Lou's Cafe**, 200 N. Main St., Galena, 815/777-4732. If you stick around for lunch or dinner, you'll want to try the homemade pies or strawberry shortcake. No, **Fried Green Tomatoes**, 1301 N. Irish Hollow Rd., Galena, 815/777-3938, Web site: www.friedgreen.com, isn't a greasy-spoon diner. It's an upscale eatery in an old brick farmstead that used to be the area's poorhouse. While you're dining on some exquisite pasta or steaks (or signature tomatoes), look around and see if you can find the marks from the old cells that housed the poor and criminally insane. For extra credit, be the first in your group to find the remnants of the shackles used to restrain inmates.

At **Grant's Place**, 515 S. Main St., Galena, 815/777-3331, you can enjoy some gourmet sandwiches while rehashing the war between the states. The Civil War–themed decorations here will certainly put you in the mood.

The **Log Cabin**, 201 N. Main St., Galena, 815/777-0393, offers arguably the best Greek food in northwest Illinois. Make sure to order the flaming *saganaki* and the shish kebab.

Vinny Vannucchi's, 201 S. Main St., Galena, 815/777-8100, is an affordable Italian restaurant that also features good seafood, salads, and even hamburgers.

LODGING

Bed-and-breakfasts are king here, but there are many other options. This is just a small sampling of the best. Bed-and-breakfasts are first, followed by resorts, hotels, and motels.

Bielenda's Mars Avenue Guest House, 515 Mars Ave., Galena, 815/777-2808, Web site: homepage.interaccess.com/~marsbb, features one elegant suite and two comfortable guest rooms, plus bikes, nightly desserts, and a great porch swing. **Early American Settlement Log Cabin Lodging**, Blackjack and Hart John Rds., Galena, 800/366-LOGS, features a dozen handmade log cabins that look rustic outside, but feature plush rooms with a full compliment of modern conveniences inside. This 78-acre property is near a wide variety of outdoor activities. **Felt Manor Guest House**, 125 S. Prospect St., Galena, 800/383-2830, offers some great weekend and midweek packages, and serves an elegant afternoon tea buffet several times a week. Take a virtual tour at www.feltmanor.com. The **Inn at Irish Hollow**, 2800 S. Irish Hollow Rd., Galena, 815/777-6000, is attached to a general store and a shopkeeper's house. Request the French Maid's Cottage and ask them to deliver your breakfast in the morning. If you're stressed out, reserve the "Five Steps to Stress Relief" package at the **Log Cabin Guest House**, Chetlain Ln., Galena, 815/777-2043. You'll be pampered with wine, cheese, fruit, candlelight, soft music, massage oils, a whirlpool bath, and a gourmet champagne dinner.

Chestnut Mountain Resort, 8700 W. Chestnut Mountain Rd., Galena, 800/397-1320, is a luxury resort in the truest sense of the word. In the countryside near Galena, visitors here can swim, ride bikes, play games, and—in winter—ski. At **Eagle Ridge Inn and Resort**, Hwy. 20 E., Galena, 800/892-2269, Web site: www.eagleridge.com, you can choose a beautifully appointed room, a villa, or a home. There are all sorts of activities, including golfing, boating, and horseback riding, plus some good shopping on-site.

The **DeSoto House Hotel**, 230 S. Main St., Galena, 800/343-6562, Web site: www.galenalink.com/desoto, is located in the middle of some of the best Galena sights. Actually, it's a sight in its own right. Listed on the National Register of Historic Places, the DeSoto was built in 1855 and has managed to keep up with the changing expectations of travelers since then. **Longhollow Point Inn**, 5129 Longhollow Rd., Galena, 800/551-5129, has great suites. It also has some very affordable rooms, all of which come with kitchenettes, private decks, and fireplaces.

Grant Hills Motel, Hwy. 20 E., Galena, 815/777-2116, was recently refurbished. Guests at this mid-range motel enjoy a heated pool, a wonderful view, and the adjacent antique auto museum.

CAMPING

Campers in the Galena area have their choice of both primitive and modern campsites. **Apple River Canyon State Park**, 8763 E. Canyon Rd., 815/745-3302, has great hiking and is just $7 per family. **Palace Campground**, 11357 Hwy. 20 W., Galena, 815/777-2466 ($25 full hook-up, $23 electric and water hook-up, $21 electric only, $18 tent sites), has everything from a heated pool and movies to miniature golf and a game room. **Lake Le-Aqua-Na State Park**, 8542 N. Lake Rd., near Lena, 815/369-4282, has 170 campsites near all sorts of outdoor activities.

PERFORMING ARTS

The days in Galena are so full, it's tempting to spend the evening lounging on a deck, watching the scenery. But if you can summon the energy to freshen up and head out for the evening, you'll be glad you did.

An Evening with General Grant is a one-man show performed by W. Paul LeGreco at different venues in Galena several times each year. To see whether he'll be performing while you're here, call 815/777-0383 or visit his

Web site at users.mwci.net/~legrecotoys. Another great local show features Mrs. Grant. It's called **The General's Lady** and is performed by Lucy Miele. For information, call 800/343-6562. The **Galena Trolley Depot Theatre**, 314 S. Main St., Galena, 815/777-1248, is the best place to see Emmy and Grammy Awards nominee Jim Post perform his one-man concerts. Shows are scheduled for Wednesday through Sunday.

Great River Road

If you have a lot of time on your hands, you can follow the Mississippi River from its origin in Minnesota to Louisiana, where it empties into the Gulf of Mexico. But if you'd just like to catch some of the prettiest parts of it, drive the Great River Road from Galena to Alton. This scenic route takes you near several state parks, locks and dams, and—at times—almost close enough to the river to cast a fishing line out the passenger-side window. You'll also travel through the Quad Cities (see Chapter 4), Navoo, Quincy, and Hannibal, Missouri. Navoo's claim to fame is that it was the home of **Joseph Smith**—the founder of the Church of Jesus Christ of Latter Day Saints. In Quincy you can visit the **Lincoln Douglas Valentine Museum**, 101 N. Fourth Street, 217/224-3355, with a great collection of old love messages. The museum is open by appointment only, and admission is free. And in Hannibal, you can see the place that inspired some of Mark Twain's best work.

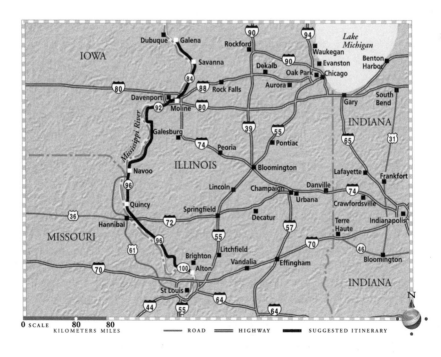

4
THE QUAD CITIES

The Quad Cities can be thought of as Rock Island and Moline, Illinois, and Bettendorf and Davenport, Iowa—four cities in two states sharing the Mississippi River as a common border. In reality, though, there are about a dozen cities and towns that make up this major metropolitan area straddling the Big Daddy of all American rivers. Ask locals what they like about the area, and the most common answer will be "small-town feel with big-city benefits." Davenport teems with nearly 100,000 people to anchor the population centers. The towns on the Illinois side maintain a feeling of intimacy. In both Moline and Rock Island you can easily park and walk to many sights, shops, and eateries.

The area is well known for its riverboat gaming, with three large boats that draw visitors from all over the Midwest. But non-gamblers will find boats for pleasure cruising (an overnight trip), often including an elegant dinner.

Travelers who like a little history with their fun will find terrific sites that memorialize one of the greatest Native American leaders to never become a chief, Black Hawk, who led fellow British sympathizers against the upstart Americans in the War of 1812 and in the Black Hawk War of 1832.

Beautiful new businesses along the riverfront retain the flavor of the old industrial buildings they now occupy, and new attractions and lodgings are nearby as well. Interstates 80, 74, and 88 all run through the Quad Cities, and the hills surrounding the Mississippi and Rock Rivers provide great scenery along the way.

A PERFECT DAY IN THE QUAD CITIES

Start at the brand-new John Deere Pavilion for an amazing walk through America's farming history, then walk two blocks south to buy handmade candies from Lagomarcino's. Stay on your feet with a short walk to Finney's for lunch, then take your pick between two great Rock Island sites for the afternoon: nature and history at the Black Hawk State Historic Site, or indoor beauty at the new Quad Cities Botanical Center. Another short drive puts you in Davenport in time for shopping in the boutiques of East Davenport and dinner at the Dock where you can leave your car during a fun evening on the boats.

SIGHTSEEING HIGHLIGHTS

★★★★ CIRCA '21
1828 Third Ave., Rock Island, Illinois; 309/786-7733
This dinner playhouse lives in the Fort Armstrong Theatre. As you might guess, it was built in 1921, and began as a vaudeville and silent movie venue. The restored theater is breathtaking, and was given a spot on the National Register of Historic Places in 1978. Ticket prices for dinner and a Broadway show are reasonable (in the $30 range), but even if you don't have the time for a show, stopping to see this ornate building is worth it.

> **Details:** *Wed matinee, Wed–Sun evening shows; wheelchair accessible. (1–3 hours)*

★★★★ JOHN DEERE PAVILION
15th St. and River Dr., Moline, Illinois; 800/747-7800
Sounds like a glorified shed with a riding mower in it, doesn't it? But this magnificent new museum and welcome center offers much more than just tractors. True, you will see everything from the earliest Deere models to huge new earthmovers parked inside and outside the brick and glass building. But this museum promises a broad look at the history of the American farmer. We saw a four-year-old boy running ahead of his family to get

Plan to spend a few bucks on genuine John Deere merchandise. By the time you get through here, everyone in the family will want to wear the green and gold!

THE QUAD CITIES

KILOMETERS   MILES   — ROAD   — HIGHWAY   ✦ PLACE OF INTEREST

SCALE

La Claire
Rapids City
Hampton
Campbell's Island
Riverdale
Bettendorf
East Moline
Silvis
Carbon Cliff
Colona

Niabi Zoo
Coal Valley
Quad-City Airport

Rock Island Co. Fairgrounds
Moline

Davenport
Rock Island
Milan

Credit Island
South Park Mall

Marycrest International University
Mississippi Valley Fairgrounds

Mississippi River

DEVIL'S GLEN RD
MIDDLE RD
STATE ST
SPRUCE HILLS DR
CENTRAL
4TH AVE
12TH AVE
30TH AVE
42ND AVE
KENNEDY DR
COLONA RD
JOHN DEERE RD
23RD AVE
7TH ST
38TH ST
18TH AVE
14TH AVE
24TH ST
31ST AVE
17TH ST
11TH ST
5TH AVE
BLACKHAWK RD
AIRPORT RD
MILAN PKWY
78TH AVE
HARRISON ST
BRADY ST
2ND ST
RIVER RD
DIVISION ST
LOCUST ST
KIMBERLY RD
NORTHWEST BLVD
ROCKINGHAM RD

To I U
A B C D E F G H J K L M N O P Q R S T

his first glimpse of the man-sized toys, and we realized why the Pavilion has quickly become such a draw for families: The building is huge, the machines are awesome, and the entire exhibition hall is interactive. Whom do you suppose was harder to convince it was time to go, the four-year-old boy or his dad?

Details: Mon–Fri 9:30–7, Sat 9:30–5, Sun 12:30–5; free; wheelchair accessible. (2 hours)

★★★★ **PUTNAM MUSEUM**
1717 W. 12th St., Davenport, Iowa; 319/324-1933

Of the many museums in the Quad Cities, locals are perhaps most proud of the Putnam Museum in Davenport. This is a history and natural science museum that has won awards for its display tracing the area's residents, from Native Americans to baby boomers. Other galleries cover animals, Asian and Egyptian cultures, and a hands-on discovery room. An amazing variety of temporary displays can be found in this beautiful, modern building.

Details: Tue–Fri 9–5, Sat 10–5, Sun noon–5; $4

The Putnam Museum is next door to the Davenport Museum of Art, also a wonderful sight. Plan to hit them both, but only if you have plenty of time and strong legs.

SIGHTS

- Ⓐ Black Hawk State Historic Site
- Ⓑ Casino Rock Island
- Ⓑ Circa '21
- Ⓒ Family Museum of Arts and Sciences
- Ⓓ John Deere Pavilion
- Ⓔ Lady Luck
- Ⓕ The President
- Ⓖ Putnam Museum
- Ⓗ Rock Island Arsenal
- Ⓘ Walnut Grove Pioneer Village

FOOD

- Ⓙ C'est Michele
- Ⓚ The Dock
- Ⓓ Finney's
- Ⓛ Iowa Machine Shed
- Ⓜ Lagomarcino's
- Ⓝ Sydney's
- Ⓞ Thunder Bay Grill

LODGING

- Ⓟ Abbey Hotel
- Ⓠ Fulton's Landing Guest House

LODGING (continued)

- Ⓡ Jumer's Castle Lodge
- Ⓢ Potter House
- Ⓓ Radisson on John Deere Commons
- Ⓢ Victorian Inn

CAMPING

- Ⓣ Illiniwek Forest Preserve
- Ⓤ Scott County Park

Note: Items with the same letter are located in the same area.

adults, $3 seniors, $2 ages 17 and under; wheelchair accessible. (2 hours)

★★★★ **ROCK ISLAND ARSENAL**
Access the island from 14th St. in Moline or State Rd. 92 in Rock Island, Illinois; 309/782-5021
If America should ever need a reminder of what a brutal civil war it fought in the middle of the 19th century, this would be one place to visit. This arsenal, built on a large Mississippi River island, was once a notorious prisoner-of-war camp. Two thousand Southern soldiers fill the Confederate Cemetery; 13,000 fill the National Cemetery. There's much more packed onto this three-mile-long island: the historic block house, a museum that includes one of the largest collections of small arms in the country, and the Davenport House (on the National Register of Historic Places).
Details: Arsenal daily 8–7, museum 10–4; most sites free; wheelchair accessible. (2 hours)

★★★ **BLACK HAWK STATE HISTORIC SITE**
Park office is at 1510 46th Ave. (Rte. 5 or Black Hawk Rd.), Rock Island, Illinois; 309/788- 9536
This 208-acre wooded preserve overlooks the Rock River. It tells the tale of Indians and settlers who struggled to live and who, at times, struggled against each other. The Hauberg Indian Museum is housed in a stone lodge built by the Civilian Conservation Corps during the 1930s, and features artifacts and realistic dioramas of summer and winter Sauk dwellings. Stretch your legs on miles of hiking trails (medium difficulty) and try to get a look at the pioneer cemetery that occupies the northwest corner of the site. Most of the headstones are broken, but it's still neat to see.
Details: Year-round daily sunrise–10 p.m.; no camping; donations are accepted for the museum, but everything else is free; wheelchair accessible. (1–2 hours)

★★★ **FAMILY MUSEUM OF ARTS AND SCIENCES**
900 Learning Center Dr. (near 18th St. and Spruce Hills Dr.), Bettendorf, Iowa; 319/344-4155
If you have kids, this is a "must visit." Locals say their children want to go back repeatedly, and your boys and girls will think this place is a blast! You'll get a break from chanting the parent's mantra ("don't

touch"), since everything is hands-on. The best part is, they'll be learning while they play. There's too much adventure to list, but our favorite is the giant tree where kids become squirrels as they crawl through holes to check out the rabbit and raccoon homes.

Details: Mon–Thu 9–8, Fri–Sat 9–5, Sun noon–5; $3 adults and children, $2 seniors; wheelchair accessible. (2 hours)

★★★ **WALNUT GROVE PIONEER VILLAGE**
Northeast of Davenport, Iowa; 319/285-9903
Operated as part of Scott County Park, this recreated nineteenth-century village features 18 historic buildings, including two log cabins, a small house full of antiques, a bank, a general store, a blacksmith shop, a saloon, and an ice-cream shop where sweaty visitors can cool off with treats. On our visit we heard an older woman say, "This is really neat," and a 10-year-old boy say, "This is really cool." They may have different ways of expressing it, but everyone finds it fascinating.

Details: Take Rte. 61 north out of Davenport to the Long Grove exit, then head east and follow the signs to Scott County Park on Saint Anne's Rd.; Apr–Oct daily 8 a.m.–sundown; donations accepted; there are ramps, but people in wheelchairs may have a hard time maneuvering around this site. (1 hour)

RIVERBOAT GAMING SIGHTSEEING HIGHLIGHTS

The Quad Cities are home to three large gambling boats, and many people visit just to take their chances on "the boats."

★★★ *CASINO ROCK ISLAND*
17th St. and the Riverfront, Rock Island, Illinois;
800/477-7747
Associated with Jumer's Hotel chain, this boat is much like the hotels—splendid in its craftsmanship. There are two lounges on three decks, free hors d'oeuvres, and $1 alcoholic beverages. This is the gaming boat that strikes us as the most "riverboatie" looking, with it's upholstered chairs and green, red, and purple interior color scheme. It's the boat most likely to make you feel as though you've stepped back in time.

Details: Boarding 9 a.m.–1 a.m. Wheelchair accessible. (4 hours)

★★ LADY LUCK
18th St. and the Riverfront, Bettendorf, Iowa; 800/724-5825

The newest boat on the Quad Cities riverfront, the *Lady Luck* offers the most gambling opportunities with more than 40 table games plus slot, video poker, and keno machines *everywhere*. Again, a nice buffet is provided, and hometown football hero Roger Craig has a sports bar on the second deck. The *Lady Luck* also offers a nonsmoking section.

Details: *Open 24 hours. Call ahead if you want to cruise; schedules depend on weather. Wheelchair accessible. (4 hours)*

★ THE PRESIDENT
Rte. 61 and Rte. 67 on River Dr., Davenport, Iowa; 800/262-8711

The biggest of all three boats (its unimaginative nickname is "The Big One"), at nearly 300 feet long and five decks tall. With 776 slot machines on board, you probably won't have to wait in line to start dumping nickels.

Details: *Open 24 hours. Wheelchair accessible. (4 hours)*

SHOPPING

With three major malls in the Quad Cities, you won't have any trouble finding the stores you like to shop back home. **Northpark Mall**, 310 W. Kimberly Rd., 319/391-4500, in Davenport is the largest mall in all of Iowa. It has a mini–roller coaster and a three-story children's play area that's made entirely of foam rubber. **Southpark Mall**, 4500 16th St., Moline, 309/797-9070, has a similar distinction. It's the largest Illinois mall outside the Chicago metropolitan area. **Duck Creek Plaza**, 852 Middle Rd., Bettendorf, 319/359-0303, isn't as big as the other two, but does have nice anchors (Talbots and Von Maur among them) and a good variety of specialty shops.

For a unique shopping experience (the kind we enjoy more when traveling) the place to go is the **Village of East Davenport**. This historic district has been a mercantile center for 150 years, and has the kind of nifty shops that seem to hold the best gifts for folks back home. One place not to miss in the East Village (as it's known locally) is **Isabel Bloom**, at 736 Federal Street. The handmade sculptures here are known around the world. The village encompasses six square blocks just off the riverfront at Mound Street. Call the central phone number, 319/322-0546, for information about the village.

Our favorite place to antique shop is **Riverbend Antiques**, 425 Brady St.,

Davenport, 319/323-8622—seven historic buildings that have been transformed into an antiquing neighborhood. The buildings are interesting, too.

FITNESS AND RECREATION

If you are visiting the Quad Cities, the best way to stay fit is by walking, running, bicycling or in-line skating the **Great River Trail**. You'll see wonderful scenery, the breeze down the river will keep you cool, and you'll locate many of the sights you will want to visit.

On the Illinois side of the river, the **Walk** stretches for about 10 miles, and on the Iowa side it runs for about six miles. It winds through parks, providing shady rest spots with a fantastic view of the river. If you want to continue your trek on the opposite bank, the **Channel Cat River Taxi**, 309/788-3360, will take you and your bike across and back again. For bike rentals try **Jerry & Sparky's Bicycle Shop**, 1819 E. Locust, Davenport, 319/324-0270.

If golf is your favorite form of exercise, you've come to the right place. The Quad Cities boast 20 public golf courses, ranging from relatively flat to some very hilly, challenging courses. The local visitor's centers can provide a list, but some of our favorites are **Glynn's Creek**, next to Scott County Park north of Bettendorf, 319/285-6444; and **Highland Springs**, Rock Island, 309/787-5814. Glynn's Creek is long, narrow, and challenging. Highland Springs will be more forgiving with your slice is but is also challenging.

Of course, the **Mississippi River** is a main source of recreation, and folks who like to fish will have opportunities to haul in some of the ugliest catfish in the world. Your best bet for fishing is to hang out with the locals along the Davenport bank just below the spillway near the President Casino.

FOOD

Let's not beat around the bush: The best place to eat in the Quad Cities is **Finney's**, 1510 River Dr., 309/797-1234. This casual, moderately priced restaurant is among the restored industrial buildings on Moline's new Riverfront, just about a block from the John Deere Pavilion. Tons of wood and exposed brick walls set the atmosphere. Original ceiling fans throughout the building all run on a single small motor, connected by long leather straps. They make their own potato chips, serve creamy draft root beer from a tapper at the bar, and make the best Reuben sandwich ever. This isn't fine dining, but it's a treat.

Another favorite, serving great steaks as well as some oddities like emu, kangaroo, and alligator, is **Sydney's**, 425 15th St., Moline, 309/736-2252. It's in the same part of town as Finney's, but might make a fine dinner choice with good prices for very nice dining. For white-tablecloth, fine French dining go to **C'est Michele**, 1405 Fifth Ave., Moline, 309/762-0585. They have three floors of dining, including a balcony that overlooks the first-floor dining area, and parking is easy. More fine dining, but on the other side of the river, can be found at **The Dock**, 125 S. Perry St. at River Dr., Davenport, 319/322-5331, overlooking the Mississippi River.

Local family-dining favorites include the **Iowa Machine Shed**, 7250 Northwest Blvd., Davenport, 319/391-2427, with country cookin' served family style; and **Thunder Bay Grill**, 6511 N. Brady St., Davenport, 319/386-2722, will make you feel like you sat down to eat in a Northwoods lodge. Neither are economical.

Finally, you must not leave the Quad Cities without visiting **Lagomarcino's**, 1422 Fifth Ave., Moline, 309/764-1814. This 90-year-old confectionery is still family run, with the second, third, and fourth generations all currently taking a hand in the business. They have fantastic ice cream, a little lunch counter, and the best chocolates in town.

LODGING

If you want to stay near **Moline's** spiffy new riverfront attractions, the **Radisson on John Deere Commons**, 1415 River Dr., Moline, 309/764-1000, is a great choice at a moderate fare. The hotel is brand new and the riverside location is great. It's next door to the MARK, home to top concert acts and the Quad Cities' semi-pro basketball and hockey teams, and across the street from the John Deere Pavilion.

Jumer's Hotel is absolutely four-star all the way. Jumer's has a small chain of hotels in the Midwest, each with a European feel. But this original **Jumer's Castle Lodge**, I-74 and Spruce Hills Dr. in Bettendorf, 800/285-8637, is the flagship. You'll pay for the beautiful decor, fantastic dining, indoor and outdoor swimming pools, and putting green, but if you're ready to treat yourself to fantastic lodgings, this has to be the place.

Around 1917, the Sisters of Our Lady of Mount Carmel moved into a beautiful monastery overlooking the Bettendorf riverfront. Today the monastery has been converted into the **Abbey Hotel**, 1401 Central Ave., Bettendorf, 800/438-7535. You'll see it on the bluff just after crossing the I-74 bridge into Iowa. One of the tiny "cells" the sisters occupied was restored as a kind of museum view of the simplest life and surroundings (including straw-mattress beds). The Abbey feels prayerful and restive and is moderately priced for such deluxe accommodations.

For travelers on a budget, the chain hotels are the best bet. But you can also find great prices, and a unique stay, at one of the Quad Cities many bed-and-breakfasts. The **Potter House**, 1906 Seventh Ave., Rock Island, 309/788-1906, has a great solarium and two baby grand pianos in the common areas. Consider **Fulton's Landing Guest House**, 1206 E. River Dr., Davenport, 319/322-4069, for its terrific location on the Iowa riverfront near the East Village. **Victorian Inn**, 702 20th St., Rock Island, 309/788-7068, has been in the family for more than 50 years. All are good values at $65 to $85 per night.

CAMPING

There are limited camping opportunities in the Quad Cities area, but these two sites offer nice accommodations. **Scott County Park** near Long Grove in northern Scott County, 319/285-9656, is a nice place to camp, has an Olympic-size pool, and is close to Glynn's Creek golf course and the Walnut Grove Pioneer Village. **Illiniwek Forest Preserve**, along Rte. 84 on the northeast side of the Quad Cities, 309/496-2620, is another county-run park with good camping spots and plenty of woods.

NIGHTLIFE

Many visitors will want no other nightlife besides the riverboat casinos (see details above), but there are many other things to do. A great comedy club called **The Speakeasy**, 1828 Third Ave., Rock Island, 309/786-7733, is home to the group Comedy Sportz. Call first as they're often sold out.

For the fan of beers 'n' bands, the popular destination is **The District** in Rock Island. Second Avenue has been blocked off to form a plaza between 17th and 19th Streets, and there are several worthy nightclubs here. Very good regional bands, and even some bigger names play the **Rock Island Brewing Company**, 309/793-1999. RIB-CO, as it's known, sells bar food, but if you want to eat, the food is much better at the **Blue Cat Brew Club**, 309/788-8247, where they brew their own tasty beers. **Chantilly Lace**, 309/793-4088, is a popular dance club that draws a lot of college kids.

PERFORMING ARTS

Make sure to check the schedule of **The MARK of the Quad Cities**, 309/764-2001, a 12,000-seat arena across the street from the John Deere Pavilion that attracts the very best music groups in the country. The **Circa '21** dinner playhouse, 1828 Third Ave., Rock Island, 309/786-7733, is a treat with its professional actors and Broadway shows.

5
ALTON AREA

"This is a real river town." You'll hear that often around Alton, and the longer you stay, the more you'll realize how true it is. The Mississippi River is the dominant life force of the area, and you wouldn't be wrong in saying that the Mississippi gave birth to this town.

At one time, Alton was a major commerce center, and even raced against St. Louis to become the big city in the area. Obviously, St. Louis won, but Alton won, too. Alton remained a charming city that holds tight to its history—a "real river town" from the days when that phrase meant visitors from all over, thriving businesses, and riverboat captains who were wealthy and popular.

Alton and her surrounding towns are building a terrific tourism industry based on the area's history. In 1673 Pere Marquette and Louis Joliet were the first white men to explore the area for the French as they tried to find out if the Mississippi led to the sea. In the area of Alton they saw the legendary painting of the Piasa (PIE-uh-saw) bird on the cliffs. This area is still known as Piasa Country, even though the original Native American painting faded from view not long after Marquette and Joliet saw it, and despite the fact that no one believes in the man-eating bird anymore.

It was just south of Alton, where the city of Wood River now sits, that Lewis and Clark established a winter training camp in 1803 before striking out on their historic, heroic exploration of the Great Northwest.

Illinois' first penitentiary was built in Alton (part of it still stands), and after being closed for its terrific filth, it reopened as a prison for captured Confederate soldiers during the Civil War. Abraham Lincoln held his final debate against Stephen Douglas here in 1858, reportedly winning the debate handily, but losing the race for United States Senate.

Alton was a key stop in the underground railroad. Its location just across the river from slave-holding Missouri was a strong enticement for some to run here, and once they arrived (usually under cover of darkness) there were several good hiding places. The abolitionist sentiment here was also the spark for what would become Alton's greatest tragedy: the murder of First Amendment hero Elijah P. Lovejoy.

The area is also known for more recent events, as in 1993, when awesome floodwaters did untold damage to Alton and her neighbors. You'll see several places around town where high water marks are proudly highlighted.

A PERFECT DAY IN THE ALTON AREA

Start with a visit to Pere Marquette State Park to see the fantastic lodge and bluff-top views, or for a challenging hike. Drive down the scenic Great River Road to the tiny town of Elsah where not just buildings, but the entire town is on the National Register of Historic Places. Stay on the River Road and head into Alton. You can see several of the historic spots here in the afternoon and still have time for the antiquing district. At night, try your hand (or at least the hand you're dealt) on the *Alton Belle* Riverboat Casino.

SIGHTSEEING HIGHLIGHTS

★★★★ ALTON MONUMENTS

There are three must-see monuments in Alton. The town has recently built a reproduction of the Lincoln-Douglas debates held here in 1858. The brick **Lincoln-Douglas Square**, Landmarks Road and Broadway, sits along the riverfront near the *Alton Belle* Riverboat Casino, where the town hall used to be before it was destroyed by fire.

The **Lovejoy Monument** seems to tower above the city as you approach it on Monument and Fourth Streets in the Alton City Cemetery. It's 93 feet tall, and sits just in front of freedom-of-the-press martyr Elijah Lovejoy's final resting place.

This may seem cheesy, but anyone visiting Alton should see the **World's Tallest Man Statue**. The people of Alton loved Robert

ALTON

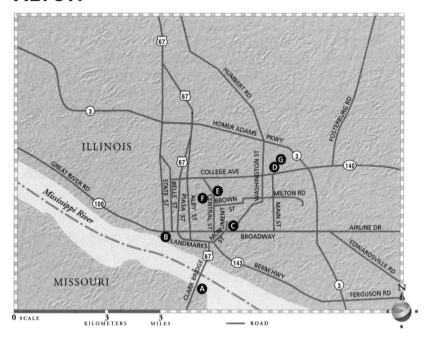

SIGHTS
Ⓐ Clark Bridge
Ⓑ Lincoln-Douglas Square
Ⓒ Lovejoy Monument
Ⓓ World's Tallest Man Statue

FOOD
Ⓔ Cane Bottom/My Just Desserts
Ⓓ Marie's Kitchen
Ⓔ Midtown Restaurant and Lounge

LODGING
Ⓕ Beall Mansion
Ⓑ Franklin House
Ⓖ Jackson House

Note: Items with the same letter are located in the same area.

Wadlow, a shy and friendly man who grew to 8 feet, 11.1 inches tall before dying prematurely at age 22. Because of his freakish size, Wadlow became something of a traveling goodwill ambassador for the community. When he died in 1940 all the town's businesses closed. Now, almost 60 years later, people still speak fondly of him. His statue, located in a park along College Avenue (Route 140) just

---

east of Main Street, will show you just how big he was, and how much people thought of him.

Details: *Free; wheelchair accessible. (15 minutes per statue)*

★★★★ **CAHOKIA MOUNDS STATE HISTORIC DISTRICT**
West of Collinsville, Illinois, on Collinsville Rd., off I-55/70 take Exit 6 to Illinois Rte. 111; 618/346-5160

This historic Indian city located near Collinsville, Illinois, has joined such internationally renowned sites as the Pyramids of Egypt, the Taj Mahal in India, and the Great Wall of China on the list of United Nations World Heritage Sites. It preserves the remains of the largest Indian city north of Mexico, and tells the story of a people who enjoyed an amazingly cosmopolitan life before the city and its people faded away around 1300 A.D. An entertaining Interpretive Center completed in 1989 explains what function was served by the many mounds built here and throughout the area.

Details: *Daily 8 a.m.–dusk; Interpretive Center open daily 9–5; suggested donation $2 adults, $1 children ages 12 and under; wheelchair accessible. (2 hours)*

★★★★ **NATIONAL SHRINE OF OUR LADY OF THE SNOWS**
442 South De Mazenod Dr., Belleville, 618/397-6700

A short drive from Alton near the city of Belleville, Illinois, is a peaceful, pastoral site that will be appreciated by people of all faiths. The National Shrine of Our Lady of the Snows was established in 1958 in a large, wooded, park-like setting. Plan to spend a few hours here, since you'll want to see the gardens with their reflecting pools, the outdoor alter and amphitheater, the church, the Lourdes Grotto, and a new piece of art meant to celebrate the 2000th anniversary of Jesus' life—called the Millennium Spire. Included on the grounds are a motel, a nice restaurant, and a children's playground, so you don't need to limit your stay to a single day. Information on daily programs and events can be found at the Shrine's Web site, www.oblatesusa.org.

Details: *Open daily including holidays; free; wheelchair accessible. (3 hours)*

★★★ **EAGLE WATCHING**

Thanks to tough laws that make it a felony to harm a bald eagle, the species has recovered with strong numbers. Thanks to the terrain, food supply, and winter climate at the confluence of the Illinois and

Call around to favorite hotels or bed-and-breakfasts in the area and ask about eagle packages. Since the birds don't come in the busy tourist season, there are good buys to be had on rooms, and the package may include bus tours and other goodies.

Mississippi Rivers, the Alton area is a fantastic place to watch bald eagles. Look for the white head and tail of the adult bird, and their huge eight-foot wingspan. Eagle season begins in December, but January is the best month to spot them.

Details: *Among the great places to eagle-watch are the Melvin Price locks and dam (just southeast of Alton near Wood River), across the Clark Bridge (on Ellis Island at the Ellis Bay Waterfowl Refuge), or just about anywhere along the Great River Rd. between Alton and Pere Marquette State Park. (2 hours)*

★★★ PERE MARQUETTE STATE PARK
Rte. 100 (the Great River Rd.) northwest of Grafton, 618/786-2331

This park encompasses 8,000 acres of rolling bluffs and natural beauty along the Mississippi River. The scenic overlooks are awesome, the hiking is challenging, and the accommodations are large and moderately priced. The Pere Marquette Lodge and Conference Center was built in the 1930s by the Civilian Conservation Corps. Recently renovated, the lodge is a beautiful site to visit, but can also be a wonderful vacation spot on its own. There are stables, a giant chess board that requires full-body participation, and indoor swimming.

Details: *Free; wheelchair accessible. (2 hours)*

★★ CLARK BRIDGE
Alton

Don't get us wrong, we're not engineer-wannabes, but this is one beautiful bridge. Completed in 1994, this cable-stay bridge is unique in the United States, and it is said to be earthquake resistant. From a distance, it looks like sails on boats.

Details: *Remember to watch the road occasionally when you cross it. You'll be tempted to look up. (1 hour)*

★ WORLD'S LARGEST CATSUP BOTTLE
800 S. Morrison Ave. (Hwy. 159), Collinsville, 618/345-5598

This is the kind of thing you want to see on your vacation, but you don't want anyone to know you actually drove any great distance to see it. So, while you're in Collinsville to see the highly educational Cahokia Mounds anyway . . . . This giant Brooks Catsup Bottle/water tower was constructed in 1949, and it looks like 1949 roadside art should look. It was restored in 1995, but we're not sure why.

Details: Free. *(1–4 minutes, depending on how long it takes your Dad to focus the camera)*

SHOPPING

The **Alton Antique District** covers a large area, roughly between Fourth Street and the Riverfront and between State Street and Monument Avenue. The heaviest concentration of stores is along Broadway (same as Route 140 and the Great River Road). It's a fairly concentrated area, so it should be easy to cover a lot of stores in a single day or afternoon. If you hit only the antique and specialty stores along or just off Broadway, you'll find more then a dozen. If your time is really tight, try the **Mineral Springs Mall**, 301 E. Broadway, where you'll find nine nice antiques shops under a single roof. Most of the shops in Alton's antique district keep the same tourist-friendly hours: Wednesday through Sunday from 11 a.m. to 5 p.m. Stop at the Convention and Visitors Bureau, Broadway and Piasa, 618/465-6676, for a guide to the shops if you don't want to miss any.

Grafton also has a few antiques shops easily spotted along Main Street. Be sure to check out **Mosby Woodworking** at 15 E. Main St., Grafton, 618/786-2223, for terrific handmade wood furniture and decorative items. The shop is known locally for its fine craftsmanship.

Finally, take a little drive out to **Eckert Orchard**, 618/786-3445, for apple products and a little rowdy, rural fun for the kids. They've got a petting zoo and playgrounds for the kids, and if you go in the winter you can cut a fresh Christmas tree. Take the Great River Road into Grafton, turn right onto Route 3, then take a left on Otterville Road.

FITNESS AND RECREATION

The single greatest source of recreation in the area is the mighty **Mississippi River**. You can boat, Jet-Ski, fish, parasail, or gamble on it; run, bike, in-line skate, hike, or bird-watch beside it. Wet or dry, you'll find plenty of fun to keep you fit.

Let's start with the wild stuff: "Anyone can parasail" says their literature.

ALTON AREA

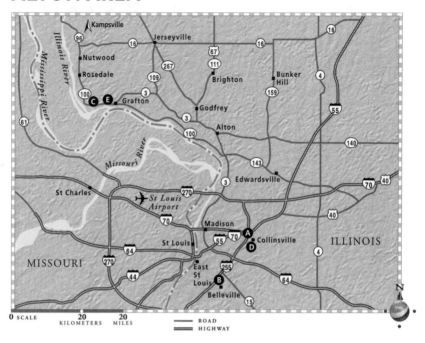

SIGHTS

- **Ⓐ** Cahokia Mounds State Historic District
- **Ⓑ** National Shrine of our Lady of the Snows
- **Ⓒ** Pere Marquette State Park
- **Ⓓ** World's Largest Catsup Bottle

FOOD

- **Ⓔ** Fin Inn
- **Ⓔ** Muriel's Cafe
- **Ⓒ** Pere Marquette Lodge

LODGING

- **Ⓔ** Ruebel Hotel
- **Ⓔ** Tara Point Inn and Cottages

CAMPING

- **Ⓒ** Pere Marquette State Park

Note: Items with the same letter are located in the same area.

Perhaps it should say, "Anyone who's *willing* can parasail." For 45 bucks, the **Loading Dock** restaurant, bar, and boat rental joint in Grafton will take you out with licensed captains and crew, and Coast Guard approved gear. You can take off and land directly from the deck of the boat that tows you around like a living kite. They promise to keep you dry, if that's the way you want it, and will even take your picture so you can brag about it later. The Loading Dock, on the riverside on the west end of Grafton, 618/786-3444, also rents pontoon boats ($200/full day) and Waverunners ($50/hour).

If you don't have a full day to spend at Raging Rivers, go after 3 p.m. and save $4 per person. Also, don't bring alcohol or wear a thong bikini. They won't let you in.

With all the water sports available on the Mississippi, who'd want to go to a water park next to the river? Just about any kid or fun-loving kid-at-heart, that's who. Just west of Grafton on the Great River Road is the **Raging Rivers Water Park**. This place has a well-deserved reputation as one of the coolest summertime places to play in the area. It has smaller, safer pools and waterslides for the little ones; and big slides, a wave pool, tube floats, and something called the Swirlpool for bigger kids. All the lifeguards are certified, and there's always an EMT on duty. Expect to spend more than $50 for a family of four, but the whole group will squeal with laughter and sleep like logs after a day here.

Ready to dry off? All along the Great River Road from Alton to Pere Marquette State Park, there's a separate path for bicycling, running, or walking. It runs right along the river at the bottom of the bluffs, so it's a fairly easy ride, and there are places to stop and rest. You don't even have to bring your own bike. Contact **Bike Route Rentals** in Grafton, in the Country Corner Fudge Shop, 321 E. Main St., 618/786-3700, to get a fairly new mountain bike.

If you want to hike, our enthusiastic vote goes to **Pere Marquette State Park**. Its 15 miles of trails pass breathtaking overlooks, and critters like deer, chipmunks, and wild turkeys can be seen by the quietest hikers. Benches along the trails will be appreciated by most. Pere Marquette also offers year-round horseback riding. Make a reservation by calling 618/786-2156.

Finally, there's a very nice golf course in Alton designed by Arnold Palmer called the **Spencer T. Olin Community Golf Course**. The 18-hole championship course is challenging, but all the amenities are there including a new electronic yardage system. Take College Avenue (Route 140) to the east side of town and turn into the Gordon F. Moore Park, then follow the signs to the golf course. Call 618/465-3111 to reserve your tee time.

FOOD

Breakfast is a special meal, no matter how late you sleep. That's why it's good to find a place that serves eggs and pancakes anytime. In Grafton, that place is

Muriel's Cafe, 22 E. Main St., 618/786-2233. The prices are cheap for breakfast or lunch, and it's clean and the food is good. Also in Grafton, try the **Fin Inn**, 1500 W. Main St., 618/786-2030. It has good seafood and good service, but great surroundings. Aquariums line the walls so that every booth has a clear view of lunker catfish, turtles, and other freshwater species. Some of the fish are huge! If you are in a wheelchair, call ahead. They can accommodate, but it'll take some special instructions.

The restaurant in **Pere Marquette Lodge**, Rt. 100, Grafton, 618/786-2331, is very nice. It's not pricey, but it is elegant, even in the rustic setting of the log and stone lodge. There's a good salad menu, and this is *the* place to get catfish. After all, you can't vacation beside the Mississippi River and not have catfish!

There are several nice tea rooms in Alton that make great lunch stops. Try **Marie's Kitchen**, 215 W. Third St., for her sandwiches served on delicious homemade bread at a fair price. A lot of the local shop owners eat here for lunch, which says a lot for her quality and value. More great soups and sandwiches can be found at **Cane Bottom/My Just Desserts**, 31 E. Broadway, 618/462-5881, but there's a catch. You must not leave without having a piece of pie. There are usually a dozen kinds of pie that have been made fresh and sinful.

For a nice dinner, one of the local picks is the **Midtown Restaurant and Lounge**, Seventh St. and Central Ave., Alton, 618/465-1321. Their specialty is fried chicken, but they also offer a good steak and are one of the few places to give "heart-healthy" options. Prices are moderate, and sometimes you even get piano entertainment.

LODGING

Alton and the entire River Bend area, as it's called, is bed-and-breakfast country. Since so many riverboat captains chose to build their homes here in the late 1800s, you'll find many stately old houses. Some of the better historic bed-and-breakfasts include the **Beall Mansion**, 407 E. 12th St., Alton, 618/474-9090, where you'll be completely pampered. The breakfasts are wonderful, full meals; and each room's bath includes a whirlpool tub. **Jackson House**, 1821 Seminary St., Alton, 618/462-1426, is charming with its wraparound front porch (the perfect place to sip iced tea), and the prices are reasonable. If you want to stay in a place with a terrific history, choose the **Franklin House**, 208 State St., Alton, 618/463-1078. This brick building was once a hotel where Abraham Lincoln stayed before his final debate against Stephen Douglas. Period furnishings make it a charming bed-and-breakfast.

Not all great bed-and-breakfasts have to be old, and one of the most awesome is **Tara Point Inn and Cottages**, I Tara Point Ln., Grafton, 618/786-3555. As you drive southwest through town on the Great River Road, look up. On the bluff above you'll see Tara Point, looking as though it hangs over the edge. The point provides a breathtaking view of the river and surrounding woodlands.

The **Ruebel Hotel**, 217 E. Main St., Grafton, 618/786-2315, was established in 1884, and still has the feel of that era thanks in part to the resident riverboat captain who greets and mingles with guests. A large staircase leads up to second-floor guest rooms, and the attached saloon is dominated by a walnut bar purchased at the St. Louis World's Fair in 1904. It's all been beautifully restored recently, and the second-floor deck now includes a hot tub.

CAMPING

Pere Marquette State Park is the best choice for camping. Along with the amenities listed previously, Pere Marquette offers full-hookup campsites and several tentsites that include electricity. If you don't want to pack your gear, try their rent-a-camp. It includes everything you'll need except groceries, clothes, and toiletries. If that's too rough, rent a beautifully appointed cabin.

NIGHTLIFE

The *Alton Belle* **Riverboat Casino**, on the downtown riverfront, 800/336-7568, draws many visitors to the area for the excitement of gaming. Unlike other riverboat casinos in neighboring states, this one actually cruises when the weather allows. Boarding takes place each day on even hours, with the last boardings at 2 a.m. weekdays and 3 a.m. weekends. Nice breakfast, lunch, and dinner buffets are available in a white-tablecloth setting.

Live music, cold drinks, good food, and a lot of fun are all packed into **Fast Eddies Bon-Air**, 1530 E. Fourth St., Alton, 618/462-5532. Fast Eddie's has become famous, both locally and nationally, for its cheap beer and cheap food. Half-pound burgers are less than a buck!

PERFORMING ARTS

Alton's Little Theater, 2450 N. Henry, 618/462-3205, offers local productions of plays and musicals. **Piasa Productions Dinner Theaters**, 101 Alton Square, 800/324-9608, provides dinner and a show.

6
SOUTHWEST ILLINOIS

Put on your hiking boots, we're going exploring! The southern tip of Illinois is an outdoor enthusiast's dream playground with its unusual diversity of terrain, plants, and animal life. Most of the area is included in the Shawnee National Forest that stretches across the state from the Ohio River to the Mississippi. This land, untouched by glaciers, includes a piece of the Ozarks and the Shawnee Hills, but it also includes an area of cypress swamps and the low-lying delta of the Mississippi and Ohio Rivers.

You'll find that recreational opportunities are as diverse as the landscape. The region offers great hunting and fishing, camping, hiking, equestrian trails, boating and canoeing, hiking, snowmobiling, and just about anything else you'd want to do outdoors. This is Illinois at its rustic best. If the days of Daniel Boone strike a chord of romance, come here to touch and smell the adventure.

That's not to say that there aren't cities. Carbondale (the home of Southern Illinois University), Herrin, and Marion are clustered together around Crab Orchard Lake, providing an abundance of lodging and cultural activities. If you prefer to see the outdoors, but not wallow in them, consider a stay in town. But if you're ready to discover caves and learn how the river pirates used them as hideouts, see a modern working mine from 600 feet below ground, and hike across a rare natural rock bridge—in short, if you're ready for an adventure—then you're ready for Southwest Illinois!

A PERFECT DAY IN SOUTHWEST ILLINOIS

Begin your day in the Giant City Lodge where you spent the night in rustic comfort. Breakfast here, then head out to the Trail of Tears State Forest for a hike. Stop by the Pamona General Store to pick up everything you'll need for a nice picnic lunch at Alto Vineyards. After lunch, take the steep drive up to see the view from the Bald Knob Cross. It's a short drive into Carbondale for a nice dinner at Bistro 51, then head to Shryock Auditorium on the Southern Illinois University campus for the symphony or a play.

SIGHTSEEING HIGHLIGHTS

★★★★ FORT MASSAC STATE PARK MUSEUM
1308 E. 5th St., Metropolis, 618-524-9321

Illinois' first state park remains one of the most heavily used, thanks in part to its historical significance, very good maintenance, and the museum. It all adds up to one of the most educational state park experiences in Illinois. The 1794 American fort that was built to protect the region against the Spanish has been recreated, providing the site for one of the best reenactment weekends in the state every October. Hundreds of people recreate battles, race in voyageurs' canoes, exhibit crafts, and do all they can to show what life was like in the early 1800s. The museum tells the tale of the many people who occupied this site, and has the artifacts to back up their stories. Be sure to see the **George Rogers Clark** statue inside the park, too.

Details: Daily 9:30–5:30; free; wheelchair accessible. (1–2 hours)

★★★★ NATIONAL COAL MUSEUM
One mile south of Rte. 149 on Rte. 37 (Logan Rd.), West Frankfort, 618/937-2625

This is the only vertical-shaft coal mine in the country that's open to the public, and it'll take you 600 feet underground. Sound creepy, dirty, and a little claustrophobia-inducing? Don't let the descending "cage ride" scare you. It's surprising how spacious and well lit it is down there, and you'll definitely be impressed by the work. Inside the museum you'll find more information and interesting artwork and artifacts.

Details: Daily 9–5; $10 adults, $8 seniors and children ages 15 and under, $7 retired miners; wheelchair accessible. (1½ hours)

SOUTHWEST ILLINOIS

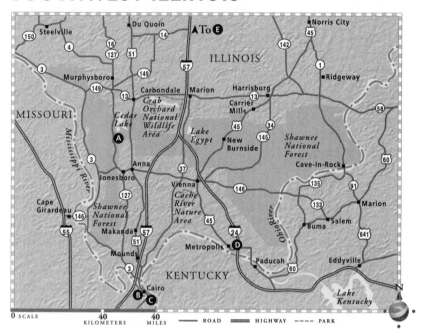

SIGHTS

- **Ⓐ** Alto Vineyards
- **Ⓐ** Bald Knob Cross
- **Ⓑ** City of Cairo
- **Ⓒ** Fort Defiance State Park
- **Ⓓ** Fort Massac State Park Museum
- **Ⓔ** National Coal Museum
- **Ⓓ** Superman Museum

Note: Items with the same letter are located in the same area.

★★★ **ALTO VINEYARDS**
8515 Rte. 127 N., Alto Pass, 618/893-4898

This is the largest of four excellent wineries in the area. A real connoisseur will want to follow the well marked Shawnee Hills Wine Trail to all four. But if you want to visit just one for a taste of the area's multiple award-winning products, choose Alto. They've been making wines since 1988, and have 10 acres of vines that produce a variety of

French/American hybrid grapes. The result: more than 150 medals in international competitions. The vineyards are a great place to taste wines, select from a variety of cheeses, stroll the grounds, and perhaps have a picnic. Gifts and local crafts are also offered in their shop. *Details: Open year-round Sun–Fri 1–5, Sat 10–5. Free; wheelchair accessible. (1 hour)*

★★★ CITY OF CAIRO
14th and Washington Aves., 618/734-1019

The southern tip of Illinois is known as "Little Egypt," probably because after a drought in the 1830s the only grain available was in the south, and northern farmers likened themselves to the Old Testament characters who chose to go to Egypt rather than starve. Cairo, then, is a fitting name for this southernmost city. It's a place with a tremendous history of floods, hardship, and strategic importance during the Civil War. This town is on the National Register of Historic Places, and among its important sites is the **Cairo Custom House**, built in 1872 and containing Civil War–era artifacts. *Details: Mon–Fri 10–3; donations accepted; wheelchair accessible on first floor only. (2 hours)*

★★★ SUPERMAN MUSEUM
611 Market St., Metropolis, 618/524-5518

The city of Metropolis has claimed Superman as its favorite son for a long time, but the bronze statue you see in the square downtown is relatively new. This was the 1993 replacement of the old "primary colors" statue, and folks still talk about which one they like best. In the museum you'll find goodies like the original costume worn by George Reeves in the 1950s television show, plus movie props, comic books, and toys that are probably worth a fortune. *Details: Daily 9–6; $3 per person, ages 5 and under free; wheelchair accessible. (1 hour)*

★★ BALD KNOB CROSS
Follow the signs west out of Alto Pass, 800/248-4373

Many people see this huge cross shining on a distant hillside at night and drive miles to find it. Make the trek during the day and save yourself a lot of confusion. This white porcelain cross stands 111 feet above the highest point in southern Illinois as a monument to peace. The steep, curvy road to the cross requires that you pay attention, but once you're on the top, you'll find a visitors center with information.

Details: *Free; partially wheelchair accessible. (1 ½ hours including the great drive from Alto Pass)*

★★ **FORT DEFIANCE STATE PARK**
Two miles south of Cairo on U.S. 62

The historic significance of this site lies in its strategic location at the confluence of the huge Mississippi and Ohio Rivers. This was General Ulysses S. Grant's staging area in the Civil War, a perfect spot to guard the southern point of "free" territory and ensure that union supplies could be shipped. With the nearby town of Cairo, this became a main supply station for Union troops. Today there's no camping allowed, but it's a great place to hike and learn a little Civil War history. It's also the perfect vantage point for watching the two rivers meet, especially if you climb onto the memorial structure.

Details: *Dawn–dusk; free; not completely wheelchair accessible. (1 hour)*

SHOPPING

You'll find good antique shopping in southern Illinois, and lots of arts and crafts. Visit **Austin's of Alto Pass**, on Alto Pass Rd. just southwest of town, 618/893-2206, for all of these. It's set in an early 1900s schoolhouse.

The **Associated Artists Gallery**, 213 S. Illinois Ave., Carbondale, 618/457-4743, houses art by a number of local artists. Some 40 members supply paintings, sculpture, jewelry, pottery, and more, and it's all on display and for sale.

The **Boardwalk** in Makanda, 618/457-8508, is a great place to shop. The whole town has an artsy feel, and walking the boardwalk is like sneaking onto a movie set. About 25 shops carry work by local artists and craftspeople.

Rotkappchen, 1296 Post Oak Rd., Campbell Hill, 618/426-3445, is a lovely store in a beautiful setting. Fine china, sterling silver, books, cards, and pottery, all with a Scandinavian flair, might not be expected in this part of Illinois.

If there's anything you need for wilderness adventures, **Shawnee Trails Wilderness Outfitters**, 222 W. Freeman (in the Campus Shopping Center), Carbondale, 618/529-2313, probably has it. They well stocked on everything you need to enjoy the Shawnee National Forest.

Finally, don't miss the **Pamona General Store**, Poplar and Main Sts., Pamona, 618/893-2997. This place has been in business since 1876, although the current building is relatively young, built in 1917. This is also a great place to grab a soda-fountain treat on a hot day.

FITNESS AND RECREATION

The opportunities for hiking, hunting, fishing, boating, canoeing, and discovery are limitless in the Shawnee National Forest area. You can virtually set off in any direction and be lost in the wilderness within just a few minutes.

Ferne Cliffe State Park, just east of I-57 at exit 40, 618/995-2411, is one of the best places to hike in the state. It has 10 trails that vary in their difficulty, but even the easy trails take you by waterfalls and rock overhangs. **Trail of Tears State Forest**, 618/8336125, near Jonesboro, is a great hiking spot with an awful history. Make sure to see the totem pole there that commemorates the deadly march of the Cherokee and other Indian nations from their homelands to reservations in Oklahoma. The group spent a winter just south of here.

Special spots for fishing include the three lakes and several small ponds in the **Crab Orchard Lake Recreation Area**, between Carbondale and Marion, 618/997-3344, where boating and waterskiing are also popular. **Lake Murphysboro State Park**, two miles west of Murphysboro, 618/684-2867, has good largemouth bass fishing. Nearby **Kincaid Lake**, 618/687-4914, is one of the only lakes in the state that stays cool enough to successfully stock muskie. The recreation area includes a beach and good hiking trails.

Giant City State Park, just east of Jonesboro, 618/529-4110, is another great place to hike and has huge rock formations that look like buildings in a "giant city." Stables at this park provide trail rides and wagon rides.

Kosmic Acres Stables and Rentals, Prospect St. in Alto Pass, 618/893-2347, takes groups of up to four people for horseback trail rides.

To canoe the bald cypress bayou along the Cache River contact **Cache Core Canoes** in Ullin, 618/845-3817.

FOOD

While it's true there aren't many opportunities for fine dining in southern Illinois, you can find good places to eat, and a variety of foods. Two of the nicest places are **Bistro 51**, 227 W. Main St., Carbondale, 618/549-9700; and the moderately priced **Martha and Mary's Tea Room**, 16th and Walnut, Murphysboro, 618/687-1125, which is open for lunch every day, but dinner only on Friday and Saturday. The **Bald Knob Dining Room** in the Giant City

SOUTHWEST ILLINOIS

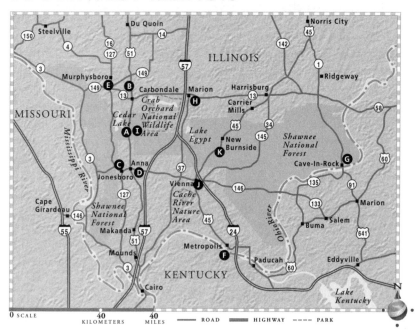

FOOD

A Bald Knob Dining Room
B Bistro 51
C Cerro de la Silla
D Depot Restaurant
B El Bajio Mexican Restaurant
E Martha and Mary's Tea Room
B Pagliai's Pizza
B Tres Hombres Mexican Restaurant

LODGING

F Amerihost Players Riverboat Hotel
G Cave-in-Rock
H Motel Marion
H Old Squatt Inn
I State Park Lodges
J Triple T Cedar Lake Ranch

CAMPING

K Camp Ondesonk
A Fort Massac State Park
F Giant City State Park
E Lake Murphysboro State Park
D Trail of Tears State Forest

Note: Items with the same letter are located in the same area.

State Park Lodge, Makanda, 618/457-4921, serves a full menu of steaks, prime rib, and seafood at reasonable prices. Just outside of Trail of Tears State Forest there's a good Mexican restaurant called **Cerro de la Silla**, on the square in Jonesboro, 618/833-8833. The **Depot Restaurant**, 124 E. Davie St., Anna, 618/833-7124, serves Cajun food, but you can also get a good steak for a good price.

As a college town, Carbondale has a few good restaurants that cater to younger tastebuds. **Tres Hombres Mexican Restaurant**, on the square in downtown Carbondale, 618/457-3308; **El Bajio Mexican Restaurant**, 1010 E. Main St., 618/529-1648; and **Pagliai's Pizza**, 515 S. Illinois St., Carbondale, 618/457-0321, are each competitively priced. Our pick is Tres Hombres for a quick burrito.

LODGING

The nicest places to stay in southern Illinois are the **State Park Lodges** at **Giant City** near Makanda, 618/457-4921; **Trail of Tears** in Jonesboro, 618/833-4910; and **Cave-in-Rock**, near the little town of Cave-in-Rock, 618/289-4545. Each place has a rustic lodge made of stone and logs, but each also coddles you in very nice accommodations with amenities like fireplaces and swimming pools. There are also cabins to rent that are very nice and relatively secluded. There are other places to rent cabins, each with their own flavor. The **Old Squat Inn**, 14242 Liberty School Rd., Marion, 618/982-2916, will put you up in a cabin so rustic it looks like Granny Clampett should be sitting on the porch drinking from a jug. The **Triple T Cedar Lake Ranch** near Vienna, 618/695-2600, also has cabins, and a dining hall and occasional entertainment make it interesting.

If you plan on visiting the gambling boat near Metropolis, book a room in the **Amerihost Players Riverboat Hotel**, 203 E. Front St., Metropolis, 618/524-5678. This is a very comfortable hotel that's in the same complex as the boat and Merv Griffin's Theater. For less expensive rooms try the **Motel Marion**, 2100 W. Main St., Marion, 618/993-2101, where they have a whopping 45 rooms and a pool.

CAMPING

If the weather's nice, this is the way to go. Camping is everywhere in southern Illinois and the amenities provided by the state's park system assure reasonable comfort, safety, and a lot of fun. Several provide specialty areas like horse camps, and most have tent sites that must be accessed without the help of your motorized vehicle. Camping with children may require a private campground, as these tend to have more snack bars and pools, but these places are generally more expensive, with less attractive campsites. Playground equipment is located near most of the campsites. Camping fees for all of Illinois' state parks range from $6 for walk-in sites to $11 for RV sites with electricity and pads.

Trail of Tears State Forest, Jonesboro, 618/833-4910, is a great place for tent campers because it doesn't accommodate the motor-home crowd. In fact, all the campsites are class C or D, meaning they have fire rings and possibly a picnic table, but not much else. Some sites have log shelters and privies, but this is definitely a place for the nonsqueamish.

Giant City State Park, Makanda, 618/457-4836, is a favorite in part because of its location near great fishing lakes and the sights at Pamona and Alto Pass, but also because of its terrific restaurant, lodge, and cabins. It's also one of the best parks in the system for campers in wheelchairs.

Fort Massac State Park, Metropolis, 618/524-4712, has camping facilities best suited to the RV crowd. The fort and related historical activities bring in a lot of people, so there can be moderate traffic at times.

Lake Murphysboro State Park, Murphysboro, 618/684-2867, may be the state park to choose if you're camping with children. It's just a short drive on Route 149 back into town where there's a little amusement park with go-carts, ice cream, and miniature golf.

One of the most interesting campgrounds we've found is **Camp Ondesonk**, off Rte. 45, 10 miles north of I-24 near Ozark, 618/695-2489, where you can camp in three-sided "tree houses," or even under a rock overhang. They host summer camps for kids, so they generally only take the public in the spring and fall. The fee is $3.75 per person plus a $25 deposit on the tree houses with a two-week reservation. They can also supply meals if you let them know ahead of time.

NIGHTLIFE

You may need nothing more than the stars above for nightlife activities, but when the hankering for civilization gets too strong, run into town for a little artificial fun.

For a slightly different pace, put on your best cowboy boots and head to **Kickin' Country Dance Barn**, four miles west of Vienna on Rte. 146, 618/658-8084, where the music is country, the drinks are nonalcoholic, and everybody dances.

Player's Riverboat Casino, Merv Griffin's Landing, Metropolis, 800/524-5518, is four decks of slot machines, video poker, and other gaming.

PERFORMING ARTS

The **Shryock Auditorium**, at Southern Illinois University, Carbondale, 618/453-3379, is a gorgeous facility with near-perfect acoustics that houses all kinds of performing arts. Likewise, the **McLeod Theater**, in the Communications Building at SIU, 618/453-3001, stages six major productions plus Summer Playhouse shows. **Southern Illinois University Arena**, Carbondale, 618/453-5341, is the place to see large productions and big-name bands.

Merv Griffin's Theater, on the landing, 618/524-2628, is a 350-seat state-of-the-art theater that brings Las Vegas entertainment to southern Illinois.

7

SPRINGFIELD AREA

There's a lot going on in Springfield, Illinois. A city of well over 100,000 people, Springfield is a hub of educational and medical services for central Illinois. It's the state capital, so there's always a flurry of activity in the spring and fall when the legislature's in session. It's the headquarters of no fewer than 12 insurance companies that do business across the nation, and state and regional associations like to have headquarters here to be close to politicians they hope to influence. But all of that matters not one iota here. Not a bit, because the reason Springfield attracts a million visitors a year is singular: Abraham Lincoln. Lincoln is everywhere here—in the historic sites, in the names of businesses and in their assurances of quality ("Honest!"), and on the tips of politicians' tongues who take every opportunity to quote the Great Emancipator.

The commercialization of Lincoln's memory is tiring, but understandable, considering Lincoln's ties to the area. He led a group of legislators known as the Long Nine (they were all really tall) who shoved through legislation to move the state capitol here in 1837. The only home Lincoln ever owned is here, preserved for generations to stroll. It's where three of his four sons were born and was his home base for all of his political career.

Come to Springfield and have fun. It's a grand host of a city. Learn all you can about Abraham Lincoln and use the historic sites to get a *feel* for who he was. When you leave you'll know the heartache America felt in April of 1865, when the man who saved "the American experiment" for all of us was killed; and you'll know the pride we Illinoisans feel to be able to claim him as one of our own.

A PERFECT DAY IN THE SPRINGFIELD AREA

Before you even leave on vacation, make sure to get everyone in your family—or your group—to read a different book about Lincoln's life. That way you'll all be able to offer insights on him as you tour the places he lived, worked, and played. Start your tour where he did—in New Salem. Then drive back into town and visit his home and law office. Take a lunch break at Norb Andy Tabarin, then take a break from sightseeing to splash around at Knight's Action Park. Make sure to leave the park early enough to clean up for a visit to Lincoln's tomb in time for the moving flag ceremony.

SIGHTSEEING HIGHLIGHTS

★★★★ LINCOLN-HERNDON LAW OFFICES
Sixth and Adams Sts., just across from the historic Old State Capitol, 217/785-7289
In the years before Abraham Lincoln became the 16th president of the United States, he was a locally famous attorney. This restored law office should not be missed by visitors eager to get a feel for Lincoln's life in Springfield. The first floor (a store in Lincoln's day) now holds several Lincoln artifacts, and shows a short film on the history of the building. The stairs to the second-floor law offices have been restored for safety reasons, but the offices themselves are wonderfully rustic. You can imagine Lincoln's law partner getting upset with his famous friend's squealing children, the sound bouncing off the wooden walls.
Details: Mar–Oct daily 9–5, Nov–Feb daily 9–4; donations accepted; wheelchair accessible. (1 hour)

★★★★ LINCOLN HOME NATIONAL HISTORIC SITE
Eighth and Jackson, Springfield, 217/492-4241, ext. 221
With the resources of the National Park Service behind the upkeep of the only home Lincoln ever owned, this is a beautiful site. Many of the furnishings inside belonged to the Lincolns, and others are period pieces that add to the genuineness. You'll wonder how lanky old Abe Lincoln ever moved through the tight house without bumping his head

SPRINGFIELD

0 SCALE 150 METERS 1000 FEET   ——— ROAD   ✖ POINT OF INTEREST

SIGHTS

- **A** Dana-Thomas House
- **B** Dean House
- **C** Lincoln Home National Historic Site
- **D** Lincoln-Herndon Law Offices

FOOD

- **E** Cafe Brio
- **F** Gumbo Ya-Ya's
- **G** Norb Andy Tabarin

LODGING

- **H** Henry Mischler House
- **I** Inn at 835
- **J** Mansion View Inn
- **K** Renaissance Hotel

---

and knocking things over, and you'll wonder how this house ever could have been considered "state of the art." The surrounding four blocks are being restored to recreate Lincoln's neighborhood, but this will still be the treasure.

Details: *Daily 8:30–5:30; free, but you must have a ticket from the Lincoln Home Visitor's Center (426 S. Seventh St.). (1 hour)*

★★★★ LINCOLN'S NEW SALEM STATE HISTORIC SITE
Rte. 97, two miles south of Petersburg, 217/632-4000

In the spring of 1831, 22-year-old Lincoln piloted a flatboat full of goods to New Orleans for a man named Offutt who later started a store in New Salem. Upon his return, Lincoln stayed in New Salem to clerk at the store, and stayed in the little town for six years. His first campaign for the State House of Representatives commenced the following year. Despite losing, Lincoln made the contacts that landed him the postmaster's job in 1833. Today New Salem is a recreation of the town as it was then, with costumed interpreters playing the parts of residents. Some artifacts are still there, such as the copper kettle one resident used to make felt hats.

Details: Mar–Oct daily 9–5, Nov–Feb daily 8–4; donations accepted; visitor center is wheelchair accessible, but most historic buildings are not. (2 hours)

★★★★ LINCOLN TOMB STATE HISTORIC SITE
Oak Ridge Cemetery, Springfield, 217/782-2717
The monument that dominates beautiful Oak Ridge Cemetery was completed in 1874 with public donations, and while the exterior can't compete with the inside as a compelling sight, it is interesting and you might want to find a shady tree to sit under and just look around for a while. Inside there are several reproductions of Lincoln statues that show him at different stages of his career, and the actual burial marker is extremely moving. On Tuesday nights in the summer a reactivated Civil War infantry unit retires the flag in a ceremony from 7 to 8.

Details: Mar–Oct daily 9–5, Nov–Feb daily 9–4; free; wheelchair accessible. (1 hour)

★★★ DANA-THOMAS HOUSE
301 E. Lawrence, Springfield, 217/782-6776
He was young and relatively unknown, but after remodeling this house for socialite Susan Lawrence Dana in 1904, Frank Lloyd Wright became an architectural star that seemed to burn brighter all the time. The Dana-Thomas House is thought to be the finest example of Wright's early work, and a terrific example of his prairie style. Wright also designed the furniture and glass used in the windows and doors.

Details: Wed–Sun 9–4; suggested donation $3 adults, $1 children ages 3–17; visitor center and first floor wheelchair accessible. (1 hour)

★★★ DEAN HOUSE
Eighth and Jackson Sts., Springfield, 217/492-4241

The Dean House is, in our opinion, a required stop for those touring Lincoln sites. This house was in its present location across from Mr. Lincoln's home when he left for Washington in 1861. Today the house serves as a gallery space to the exhibit *What a Pleasant Home Abe Lincoln Has*. The exhibits, most of which consist of pictures with quotes and captions, explore the influences that shaped Lincoln, and explain what he believed. Most folks pass by the Dean House, and there may be no one inside, but it's a self-guided tour that will add immeasurably to your Springfield visit.

Details: *Hours same as the Lincoln Home National Historic Site; free; wheelchair accessible. (1 hour)*

★★ HENSON ROBINSON ZOO
1100 E. Lake Dr., Springfield, 217/753-6217

The Henson Robinson Zoo isn't very big, but it's in a nice setting along Lake Springfield, and they pack a lot in their 14 acres with some 300 animals and several endangered species. Kids are allowed to pet the animals in the Barnyard area. There are new cheetah and red wolf exhibits, a tropical birdhouse, and a building dedicated to nocturnal animals.

Details: *Mid-Apr–mid-Oct daily 10–5, extended hours Tue and Thu Jun–Aug; $2 adults, 75¢ children, under age 3 free; wheelchair accessible. (1 ½ hours)*

★★ WASHINGTON PARK
MacArthur Blvd. and S. Grand Ave., Springfield
217/753-6228

This large city park a few blocks west of downtown has two good attractions. The first, the **Botanical Gardens**, is housed in a domed conservatory. You'll find thriving tropical foliage here even in the dead of winter, and rose gardens in the appropriate season. A favorite display is the scent garden.

Also in the park, and the second big attraction, is the **Thomas Rees Memorial Carillon**, the third-largest bell tower in the world. You can tour the inside of the tower, or view the gardens and reflecting pool that surround it on the outside.

Details: *Botanical gardens: Mon–Fri noon–4, Sat–Sun noon–5; free; wheelchair accessible. Thomas Rees Memorial Carillon: 217/753-6219; Jun–Aug Tue–Sun noon–8, weekends only spring and fall, closed in winter; wheelchair accessible. (1 hour for both)*

SHOPPING

The downtown area of Springfield has many unique stores. **Tinsley Dry Goods**, 209 S. Sixth St., Springfield, 217/525-1825, is an old-time store that's worth a visit even if you don't need a sack of flour. **Bachman and Keefner Drug Store**, 530 E. Capitol Ave., Springfield, 217/523-2431, is one of those drug stores that can dish up a green river and a sandwich at the same time they fill your prescription. **Prairie Archives**, 522 E. Adams, Springfield, 217/522-9742, is a used bookstore heavy on Lincoln and Illinois history books, with other neat things like historic political buttons. The gift shop in the **Lincoln Home Visitor Center**, 426 S. Seventh St., Springfield, 217/492-4241, ext. 221, is a great place to pick up Lincoln-related items. They have a terrific selection of the newest and best books on Lincoln. **Penny Lane**, 2901 S. MacArthur Blvd., Springfield, 217/787-2996, is a great place to take teenagers. It has a wide variety of posters, bumper stickers, incense—anything to make a bedroom or dorm room a cool place to hang.

If you want to do some power-shopping, **White Oaks Mall**, Wabash Ave. and Veteran's Pkwy., Springfield, 217/787-8560, has well over 100 stores, and is surrounded by strip malls that carry just about anything you could want.

FITNESS AND RECREATION

Golf is a big sport in Springfield, so if you want to play it's best to make reservations as early as possible. Thankfully, there are eight public courses in the area. **The Rail**, 1400 S. Clubhouse Dr., Springfield, 217/525-0365, is home to the LPGA's Rail Classic. It's beautiful and challenging, and is by far the most widely acclaimed course around.

Lake Springfield is the place for water sports, and the eight parks that surround the lake provide picnic areas and baseball diamonds with views and a breeze. **Lake Springfield Marina**, 7100 Woodland Trl., Chatham, 217/483-3625, rents everything from canoes and paddleboats to personal watercraft and pontoon boats, with hourly, half-, or full-day rates.

The **Lost Bridge Bike Trail**, 217/789-2155, runs five miles along an old railroad line, and is used by both mountain bikers and walkers. It connects the east side of Springfield to the town of Rochester, where you'll find water and toilets in the city park.

Sanchris State Park, Rochester, 217/498-9208, is a 15-minute drive from Springfield and offers three miles of easy hiking trails, picnic areas, boating, and some of the best largemouth bass fishing in the state.

Kids love **Knights Action Park**, 1700 Recreation Dr., Springfield, 217/546-8881, for its water slides, miniature golf, go-karts, and the "wild river

SPRINGFIELD AREA

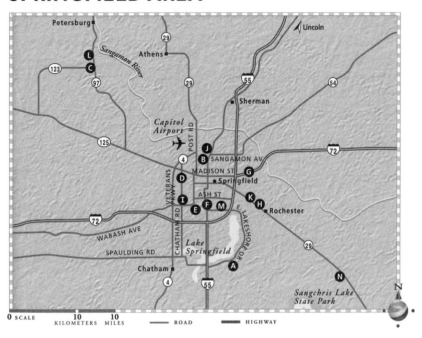

SIGHTS

Ⓐ Henson Robinson Zoo
Ⓑ Lincoln Tomb State Historic Site
Ⓒ Lincoln's New Salem State Historic Site
Ⓓ Washington Park

FOOD

Ⓔ Barrel Head
Ⓕ Cancun
Ⓖ Chesapeake Seafood
Ⓗ Jolly Tamale
Ⓘ Sebastians

LODGING

Ⓙ Country Dreams Bed and Breakfast
Ⓚ Hilton Hotel

CAMPING

Ⓛ Lincoln's New Salem Campground
Ⓜ Mr. Lincoln's Campground
Ⓝ Sangchris Lake State Park

ride" on fancy inner tubes. At $13.95 per person ($9.95 for kids under four feet tall), taking the family can add up to a good buck, but you'll earn a lot of brownie points.

FOOD

The great thing about Springfield's restaurant scene is that it's so unconventional. You're in for a big surprise if you go to **Gumbo Ya-Ya's**, 700 E. Adams St., Springfield, 217/789-1530, in jeans and a T-shirt, because this is one of the finest restaurants in town. The selections range from Cajun-fried mudbugs (crawfish) to blackened steak and pasta, and include terrific fish selections like grilled swordfish steaks. The fact that Ya-Ya's is at the top of the tallest building in town (the Hilton Hotel) just adds to the experience.

Cafe Brio, 524 E. Monroe, Springfield, 217/544-0574, is another fun place. One journalist in town calls it "Asian-Mexican fusion, with urban garage sale decor." It's a mid-priced establishment that doesn't require a change of clothes, and a lot of folks would call this their favorite restaurant in the city.

The **Norb Andy Tabarin**, more commonly called Norb Andy's, 518 E. Capital Ave., Springfield, 217/523-7777, is where the politicians hang out. It's not unusual to hear a couple of state reps debating the latest legislation over one of Norb's famous "Horseshoes," a choice of meats covered in French fries then drowned in a cheese sauce. Your doctor wouldn't recommend it, but everybody has to try it once.

Sebastians, 2106 Chatham Rd., Springfield, 217/789-8988, is a dimly lit fine-dining romancer. **Chesapeake Seafood**, 3045 E. Clearlake Ave., Springfield, 217/522-5220, is our choice for the best seafood in town. Prices are reasonable, and they've resurrected their fantastic brunch-buffet deal. The **Barrel Head**, 1577 W. Wabash Ave., Springfield, 217/787-2102, is a bar and grill with better-than-average bar food. Get some appetizers here—they're great.

Cancun, 2849 S. Sixth St., Springfield, 217/753-0088, is a very good and moderately priced family-owned Mexican restaurant. On the other hand, the **Jolly Tamale**, 803 S. Dirksen Pkwy., Springfield, 217/523-2345, serves Mexican food that's just plain cheap. Let's face it, there's a time and place for everything.

LODGING

The nicest hotels in Springfield are chains. In fact, it's hard to find accommodations that aren't part of a national chain. The best ones are the **Hilton Hotel**, 700 E. Adams St., 217/789-1530, and the **Renaissance Hotel**, 701 E. Adams

St., 217/544-8800. Both are downtown, within easy walking distance of many of the area's sights. The Hilton is the more reasonable of the two, unless you opt for its $500 presidential suite.

The are a few nice bed-and-breakfasts in town. The **Henry Mischler House**, 802 E. Edwards, 217/523-0205, is just a block south of the Lincoln Home site, and is a historic home itself with a terrific marble fireplace, private baths, and full breakfasts. The **Inn at 835**, 835 S. Second St., 217/523-4466, is just the place for travelers who want to be pampered. Whirlpool baths, fireplaces, and a wine and cheese hour in the evening set this 1909 national historic landmark building apart. **Country Dreams Bed and Breakfast**, 3410 Park Ln., Rochester, 217/498-9210, makes no apologies for not being historic. Built in 1997 in a rural area just minutes from Springfield's sights, it revels in being brand-new. Here, beautiful farmland surrounds you, the whirlpool baths and fireplaces warm you, and the hosts befriend you.

For an economical night's stay, choose the **Mansion View Inn**, 529 S. Fourth St., 217/544-7411. Nice rooms start at $50; suites at $79. And yes, you can see the executive mansion from many of the rooms.

CAMPING

Anglers who want to camp should go to **Sangchris Lake State Park**, 9898 Cascade Rd., Rochester, 217/498-9208. With 200 camping sites and more than 3,500 acres, the park easily accommodates the swarms of people that come for the excellent crappy and largemouth bass fishing.

Lincoln's New Salem Campground, Rte. 97 near Petersburg, 217/632-4003, is a nice place to camp. If you really want to spend some time at New Salem (and there's usually quite a bit going on there with reenactments and historical plays in the evening), this is a good choice for accommodations. **Mr. Lincoln's Campground**, 3045 Stanton Ave., 217/529-8206, is a medium-size campground that provides amenities like showers, laundry, and a sauna.

NIGHTLIFE

For dancing, try a couple of the "three o'clock bars": **On Broadway**, 210 Broadway, 217/523-0210, or **Mr. J's**, 1033 W. Wabash Ave., 217/546-5011. Other good bars include **Brewhaus**, 617 E. Washington, 217/525-6399, with its huge variety of beers and impressive selection of scotch; and **The Alamo**, 115 N. Fifth St., 217/523-1455, where live blues music hits the stage every Monday night.

PERFORMING ARTS

If you're in Springfield in the summer, try to arrange a romantic outdoor evening with the **Springfield Muni Opera**, 217/793-6864. It's especially nice when the stars are shining. **Sangamon Auditorium**, on the campus of the University of Illinois at Springfield, 217/786-6160, offers live music and theater in a very comfortable 2,000-seat auditorium. Back at Lincoln's New Salem, **Theater in the Park**, 800/710-9290, offers evening performances on the weekends that are entertaining, funny, and educational. Usually the shows are about Lincoln, of course. If it rains, the show moves inside the visitors center.

8
CHAMPAIGN-
URBANA AREA

They're called the twin cities because they share a common border, but they're related in a more vital way as cohosts to the flagship campus of the University of Illinois. The campus, nestled in a sea of farm fields, offers area residents and visitors all the educational, cultural, athletic, and entertainment facilities you would expect at a Big Ten university. The state's most famous son, Abraham Lincoln, signed the legislation that gave grants of land to several states to create universities, including the Illinois Industrial University. The school is now best known for its engineering and agriculture programs, as well as its library, which is the largest public university library system in the nation.

What the Champaign-Urbana area lacks in theme parks and historic sites, it makes up for with special events (see Festivals section in this chapter). Plus, you're never far from food in the area—a recent national survey found that C-U has more restaurants per person than anywhere else in the nation.

A PERFECT DAY IN THE CHAMPAIGN-URBANA AREA

If you like a hearty breakfast, start at Ott's Drive-In, then head to the Octave Chanute Aerospace Museum for a glimpse into the history of military aviation. For lunch, toss a coin. If it's heads, go to Radio Maria's; tails, go to Silver Creek.

Explore the U of I campus in the afternoon; stop at the welcome center for a guided tour or head straight to one of its three museums: Krannert Art Museum, Natural History Museum, or Spurlock. When you've had all your brain can absorb in one sitting, drive to Allerton Park—great for sunset viewing. Dinner at nationally acclaimed Timpone's will leave you feeling pampered, as will a night at Lindley House.

SIGHTSEEING HIGHLIGHTS

★★★★ ALLERTON PARK
R.R. 2, Monticello, 217/762-2721
A nearly 1,800-acre estate, the former Robert Allerton residence was donated to the University of Illinois more than 50 years ago. The formal gardens on the grounds are filled with exquisite sculptures and statues. The home is now used as a conference center, but is open to the public a few days in December for a Christmas decoration tour.
    Details: Park open daily 8 a.m.–sunset, visitors center open daily 8–5; free; wheelchair accessible. (1 hour)

★★★★ KRANNERT ART MUSEUM AND KINKEAD PAVILION
500 E. Peabody Dr., Champaign, 217/333-1860
If you want to find a bigger art museum in Illinois, you'll have to go to Chicago. Even there, however, you won't find a better museum for its size than the U of I's Krannert. The dozen or so galleries contain a collection that includes works by Picasso, Renoir, and Andy Warhol.
    Details: Tue and Thu–Sat 10–5, Wed 10–8, Sun 2–5; free; wheelchair accessible. (1 hour)

UNIVERSITY OF ILLINOIS AT URBANA-CHAMPAIGN SIGHTSEEING HIGHLIGHTS

Established in 1867, the flagship campus of the U of I system started with just 77 students and two faculty members. Today more than 35,000 people from the 50 states and more than 100 countries study here each year. Guided tours of the campus are available through the visitors center at the Levis building at 919 W. Illinois, 217/333-0824, though they tend to be geared toward prospective students. The daily tour of the Altgeld Chimes is a must-see as well as a must-hear.

CHAMPAIGN-URBANA

N

HIGH CROSS RD

130

150

AUGERVILLE RD

BROWNFIELD RD

74

PERKINS DR

45

UNIVERSITY AVE

WASHINGTON ST

PHILO RD

WINDSOR RD

150

Urbana

CUNNINGHAM AVE

MAIN ST

150

VINE ST

Crystal
Lake
Park

K

RACE ST

RACE ST

H Q
U

Fairgrounds

COLER AVE

FLORIDA AVE

LINCOLN AVE

A

LINCOLN AVE

GREGORY ST
MATHEWS AVE

E
C S F
T
4TH ST

Peabody DR

B
Stadium

ST MARYS RD

University
of Illinois

N V

MARKET ST

WASHINGTON ST

Amtrak
Station

I
1ST ST

O

NEIL ST

D

P

WALNUT ST

J

45

R

STATE ST

PROSPECT AVE

TOWN CENTER

BLOOMINGTON RD

150

Champaign

CHURCH ST

UNIVERSITY AVE

SPRINGFIELD AVE

GREEN ST

KIRBY AVE

WINDSOR RD

74

BRADLEY AVE

MATTIS RD

M

Dodds
Park

G
Parkland
College

SOUTHWOOD DR

150

57

DUNCAN RD

72

57

—×—	PLACE OF INTEREST
═══	HIGHWAY
———	ROAD

0 SCALE 2 KILOMETERS

2 MILES

★★★ CURTIS ORCHARD
From Champaign head south out of C-U on Duncan Rd. and follow the apple-shaped signs, 217/359-5565

This working apple orchard with a huge pumpkin patch and more is a favorite with children, who love the snow-fence maze, petting zoo, barnyard play structure, horse rides, and, inside the orchard's store, the real donut-making machine. Excellent fruits, juices, ciders, preserves, caramel apples, and donuts are made fresh daily. The pumpkins are great, too.

Fall and winter visits to campus are an excellent time to attend sporting events, concerts, and theater shows at Illinois. For schedules of events, call 217/333-5000 or 217/333-6280, or check their Web site at www.uiuc.edu.

Details: *Aug–mid-Dec Mon–Sat 9–5:30, Sun noon–5; extended hours in Oct; free; treats are reasonably priced. (1 hour)*

★★★ MUSEUM OF NATURAL HISTORY
1301 W. Green St., Urbana, 217/333-2517

This national historic place on the Illinois campus houses anthropological, botanical, geological, and zoological exhibits. If there's a specimen you want to see that isn't displayed, just ask and someone will find it for you in the research room.

Details: *Mon–Sat 9–4:30; free; wheelchair accessible. (1 hour)*

SIGHTS
- **A** Hartley Gardens Arboretum
- **B** Krannert Art Museum and Kinkhead Pavilion
- **C** Museum of Natural History
- **D** Orpheum Children's Science Museum
- **E** Spurlock Museum of World Cultures
- **F** University of Illinois Library
- **G** William M. Staerkel Planetarium

FOOD
- **H** Courier Cafe
- **I** Fiesta Cafe
- **J** Kennedy's
- **K** Lil' Porgy's Bar-B-Que
- **L** Merry Ann's Diner
- **M** Original Pancake House
- **N** Papa Del's Pizza
- **O** Po Boy's Bar-B-Que
- **P** Radio Maria's
- **Q** Silvercreek
- **R** The Ribeye
- **S** Timpone's

LODGING
- **T** Illini Union
- **U** Jumer's Castle Lodge
- **V** Lindley House

★★★ OCTAVE CHANUTE AEROSPACE MUSEUM
1011 Pacesetter Dr., Rantoul, 217/903-1613

Here you can sit in the cockpit of a B-52 or walk inside a "Minute Man" intercontinental ballistic missile silo to learn more about military aviation. This former aircraft hanger at the old Chanute Air Base is now home to a huge collection of planes and other military equipment, as well as hands-on exhibits and flight simulators. If you come with someone who has served a stint in the military, expect to stay a long time.

Details: *Web site: www.cu-online.com/~leonhard/chanute/; weekdays 10–5, Sat 10–6, Sun noon–5, closed Tue; $3.50 adults, $2.50 seniors, $2.50 students ages 12–17, $1.50 children under 12, age 3 and under free; wheelchair accessible. (2 hours)*

★★★ ORPHEUM CHILDREN'S SCIENCE MUSEUM
364 North Neil St., Champaign, 217/352-5895

For several decades, the Orpheum Theatre was one of the hottest entertainment spots in the twin cities. Today, the Orpheum Children's Science Museum is home to a hands-on children's museum that proves learning is fun. Exhibits include a dinosaur dig, live snakes, and a water tornado.

Details: *Web site: www.m-crossroads.org/orpheum; Wed–Sun and school holidays 1–5; $3 adults, $1 children ages 2–18, ages 2 and under free; wheelchair accessible. (2 hours)*

★★★ SPURLOCK MUSEUM OF WORLD CULTURES
Corner of California and Gregory, Urbana, 217/333-2360

The University's Spurlock Museum traces the history of man. The well-organized displays include a recreated Egyptian tomb, one of the earliest known fragments of the Biblical Book of James, and delicate Roman glassware.

Details: *Mon–Fri 9–5, Sun 2–5, closed summer; free; wheelchair accessible. (1 hour)*

Editor's Note: *The museum has been temporarily closed and will move to a new facility in late 1999. For the most current information on this sight, make sure to call before visiting.*

★★ WILLIAM M. STAERKEL PLANETARIUM
2400 W. Bradley Ave., Champaign, 217/351-2446

Parkland Community College's planetarium is the second largest in the

state. It features a Zeiss Star projector that creates 7,600 stars, plus—
of course—the sun, moon, and a variety of planets. This is a great
place to learn about the prairie sky.

Details: Shows Thu–Sat 7, 8, and 9 p.m.; matinees Sat 11 a.m.,
noon, and 1 p.m.; $3 adults, $2 seniors, students, and children ages 12
and under; $4 all seats for light shows, $1 all seats for science lectures;
wheelchair accessible. (1 hour)

★ HARTLEY GARDENS ARBORETUM
**Corner of Lincoln and Florida Aves., Urbana,
217/333-9355**

This working laboratory is probably the most fragrant and colorful
one on the U of I campus. The hundreds of bedding plants are pre-
sented along gravel walks with plenty of benches for watching butter-
flies or just imagining the possibilities of your own garden when you
return home.

Details: Daily during daylight hours; free; wheelchair accessible.
(1/2 hour)

★ UNIVERSITY OF ILLINOIS LIBRARY
408 W. Gregory Dr., Urbana, 217/333-2290

If you've had trouble finding information on anything, stop by the
University of Illinois Library. It's the largest public academic library in
the nation, and the undergraduate portion is famous for being built
underground so it wouldn't throw shade on the experimental farm
plot next door!

Details: Mon–Thu 8 a.m.–midnight, Fri 8–6, Sat 9–6, Sun 1–midnight; free; wheelchair accessible. (1 hour)

EVENTS

Just about every weekend of the year, some community or organization is holding a festival or celebration here. Even the university gets into the act with the
popular **Engineering Open House** and **Agriculture Open House**, which
feature lots of hands-on displays including a cow equipped with a special hole
in its stomach so folks can stick their hand inside and learn about digestion. Both
campus events are in early March.

In Arcola the **Raggedy Ann and Andy Festival** in mid-May pays tribute
to the creator of the Raggedy Ann doll, Johnny Gruelle. You can even enter a
look-alike contest if you're handy at making costumes. In mid-September, the

annual **Broomcorn Festival** attracts thousands of people to town, many of whom come to watch the famous "Lawn Rangers" precision lawnmower squad perform their antics.

Danville attracts a crowd to its annual **Oldsmobile Balloon Classic** each June. A shuttle system prevents parking hassles. Also in June in Danville, are the decades-old **Turtle Races**, featuring box turtles sponsored by area businesses and individuals.

Rantoul hosts the **U.S. Hot Air Balloon National Championship** in August, with hundreds of balloons and balloonists competing for prizes; plus an air show, live entertainment, and a carnival.

The "Sweetcorn Capital of the World" (a.k.a. Hoopston, Illinois) hosts arguably the best free food event anywhere. People show up for the **Hoopston Sweetcorn Festival** every Labor Day weekend to fill their empty coolers, garbage bags, and turkey roasters with this sweet, midwestern gold. Urbana also hosts its own **Urbana Sweetcorn Festival**. It's not as large as Hoopston's, but offers plenty of corn cooked on an old-fashioned steam engine.

In December, the **Kris Kringle Craft Show** fills the university's Assembly Hall with handcrafted Christmas items at great prices.

SHOPPING

The must-shop sites in Champaign are **Church Street Square**, corner of Church and Randolph Sts., 217/352-9517, for unique gifts and handcrafted clothing; **Rick Orr Florist**, 122 N.Walnut, 217/351-9299, to see the artistry of this nationally-acclaimed floral designer; and the **Larry Kanfer Gallery**, 2503 S. Neil St., 217/398-2000, where you can find a little piece of the prairie to take home with you.

The biggest retail outlet in the area is south of town. The **Factory Stores at Tuscola**, D200 Tuscola Blvd., 217/253-2282, use the motto, "Shop like crazy, save like mad," and with more than 60 manufacturers' outlets, that's just what customers here do. Stores include Jones New York, Tommy Hilfiger, and Nine West.

To the north, shoppers in downtown Rantoul will find that the old train station is now **Friends**, 217/892-2295, a great little mall filled with antiques and crafts. Also on Sangamon Avenue is **Deena's Style Shop**, 217/892-4997, a wonderful women's-clothing boutique where they still know what personal service means.

For something different, **Gordyville USA**, Rte. 136 east of Rantoul, 217/568-7117, has flea markets, craft shows, and horse auctions.

FITNESS AND RECREATION

In Urbana, **Crystal Lake Park**, 217/367-1536, is a good place to jog, fish, play, or canoe. Ice-skating and sledding are popular activities in the winter. **Lake of the Woods**, Mahomet, 217/586-3360 is the locals' favorite nearby getaway. You can fish, swim, walk, golf, picnic, and boat here. There's also a museum on early America and a beautiful botanical garden.

Kickapoo State Park near Danville, 217/442-4915, offers outdoor enthusiasts opportunities for fishing, hunting, boating, and horseback riding. **Moraine View State Recreation Area** near LeRoy (LEE-roy), 309/724-8032, is—like many state parks here—another gift from our long-gone glacier friends. These long ridges are perfect for horseback riding and hiking. There's also a lake that's stocked—to the gills! The **Middle Fork Forest Preserve** near Penfield, 217/595-5432; and the **Salt Fork Forest Preserve** near Homer, 217/896-2455, are nice places to swim, fish, hike, and picnic. The **Middle Fork State Fish and Wildlife Area**, 10906 Kickapoo Park Rd., Oakwood, 217/442-4915, is a part of the National Wild and Scenic Rivers system. As long as the water is high, canoeing here is a rush. In fact, sometimes the water moves so fast it's challenging.

The two nicest public golf courses in the area are **Hartwell C. Howard Golf Course** at Lake of the Woods, 217/586-2183, and **Brookhill Golf Course** on North Maplewood in Rantoul, 217/893-1200.

If the weather isn't good for outdoor activities, the **University of Illinois Armory**, 505 E. Armory in Champaign, has an indoor running track, and the local **YMCA**, 500 W. Church in Champaign, 217/359-9622, has an indoor public pool. One of the nicest spa facilities in the Midwest is the **Heartland Health Spa**, north of Champaign-Urbana in Gilman, 800-545-4853, where they specialize in fitness and self-confidence building. Hone your skills on their "Adventure Course," which features a climbing wall, tightropes, and a trapeze.

FOOD

With literally hundreds of restaurants in the area, you can always find something to eat. If you want something really good, though, here are a few suggestions. Good early morning spots are: **Merry Ann's Diner**, 1510 S. Neil St., Champaign, 217/352-5399 (inexpensive and open 24 hours); and the **Original Pancake House**, 1909 W. Springfield Ave., Champaign, 217/352-8866, which serves just about anything considered part of the pancake family.

For lunch: **Ott's Drive In**, 400 N. Century Blvd., Rantoul, 217/893-1100, specializes in 50s-style diner food—burgers, shakes, and fries, all made from

CHAMPAIGN-URBANA AREA

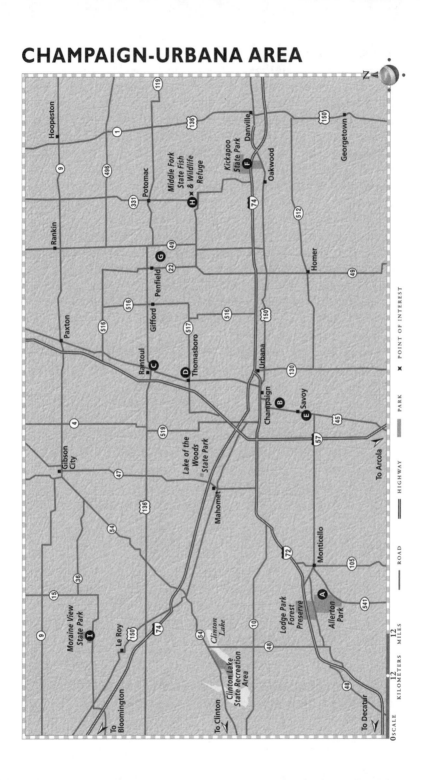

scratch. **Courier Cafe**, 111 N. Race St., Urbana, 217/328-1811, has an excellent pay-by-the-ounce salad bar. The best barbecue bargain in the twin cities is at either **Lil' Porgy's Bar-B-Que**, 101 W. University Ave., Urbana, 217/367-1018 (also at 1917 W. Springfield Ave., Champaign, 217/398-6811); or—if you're a real hot-food lover—**Po Boy's Bar-B-Que**, 58 E. Columbia Ave., Champaign, 217/352-5521.

Radio Maria's, 119 N. Walnut, Champaign, 217/398-7729, is the one of the most upscale lunch options in the area. Food here has a Caribbean flair.

Dinner options are numerous, too. For a casual meal at a great price, **Fiesta Cafe**, 216 S. First St., Champaign, 217/352-5902, has authentic Mexican food—and lots of it. Don't leave C-U without trying **Papa Del's Pizza**, 206 E. Green St., Champaign, 217/359-7700. It's pricey and may take an hour to arrive, but once you try it no other pizza you have will ever taste good.

In the Midwest, people love their corn-fed beef, and the best place to find that in Champaign is **The Ribeye**, 1701 S. Neil St., 217/351-9115.

For fine dining choose from: **Kennedy's**, 1717 S. Philo Rd., Urbana, 217/384-8111, with a wide selection of gourmet entrées; **Silvercreek**, 402 N. Race St., Urbana, 217/328-3402, the community's first completely smoke-free restaurant, with great free-range chicken; and **Timpone's**, 710 S. Goodwin Ave., Urbana, 217/344-7619, a nationally recognized Italian restaurant.

LODGING
Some of the best accommodations in the area are found at independent hotels and bed-and-breakfasts. **Jumer's Castle Lodge**, at Lincoln Square Mall in Urbana, 800/AT-JUMERS, is a reasonably priced Bavarian-style hotel. The chairs in the hotel's dining area have such high-backs that a table of four becomes a private room. The **Illini Union**, 1401 W. Green St., Urbana, 217/333-0161, is affordable and within walking distance of most U of I sights.

SIGHTS
- **A** Allerton Park
- **B** Curtis Orchard
- **C** Octave Chanute Aerospace Museum

FOOD
- **C** Ott's Drive In

LODGING
- **D** Burke's Country Inn
- **C** Fanmarker Inn
- **C** Rantoul Motel
- **E** Shurts House Inn Bed and Breakfast

CAMPING
- **F** Kickapoo State Park
- **G** Middle Fork Forest Preserve
- **H** Middle Fork State Fish and Wildlife Area
- **I** Moraine View State Park

Note: Items with the same letter are located in the same area.

AMISH COUNTRY

About 30 minutes south of Champaign you'll find several communities with an Amish flavor, including Arcola, whose welcome center is located at the train station, 800/336-5456; Arthur, 106 E. Progress, 800/72AMISH; Caldwell; Chesterville; and the Rockome Gardens Theme Park, just west of Arcola, 800/549-7625.

Hand-crafted furniture (especially cabinets), leatherwork, and quilts are all specialties here, as are pies, preserves, cheeses, and other foods, all of which are made from scratch. A horse and buggy is still the preferred transportation mode for many folks around here, so always observe the speed limits and watch for safety triangles on the backs of buggies. And remember that many members of the Amish faith prefer not to be photographed.

Lindley House, 312 W. Green St., Urbana, 217/384-4800, Web site: www.shout.net/~lindley, is a Victorian-style house filled with character and grace. **Shurts House Inn Bed and Breakfast**, 1001 N. Dunlap, Savoy, 217/398-4444, offers luxurious accommodations, plus an on-site restaurant, pub, and gift shop.

In Rantoul, the **Fanmarker Inn**, 200 Linden Ave., 217/893-1234, is a former dormitory that served the old Chanute Air Force Base. It's been remodeled into a comfortable hotel, with a good restaurant that bears the same name nearby. The **Rantoul Motel**, 301 N. Century Blvd., 217/893-1415, is a recently refurbished motel that was built when Century/Route 45 was the main highway in the area. In fact, the rooms still have Murphy beds in the walls. **Burke's Country Inn**, 2474 N. County Rd. 1100 E., Thomasboro, 217/643-7257, has four inexpensive guest rooms on a small kid-friendly farm.

CAMPING

Northeast of C-U, the **Middle Fork Forest Preserve** near Penfield, 217/595-5432, has plenty of campsites—primitive or with electrical hook-ups. **Kickapoo State Park**, **Middle Fork State Fish and Wildlife Area**, and **Moraine View State Park** all have wonderful camping options—in addition to the recreational activities mentioned earlier. Sites fill quickly, so call well in advance. All campgrounds are wheelchair accessible.

NIGHTLIFE

To hear local artists on their way to the big show, try **Mabel's**, 613 E. Green St., Champaign, 217/328-5700, in the heart of Campustown. For stand-up comedy, **T.K.Wendl's**, 1901 S. High Cross Rd., Urbana, 217/367-2255, brings in nationally known comics to accompany the silly people who already live here.

PERFORMING ARTS

Theater plays a big role in the nightlife of Champaign-Urbana. With one of the nation's best fine arts schools at the university, there's no shortage of talented actors. You can see many of them at the **Krannert Center for the Performing Arts**, 500 S. Goodwin, Urbana, 800/527-2849. The **Station Theatre**, 223 N. Broadway, Urbana, 217/384-4000, stages several productions each year featuring up-and-coming local actors. The **Virginia Theater**, 203 W. Park Ave., Champaign, 217/359-1483, is home to the community theater group, and hosts several gospel performances each year.

If you like classical music, the **Champaign-Urbana Symphony** at the Krannert Center presents world-class performances in one of the most acoustically perfect halls in the world.

9
CRAWFORDSVILLE
AREA

The Crawfordsville area has historic attractions that specialize in entertaining you while they sneak in a lot of information (that you'll find yourself using at dinner parties for a long time after you visit). The area also offers many great outdoor activities—hiking and canoeing are our favorites. Plus, the people here celebrate everything. Strawberries, the Civil War—you name it, there's a party for it.

The area's scenery is truly inspiring. In fact, it helped put General Lew Wallace in the mood to write his most famous novel, *Ben Hur*, which for years was required reading of every high school student in town. For that reason most adults in the community can recount all the fine points of the novel. The folks southwest of Crawfordsville can answer just about any question about covered bridges, including why they're sometimes called "kissing bridges." Answer: They gave young lovers some rare moments of privacy. By the way, they're still pretty good for that today.

A PERFECT DAY IN THE CRAWFORDSVILLE AREA

After a hearty breakfast at Arthur's, visit the Ben Hur Museum, Lane Place, and the Old Jail Museum. Lunch at Little Mexico, then take the scenic drive to Rockville. Explore Billie Creek Village, then take a covered-bridge tour. Stop at

Turkey Run State Park and hike whichever trail interests you, then hop in the car for an evening feast at the Beef House.

SIGHTSEEING HIGHLIGHTS

★★★★ BEN HUR MUSEUM
Pike St. and Wallace Ave., Crawfordsville, 765/362-5769

This tiny museum is the former study of General Lew Wallace, a renaissance man who did everything from writing one of the best selling novels in history (*Ben Hur*) to signing the death warrant of Billy the Kid (when Wallace was governor of the New Mexico territory). Kids' favorites are the soldier's uniform from the *Ben Hur* motion picture and the painting of a Turkish princess (with eyes like the Mona Lisa).

Pack a sack lunch and a blanket and enjoy picnic on the grounds here. An entire city block is filled with trees and gorgeous landscaping.

Details: *Apr–May and Sep–Oct Tue–Sun 1–4:30, Jun–Aug Wed–Sat 10–4:30, Sun and Tue 1–4:30; $2 adults, 50¢ children ages 6–12, ages 5 and under free. (1 hour)*

★★★★ BILLIE CREEK VILLAGE
State Rd. 36, just east of Rockville, 765/569-3430

A turn-of-the-century-style village, these 30 historic buildings and three covered bridges offer the setting for a thorough representation of prairie life as it was in the 1800s. There's a schoolhouse, livery stable, machine shed, sorghum mill, and broom shop, among others. You'll also find folks performing the duties and chores that were necessary to keep a small town viable more than 100 years ago.

Details: *Daily 9–4; $3.50 per person, $5 during major festivals, ages 4 and under free; free admission from Nov 1–May 1; wheelchair accessible. (½ day)*

★★★★ COVERED-BRIDGE TOURS
Pick up maps at any travel-brochure rack in the area or call either the Parke County Convention and Visitors Bureau, 765/569-5226

With more than 40 covered bridges in the area, you could spend a couple of days just trying to visit them all. We suggest a more leisurely approach—use bridge routes to get around while you're here and you'll probably see most of them. You might think that seeing one is sufficient, but each has its own individual and unique features and personality (some of them span waterfalls, one is allegedly haunted, and another has a load of fossils around it).

Details: *Another contact is the Putnam County Convention and Visitors Bureau, 765/653-8743. Web site: www.coveredbridges.com. (2 hours)*

★★★★ **LANE PLACE HISTORIC HOME**
212 S. Water St., Crawfordsville, 765/362-3416
If you didn't sleep your way through U.S. History 101, you'll remember Henry Lane was one of the people who helped form the Republican party and, later, helped Abraham Lincoln get to the White House as the party's first presidential candidate. The cane Mr. Lane used when he danced a jig after the victory is still in the coat tree in his hallway, as is the top hat he wore as an honorary pall bearer at the assassinated hero's funeral. This is one of the best antebellum homes

LEW WALLACE STUDY

Indiana Tourism Division

you'll ever tour, partly because it's recreated so beautifully, and partly because the rooms aren't roped off, allowing you to actually wander through them.

Details: *Tours Tue–Sun at 1, 2, and 3 p.m.; $3 adults, 50¢ children ages 6–12, ages 5 and under free. (1 hour)*

★★★ BRIDGETON GRIST MILL
Overlooks the historic Bridgeton Bridge, Bridgeton, 812/234-1520

The owners of this historic mill describe it lovingly as "the largest antique in Indiana." When they bought it, they learned it was also the oldest continuously operating mill west of the Allegheny Mountains. But with just one piece of machinery in working order, it was about to lose its title. So they began a major restoration effort, and now they grind about 10,000 pounds of corn, wheat, buckwheat, and rye each year.

These folks are experts at their trade, and they're so enthusiastic about it that by the time you leave here you'll want to find your own mill!

Details: *Open during major festivals, by appointment, or anytime the owners are there; free, although donations are accepted. (1 hour)*

★★★ ERNIE PYLE STATE HISTORIC SITE
One mile north of U.S. 36 on State Hwy. 71, 765/665-3633

The Quonset hut visitors center wasn't here when Ernie was born, but the folks who run this site thought it would be an appropriate way to celebrate the life of the great World War II journalist. You can read his newspaper columns, as well as his personal letters, and learn what made him such an important chronicler of the war.

Details: *Mid-Mar–mid-Dec Tue–Sat 9–5, Sun 1–5; free; wheelchair accessible. (1 hour)*

★★★ OLD JAIL MUSEUM
225 N. Washington St., Crawfordsville, 765/362-5222

It would be bad enough to go to jail, but imagine being stuck in a cell with *no* door. That's what it was like for hundreds of prisoners at the Rotary Jail of Montgomery County from 1882 until 1939. You could get into and out of this two-story pie-shaped jail only if someone hand cranked the 54,000-pound unit around so your cell was facing the

CRAWFORDSVILLE

N

SHADY LN

INDIANAPOLIS RD

32

136

JCT

ENGLEWOOD DR

DARLINGTON AV

GRACE AV

FREMONT ST

CANBY ST

Municipal
Golf
Course

ELMORE AV

I

OAK ST

PINE ST

WOODLAWN PL

MILL ST

JEFFERSON ST

COLLEGE ST

JOHN ST

DANVILLE AV

WHITLOCK AV

A WALLACE AV

E

ELM ST

B WATER ST

H

CHESTNUT ST

ELMORE AV

To 74

231

43

F

WASHINGTON ST

L

C

G To

WALNUT ST

Elston Park

GRANT AV

K

Sugar Creek

LAFAYETTE AV

Wabash College

D

CRAWFORD ST

COVINGTON ST

MARKET ST

MAIN ST

M

PIKE ST

WABASH AV

JENNISON ST

WEST ST

BARR ST

WAYNETOWN RD

J

BERRY ST

POINT OF INTEREST

PARK

HIGHWAY

ROAD

0 SCALE

.5 MILE

KILOMETER

.5

door. Just seven of these types of jails were built, and this is the only one that still works.

Details: Apr–May and Sep–Oct Wed–Sun 1–4:30, Jun–Aug Wed–Sat 1–4:30 and 10–4:30; free, although donations are accepted; first floor wheelchair accessible. (½ hour)

★★ WABASH COLLEGE
502 W. Wabash Ave., Crawfordsville, 800/345-5385

A small, private, men's liberal arts institution, Wabash College is the academic home of more than 800 students each year. Many of its buildings are historically significant. The best way to see them is to stop at the admission center and pick up a map.

Details: Web site: www.wabash.edu/; wheelchair accessible. (½ hour)

★ WALKING TOUR OF ELSTON GROVE
412 E. Main St., Crawfordsville, 800/866-3973

This historic section of Crawfordsville was home to the most prominent folks in town back in the late 1800s and early 1900s. The best place to start the tour is at the visitors bureau, since they have the tour maps.

Almost all the 45 buildings on the tour are private homes, so you can't go inside, but Lew Wallace Study, Lane Place, Montgomery County Visitors and Convention Bureau, and St. John's Episcopal Church all welcome visitors.

Details: Best viewing is during daylight hours; free; the 1 ½-mile tour route is wheelchair accessible. (2 hours)

SIGHTS
Ⓐ Ben Hur Museum
Ⓑ Lane Place Historic Home
Ⓒ Old Jail Museum
Ⓓ Wabash College
Ⓔ Walking Tour of Elston Grove

FOOD
Ⓕ Arthur's
Ⓖ Dog and Suds
Ⓗ Little Mexico
Ⓘ Mugsy Malone's
Ⓙ Uncle Smiley's

LODGING
Ⓚ Lew Wallace Inn
Ⓛ Riviera Motel
Ⓜ Sugar Creek Queen Anne Bed and Breakfast

CAMPING
Ⓐ KOA Campground

Note: Items with the same letter are located in the same area.

EVENTS

There are just about as many festivals in this area as there are covered bridges. The granddaddy of them all is the **Parke County Covered Bridge Festival**, held at Billie Creek Village in mid-October. You can ride an antique carousel, stuff yourself with the same foods that endowed Abe Lincoln with the energy to split rails, and watch what seems like a million craft demonstrations. Billie Creek Village hosts some sort of special event just about every weekend, including the **Parke County Maple Syrup Festival** (primitive and modern syrup making demonstrations) in late February and early March, the **Spinners and Weavers Spin In** and **Civil War Days** in early June, and the **Parke County Covered Bridge Christmas** in early December.

Crawfordsville hosts the **Strawberry Festival** in mid-June, with lots of kids' activities and tons of strawberry treats. Frankfort celebrates the food that shares its name with the annual **Hot Dog Festival** in late July; and folks in Mansfield go on a mushroom hunt, auction mushrooms, and eventually end up eating them all at the **Mansfield Mushroom Festival** in late April.

SHOPPING

This place is crawling with antiques. Many of the shops handle what you might call bric-a-brac-type items, and some offer everything from furniture to fine china to glassware. The best places to browse for all of the above are **Cabbages & Kings Antique Mall**, 124 S. Washington St., Crawfordsville, 765/362-2577; and the **Covered Bridge Mall**, on the east side of the square in Rockville, 765/569-3145. For handcrafted items made using the same techniques that were employed a hundred years ago, go to the **Billie Creek General Store** in Billie Creek Village, 765/569-0252. With products from more than 80 crafters, you can buy everything from lye soap, homemade jellies, and tinware to Amish quilts, homemade fudge, and maple syrup.

FITNESS AND RECREATION

Shades State Park, 15 miles southwest of Crawfordsville on State Hwy. 234, 765/435-2810, and **Turkey Run State Park**, on U.S. 47 just north of Marshall, 765/597-2635, are the homes of breathtaking sandstone formations under the shady canopy of magnificent trees. Both parks offer a variety of scenic hiking trails for people of all skill levels.

Sugar Creek flows along both parks, and a canoe trip down the creek offers some fantastic views of the sandstone cliffs. **Clement Canoes**, 613 Lafayette Ave., Crawfordsville, 765/362-2781, has canoe and kayak trips ranging from three hours to two days. For a lazy float, there are five-hour tubing trips. When the creek's too high for canoeing, they offer four-hour rafting trips instead. Inside Shades State Park is the **Pine Hills Nature Preserve**, another nice place to enjoy the flora and fauna. **Lake Waveland**, Hwy. 47 S. just outside of Waveland, 765/435-2073, and **Raccoon State Recreation Area**, 160 S. Raccoon Pkwy. in Rockville, 765/344-1412, both offer fishing, swimming, and other outdoor fun.

If the weather isn't nice and you'd still like to get some exercise, the new **Crawfordsville High School**, just off Hwy. 47 S. at 1 Athenian Dr., 765/362-2340, has an indoor walking track and a swimming pool available to the public for a small fee.

FOOD

People around here love **Uncle Smiley's** (decorated in what you might call "Early Pig"), on the west side of Crawfordsville at 205 Waynetown Rd., 765/362-0432. This restaurant is locally famous as the home of the "Big Oink"—a giant tenderloin sandwich that hangs over the plate. On the south side, Crawfordsville still has a real **Dog and Suds**, 1817 U.S. 231, 765/362-6881, with frosted mugs, car hops, and great food.

Downtown Crawfordsville offers several choices. Try Mexican food at **Little Mexico**, 211 E. Main St., 765/361-1042, where they still make their own chips and salsa, and all the meals are inexpensive and authentic. Or try **Arthur's**, 111 E. Main St., 765/364-9938, which specializes in homemade foods. Choose their deli sandwiches and hearty soups, or feast on the weekly lasagna lunch special. They also have great homemade chocolate chip cookies.

For a good deal on a big steak, head to the east side of town and try **Mugsy Malone's**, 1450 Darlington Ave., 765/362-4487. The entrées fill your plate, and the side dishes are just as hearty.

If you're in the mood for a scenic drive followed by some of the best food you'll ever eat, head to the **Beef House**, I-74 and Hwy. 63, Covington. Select your steak from the display case and let the chefs work their magic on the open-hearth charcoal pits while you enjoy a heaping salad with homemade rolls and strawberry preserves. It's definitely worth the drive.

LODGING

The Crawfordsville area is known for its wide array of bed-and-breakfasts, most of which are in historic homes and are quite affordable.

On the west side of town, **Sugar Creek Queen Anne Bed and**

CRAWFORDSVILE AREA

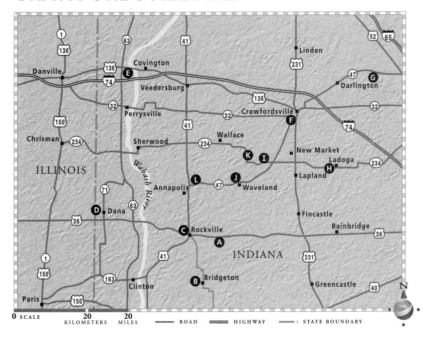

SIGHTS
ⓐ Billie Creek Village
ⓑ Bridgeton Grist Mill
ⓒ Covered-Bridge Tours
ⓓ Ernie Pyle State
   Historic Site

FOOD
ⓔ Beef House

LODGING
ⓕ Maples B&B
ⓖ Our Country Home
   Bed and Breakfast
ⓗ Vintage Reflections
   B&B
ⓘ Woods Canyon
   Resort

CAMPING
ⓙ Lake Waveland Park
ⓚ Shades State Park
ⓛ Turkey Run Park
ⓘ Wood's Canyon
   Resort and
   Campground

Note: Items with the same letter are located in the same area.

Breakfast, 901 W. Market St., Crawfordsville, 800/362-6293, is in a restored early 1900s home. The furnishings are Victorian, and they even serve afternoon tea in the rose garden.

South of town, the **Maples B&B**, 4814 Hwy. 47 S., Crawfordsville,

---

765/866-8095, has a fireplace in each room. They also have a hot tub. The aroma of quiche and homemade rolls will prevent you from sleeping the day away. At **Our Country Home Bed and Breakfast**, between Crawfordsville and Lebanon on Hwy. 47, 765/794-3139, the owners have thought of everything to ensure you have a pleasant stay. You can have a private, dinner, gaze at the stars using their telescope, or just soak in the hot tub.

A few miles southeast of Crawfordsville, **Vintage Reflections B&B**, 125 W. Main St., Ladoga, 765/942-1002, is a Queen Anne–style home with gorgeous stained glass and an upstairs veranda. The big attractions, though, are the pool and the huge breakfasts they serve every day.

For some nice possibilities in a more institutional—but still affordable—setting, the **Lew Wallace Inn**, 309 W. Pike St., 800/890-8484, is close to the Ben Hur Museum. **Riviera Motel**, 1510 U.S. 231 S., Crawfordsville, 765/362-9925, is an 18-room establishment offering a room with a double bed for just $27.

If you'd like to stay at **Woods Canyon Resort** but don't want to camp, try one of their rustic cabins instead of a tentsite. While you'll need to bring your own linens and toiletries, you will have a private bathroom with a shower.

CAMPING

You can always count on a **KOA Kampground**, and this one has everything from primitive sites to full hook-ups and cabins. Located at 1660 U.S. 231 N., Crawfordsville, 765/362-4190, this campground is near lots of attractions, and has its own playground, rec room, and swimming pool. A primitive site here runs about $16, sites with water and electricity are about $19, and sites with sewer hook-ups cost about $20.

Lake Waveland Park, has both primitive and modern campsites with showers, canoe and boat rental, tennis courts, and even a water slide. Primitive sites here run $6 each, while modern ones are $11.

If you're going to Turkey Run, one of the best places to stay is in **Turkey Run Park**. They don't have water and sewer hook-ups for RVs, but electricity is available. On-the-grid sites are $11 a night; primitives are $7.

Shades State Park also has campsites and a showerhouse, and can accommodate backpackers and canoe campers. All sites are $7.

Wood's Canyon Resort and Campground, State Rd. 234 at the Deers Mill Covered Bridge, 765/362-2781, is a pretty place to pitch your tent. It's $7 per person if you are canoeing, $8 if you aren't. All sites are primitive, but there are shower facilities and the grounds include one of the most spectacular views in the area.

NIGHTLIFE

At **Crash McClain's Sports Pub**, 1643 Eastway Dr., Crawfordsville, 765/362-5633, you can bowl, play laser tag, shoot billiards, or throw darts. The **Vanity Theater**, 122 S. Washington St., Crawfordsville, 765/362-7077, is the home of the Sugar Creek Players. They offer several live performances each year in this historic theater, and all of the shows feature local talent.

Covered-Bridge Tour

The covered-bridge route is especially breathtaking in the fall, when the leaves are so bright you have to squint. While you can follow any of the marked routes to see a few of the bridges at a time, it is possible to take in 16 in one leaf-canopied loop. You'll just need to combine a few routes for one long splash of color.

Begin in Rockville at the visitors center and take the **Red Route**. Follow it to the Mecca Bridge, then pick up the **Brown Route**. Take the Brown through the Sim Smith Bridge, then angle north on 600 West to Union Bridge. That'll put you on the **Yellow Route**, leading you to the town of Tangier (tan-jeer). There, get on the **Blue Route** (you'll be driving it backwards, so the signs may not be very helpful). Take 41 past Turkey Run State Park, then go through Marshall back to Rockville.

A note of caution: Do not try this during the Covered Bridge Festival—if you do you'll cause a decent-sized traffic jam.

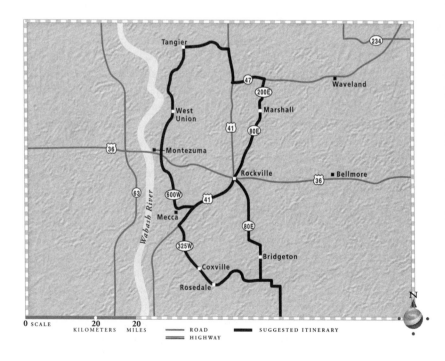

10
INDIANAPOLIS AREA

Just as listening to the *William Tell Overture* makes you think of the *Lone Ranger*, hearing the word "Indianapolis" probably makes you think "500." But while this city takes great pride in hosting the biggest car-racing event anywhere, it has many more dimensions. Sports enthusiasts can watch professional football, basketball, hockey, and tennis. The city is also home to the national governing boards of several sports, including diving, gymnastics, track and field, rowing, and synchronized swimming. Even the NCAA has decided to move its headquarters here. One of the best children's museums in the world calls Indy home. If you're looking for culture, you don't have to look far. Indy has its own world-class symphony, opera, and ballet. And there's so much good shopping, it's hard to decide where to start—and when to stop. The community is diverse, and the people here celebrate their heritage. This is also where Eli Lilly brought together some of the best scientists in the world to develop insulin, where Madam C. J. Walker created a line of cosmetics designed especially for African American women, and where researchers at Indiana University's School of Dentistry developed Crest toothpaste.

Indianapolis is one of the friendliest places you'll ever visit, and you might even find someone who knows what the word "Hoosier" really means. In fact, they're so hospitable, the folks at the visitors center built you a 13-by-13 model for downtown to keep you from getting disoriented.

A PERFECT DAY IN THE INDIANAPOLIS AREA

You must have breakfast at Le Peep's at least once, so make it today. Then go to the Children's Museum, and be there when they open. After working your way down the exhibit floors, take a load off in the CineDome and watch the current feature. Then head for Circle Centre to eat and shop till you can't take it anymore. Stop at Ybor's Martini Bar for refreshments, then drive to the Indianapolis Speedway to see the museum and take a trip around the track. Finally, dinner at Palomino is a perfect finish to the day.

GETTING AROUND INDIANAPOLIS

Most of Indianapolis is laid out like a grid, which makes it a fairly easy city to navigate. But some sections tend to get a little hairy, so a bit of patience is necessary, especially at rush hour. The Indianapolis bus system, IndyGo, is very limited and is not an extremely efficient or convenient way to travel in the city. But it is economical. The fare is only $1 to anywhere in the city and transfers are free. For more information on bus routes and fares contact the IndyGo Transit Store at 317/635-3344.

At this time, no subway or commuter train is available, so driving is probably the best way to get around the city. And surprisingly, traffic in Indianapolis is not that much of a problem, at least not compared to other cities of the same size. Indianapolis has several taxi companies, but they generally earn most of their profits from phone-ins, so it can be anywhere from frustrating to impossible to hail a taxi from the sidewalk.

SIGHTSEEING HIGHLIGHTS

★★★★ CHILDREN'S MUSEUM OF INDIANAPOLIS
3000 N. Meridian St., Indianapolis, 800/208-KIDS

If you ever tell anyone you've been to Indianapolis, one of the first things they're going to ask you is, "Did you go to that great kids' museum they have?" There's a reason it's so well known. You can touch, hear, climb, try on, and even build the exhibits. And you don't even have to bring a child with you. This place is dedicated to making knowledge fun, and it covers everything from science and math to history and language. One of the biggest attractions here is the water clock. It measures 30 feet high and uses 70 gallons of water to keep track of time. There's a great rock climb, too, but get

INDIANAPOLIS

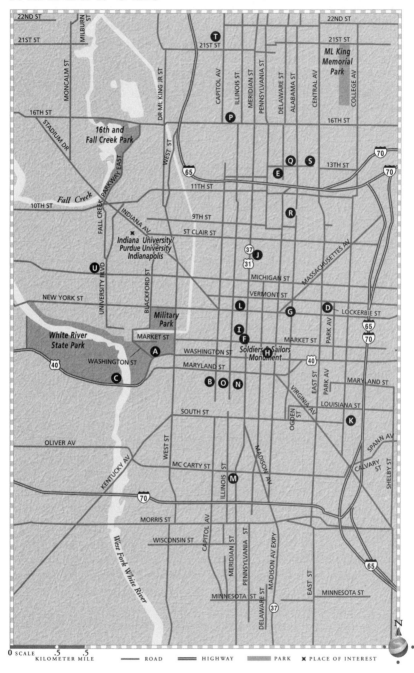

tickets for that early or you'll be left out of the fun. Schedule some time to catch a film in the CineDome Theater, attached to the museum. It certainly puts those old 3-D glasses to shame, with its domelike screen and amazing stereo that take you right into the action.

Details: *Mar–Labor Day daily 10–5, closed Mon Sep–Feb; $8 adults, $7 seniors, $3.50 children ages 2–17, ages 1 and under free, free for ages 5–8 the first Thu every month; wheelchair accessible. (3 hours)*

★★★★ **EITELJORG MUSEUM OF AMERICAN INDIANS AND WESTERN ART**
500 W. Washington St., Indianapolis, 317/636-9378

The folks who work here say the nicest compliment they can get is when a visitor says thanks for showing what Indians were really like. And at the Eiteljorg Museum, people say that all the time. The paintings, pottery, baskets, and other hand-crafted items in the museum tell a complex, beautiful, and sometimes tragic story of life for Native Americans throughout the history of the United States. The gift shop is stocked with handcrafted items that allow you to take some of the museum's beauty home with you.

SIGHTS

Ⓐ Eiteljorg Museum of American Indians and Western Art
Ⓑ Indianapolis City Center
Ⓒ Indianapolis Zoo
Ⓓ James Whitcomb Riley Museum Home
Ⓔ President Benjamin Harrison Home
Ⓕ Soldiers and Sailors Monument

FOOD

Ⓕ Alcatraz Brewing Company
Ⓖ Bazbeaux Pizza

FOOD (continued)

Ⓗ Benvenuti
Ⓑ Bertolini's Authentic Trattoria
Ⓑ Cooper's Turkey Place
Ⓘ Del Frisco's
Ⓙ Elbow Room
Ⓚ Iaria's Italian Restaurant
Ⓛ Le Peep Restaurant
Ⓗ Majestic Restaurant
Ⓑ Palomino Euro Bistro
Ⓜ Shapiro's Delicatessen Cafeteria
Ⓝ Snow Lion Tibetan Restaurant
Ⓑ Soup Masters Cafe
Ⓑ St. Elmo Steak House

LODGING

Ⓞ Canterbury Hotel
Ⓑ Crowne Plaza Union Station
Ⓟ Methodist Tower Inn
Ⓠ Old Northside Bed and Breakfast
Ⓡ Renaissance Tower Historic Inn
Ⓢ Stone Soup Inn
Ⓣ Tranquil Cherub Bed and Breakfast
Ⓤ University Place Conference Center and Hotel

Note: Items with the same letter are located in the same area.

Details: *Web site: www.eiteljorg.org; Mon–Sat 10–5, Sun noon–5, guided tours daily at 2, closed Mon Sep–May; $5 adults, $4 seniors, $2 students ages 5–17, ages 4 and under free; wheelchair accessible. (2 hours)*

★★★★ INDIANAPOLIS MOTOR SPEEDWAY HALL OF FAME MUSEUM
4790 W. 16th St., Indianapolis, 317/484-6747

To many people across the country and around the world, Indianapolis is *the* speedway. If you can't make it to Indy for the 500, at least stop by the Hall of Fame Museum and experience the next best thing. The huge collection of 500 champions and other classic cars traces the history and development of engines, aerodynamics, and style throughout driving history. Folks who have wondered what it would be like to navigate turn four and see the checkered flag announcing their victory may want to postpone their visit to the museum and instead begin with a trip around the track.

Details: *Daily 9–5 except Christmas; $2 adults, ages 15 and under free; bus tours around track $2 per person; wheelchair accessible. (1 hour)*

★★★★ INDIANAPOLIS MUSEUM OF ART
1200 W. 38th St., Indianapolis, 317/923-1331

This museum houses an extensive collection of works from the classical masters to contemporary artists. Some of the most beautiful works are the pieces from Africa and China. The large collection of J.M.W. Turner watercolors and drawings is a real treat for your eyes. So are the works from the Old Masters and the famous *LOVE* sculpture (you know—the one with the "LO" sitting on the "VE"). The museum's grounds are a work of art, too. You can stroll the trails, enjoy the botanical garden, and attend a performance at the Indianapolis Civic Theatre without leaving the property.

Details: *Tue–Wed and Fri–Sat 10–5, Thu 10–8:30, Sun noon–5; free except for selected exhibitions; wheelchair accessible. (2 hours)*

★★★★ INDIANAPOLIS ZOO
1200 W. Washington St., Indianapolis, 317/630-2001

With more than 3,000 different species of animals, the Indianapolis Zoo has a lot to offer. The zoo is home to the largest aquarium in the state, a beautiful botanical garden, and a re-created habitat for all sorts of lizards and birds called the "Desert Biome." The coolest feature of this so-called "cageless zoo," though, is the up close interaction you can have with the residents. Petting, feeding, holding, and riding are all allowed—under supervision, of course.

Details: *Daily 9–5; $9.75 adults, $7 seniors, $6 children ages 3–12, ages 2 and under free; wheelchair accessible. (4 hours)*

★★★★ JAMES WHITCOMB RILEY MUSEUM HOME
528 Lockerbie St., Indianapolis, 317/631-5885

James Whitcomb Riley lived in this house on Lockerbie Street for the last 23 years of his life. But he fell in love with the neighborhood long before he took up residence here. In fact, he even wrote a poem about the street ("For no language could frame and no lips could repeat my rhyme-haunted raptures of Lockerbie Street."). Once you visit this amazingly well-preserved home, you'll see why it meant so much to him. Filled with exquisite furnishings and all the modern conveniences of his day, it was the type of setting that would help a poet work through even the worst case of writer's block.

Details: *Tue–Sat 10–3:30, Sun noon–3:30; $2 adults, $1.50 seniors, 50¢ children ages 7–17, ages 6 and under free; first floor wheelchair accessible. (½ hour)*

★★★★ PRESIDENT BENJAMIN HARRISON HOME
1230 N. Delaware St., Indianapolis, 317/631-1898

This three-story mansion is certainly befitting a head of state. Benjamin Harrison's home is furnished in the late-Victorian style, with four of every five pieces actually from the Harrison family. While touring the rooms you'll be treated to a fascinating history of the former resident and his legacy: He's the only U.S. president ever to lose the popular vote but still gain office by winning a majority of the electoral college; his grandfather was also president; and his great-grandfather signed the Declaration of Independence.

Details: *Mon–Sat 10–3:30, Sun 12:30–3:30; $5 adults, $4 seniors, $1 students ages 16 and under, preschoolers free; first floor is wheelchair accessible. (1 hour)*

★★★ HOOK'S AMERICAN DRUG STORE MUSEUM
1180 E. 38th St., Indiana State Fairgrounds, Indianapolis, 317/924-1503

If you can remember what it was like to get all gussied up on a Saturday night and go to the local drugstore for a malt, this place will take you back there one more time. It's not just a museum honoring developments in pharmacy technology; it's also a tribute to what used to be *the* place to meet in town. It features a working soda fountain and all the candies, novelties, and souvenirs you would have expected to find there 50 years ago. There are also hundreds of antiques and collectibles to view and buy.

Details: Tue–Sun 11–4; free; wheelchair accessible. (1 hour)

★★★ INDIANA MEDICAL HISTORY MUSEUM
3045 W. Vermont St., Indianapolis, 317/635-7329

Visiting this museum makes you wonder just how archaic MRIs, sonograms, and chemotherapy will seem 100 years from now. Everything in this place was once state-of-the-art, and now many items look like the furnishings of a torture chamber from a B-grade horror movie. But they're all real, and they all played a role in the development of modern medicine. There's even a restored vintage classroom (with cane-bottom, oak chairs, and a great skylight) that was used by medical students and doctors until the mid-50s.

Details: Wed–Sat 10–4; $3 adults, $1 students ages 6–18, ages five and under free; first floor wheelchair accessible. (1 hour)

★★★ INDIANA STATE FAIRGROUNDS
1202 E. 38th St., Indianapolis, 317/927-7500

Don't let the name deceive you. The State Fair is here for about two weeks every August, but this place needs locks about as much as a 24-hour grocery. With flea markets; car, motorcycle, and boat shows; auctions; dog and cat shows; go-kart races; boxing; jewelry, guitar, computer, antique and vintage-clothing shows; wine competitions; craft sales; recreational vehicle rallies; and a variety of festivals, there's almost always something fun to see or do here. Of course, if you can visit during the Indiana State Fair, that's loads of fun, too.

Details: Call ahead for a current schedule of events; admission charge varies; wheelchair accessible. (1–3 hours)

★★ CROWN HILL CEMETERY
700 W. 38th St., Indianapolis, 317/925-8231

Some of the most famous—and infamous—people who lived

and/or died in Indiana are buried here. President Benjamin Harrison's body was laid to rest here, as were no fewer than three U.S. vice-presidents. John Dillinger is here, too, and many other people who helped shape—for better or for worse—this city, this state, and the nation through the 19th and 20th centuries. Military buffs can search for Civil War veterans, plus more than a dozen generals. Pick up a brochure for the self-guided tour, or stop at the office and ask one of the guides to accompany you.

Details: Apr–Sept daily 8–6, Oct–Mar daily 8–5, office closed Sunday; free, but guided tours are $5 adults, $4 seniors, $2 students, preschoolers free. (1 hour)

★★ GARFIELD PARK AND CONSERVATORY
2450 S. Shelby St., Indianapolis, 317/327-7184

If you like your rain forests without a restaurant attached, the Garfield Conservatory offers a pleasant re-creation of the Amazon River region. The waterfall and flowers are spectacular, and the way they're arranged gives the impression that they actually sprung up without the assistance of the park's excellent horticulture staff. The park also offers traveling exhibits and lots of flower shows and events.

Details: Tue–Sat 10–5, Sun noon–5; $2 adults, $1.50 seniors, $1 children; wheelchair accessible. (½ hour)

★★ INDIANAPOLIS CITY CENTER
201 S. Capitol Ave., Indianapolis, 317/237-5200

For an official welcome to the city, stop by the Indianapolis City Center. They have brochures, maps, and event calendars, plus a big model of the city to help you map out your adventures. The staff and volunteers can answer just about any question, and they'll even help you plan your stay. This is also the place where tours of the RCA Dome begin.

Details: Mon–Fri 10–5:30, Sat 10–5, Sun 12–5; free; wheelchair accessible. (½ hour)

★★ SOLDIERS AND SAILORS MONUMENT
Monument Circle, Indianapolis, 317/232-7615

One of the best views of the city is at the top of this memorial. That's appropriate, since the men it honors fought to preserve the Indiana way of life and the freedom you're enjoying. The monument is 284 feet tall, but getting to the top isn't bad, since you have your choice of

INDIANAPOLIS MOTOR SPEEDWAY

Indiana Tourism Division

stairs or elevator. The brand-new basement museum honors Civil War soldiers, and displays their uniforms, weapons, and equipment. And don't miss the collection of the compelling exhibit of the letters that soliers sent home.

Details: Mid-Apr–Sep Wed–Sun 11–7, rest of the year 9–5; free; wheelchair accessible. (½ hour)

★ BROAD RIPPLE VILLAGE
Neighborhood bounded by Keystone Ave., Kessler Blvd., and the White River, Indianapolis

David Letterman's always talking about growing up in Indiana, and this place was his stomping grounds as a child. His boyhood home isn't a national monument—yet—but you can go into the **Atlas Supermarket**, 5411 N. College, 317/255-6800, where he bagged groceries (and stocked canned hams, perhaps?). Even without the Letterman connection, the Broad Ripple area would be worth a spot on your itinerary. It's an interesting place to tour, and—as you'll see in this chapter's shopping section, below—there's plenty to buy. The canal that runs through Broad Ripple is home to lots of hungry ducks, so make sure you pick up something for them, too.

Details: Hours of shops and restaurants vary. (1 hour)

EVENTS

By far the biggest event ever to hit this city is the **Indianapolis 500** at the Indianapolis Motor Speedway. It started May 30, 1911, with Ray Harroun driving his "Wasp" Marmon, which was equipped with a novelty Harroun built to take the place of an on-board mechanic. It was called a rearview mirror, and—like the 500—it caught on all across the country. The race is run every Memorial Day, but the preparations and festivities begin way before then. Practice begins a week before **Time Trials**, which are held a week before the race (with **Pole Day** on Saturday and **Bubble Day** on Sunday). Throughout the practice week there are all sorts of games and activities in an event called **Fan Fest**. The final day of practice is the Thursday before the race. The **Indianapolis 500 Festival**, 800/638-4296, is a series of celebrations connected to the big race. They include a queen contest, an art exhibit, an autograph party (with the drivers), a mini-marathon (on a course that includes a lap around the track), a community day (when you can drive your car around the track and tour Gasoline Alley, Pit Row, and the Tower Terrace), a black-tie ball, a symphony concert, and a parade.

The **Brickyard 400** race is relatively new to Indy, and offers NASCAR drivers a chance to compete at Indy on the Winston Cup circuit. There are several events associated with it; for information call 800/638-4296.

The **Indiana State Fair**, 317/927-7695, is held at the fairgrounds every August. It features agricultural judging (everything from cattle and sheep to squash and roses), plus rides, exhibits, and big-name entertainment.

In August the Indianapolis Museum of Art hosts the annual **AfricaFest**, 317/236-2099. The celebration includes music, dancing, ethnic foods, arts and crafts, and plenty of activities for kids.

The best way to get up-to-date information on what's happening during your visit is by contacting the **Indianapolis Convention and Visitors Association**, 317/639-4282, Web site: www.indy.org.

SHOPPING

You like shopping? You can certainly find plenty to buy in Indianapolis. The place to start is **Circle Centre**, 49 W. Maryland St., 317/681-8000. **Nordstrom** and **Parisian** are here along with all the usual mall amenities and about 100 other stores.

Some fun neighborhoods to visit for shopping and dining are **Broad Ripple Village** and the **Massachusetts Avenue** district. One of the hottest places to shop these days is **Keystone at the Crossing—The Fashion Mall**, at the corner of 86th and Keystone on the north side of town, 317/574-4000, with a little—no a lot—of just about everything. Just down the road you'll find **Clearwater Crossing**, 4016 E. 82nd St., and **Castleton Mall**, 6020 E. 82nd St., 317/849-9993.

Even in a place as contemporary as Indianapolis, you can still find great antiques. The **Indianapolis Downtown Antique Mall**, 1044 Virginia Ave., 317/635-5336, has an eclectic array of treasures. **Vi Walker Silver**, 652 E. 52nd St., 317/283-3753, offers a variety of tea spoons and tea sets, as well as silver for your dining room. Run by the same owner and located at the same address as Vi Walker Silver is the impressive, **Furnishings**, selling furniture and decoratives for your home. **Allisonville Road Antique Mall**, 6230 N. Allisonville Rd., 317/259-7318, is a huge facility with all sorts of antiques and collectibles; and **Southport Antique Mall**, 2028 E. Southport Rd., 317/786-8246, has more than 200 separate dealers. A short drive out of Indianapolis, **Greenfield**, Indiana, is known for great antique shops, too.

Several wineries are in or near the city. **Easley Winery**, 205 N. College Ave., 317/636-4516, has wines, champagnes, gift baskets filled with indigenous items, and everything you need to set up your own wine-making operation. **Gaia Wines**, 606 Massachusetts Ave., 317/634-WINE, offers wines, tours, wine- and grape-related gifts, food tasting platters, and some heavenly desserts. Just outside Indianapolis, **Chateau Thomas Winery**, 6291 Cambridge Way, Plainfield, 888-761-WINE, has free wine tasting, as well as gourmet cheeses and wonderful food and gifts. They'll even create a personalized wine label for you.

FITNESS AND RECREATION

The most popular park in Indianapolis is **White River State Park**, 801 W. Washington St., 317/634-4567. This downtown park has much to offer, from traditional, tree-filled, picnic-style settings to a number of contemporary, hi-tech attractions including an **IMAX Theater**, 317/233-4629, the **Indianapolis Zoo**, and the **Eiteljorg Museum of American Indians and Western Art**. The must-see at this park is the half-mile **River Promenade**, a limestone path that traces the river. The stone carvings along the path add interest and detail to an already beautiful place.

For real fitness junkies, the **National Institute for Fitness and Sport**, 250 N. University Blvd., 317/274-3432, is open to the public as a fitness center, and includes basketball courts, exercise rooms, an indoor track, and a weight room. The **Indiana University Natatorium**, 901 W. New York St., 317/274-3518, is also open to the public.

Eagle Creek Park, 7840 W. 56th St., 317/327-7110, is on the west edge of town, and has walking and biking trails, a huge reservoir (where you can canoe, kayak, sail, fish, or swim), playgrounds, and even a 27-hole golf course. The park is also home to several international rowing competitions, but most folks just think of it as a wooded first-class getaway.

Indianapolis Parks Department Bike and Fitness Trails are scattered throughout the city in a variety of parks. Call 317/327-7275, and ask about the **Indianapolis Greenways** to find the one nearest your hotel. All are open from dawn to dusk, and all but one (Eagle Creek Park) are free. The federal "Rails-to-Trails" program gets credit for the **Monon Trail** (one of the city greenways), which has become a popular biking, walking, jogging, and skating path through town.

For some seriously retro-style fun, try duckpin bowling at **Action Bowl**, 325 S. College Ave., 317/632-2879. This isn't the kind of bowling you remember from your high school gym class. In this game you try to knock down undersized pins with a wooden ball the size of a softball. The good news is you get an extra turn every frame. It's not exactly easy, but it is a hoot!

In-line skaters might want to call the **RCA Dome**, 100 S. Capitol Ave., 317/237-DOME, for information about public skating times in the dome. You can ice skate—in season—at **Perry Ice Rink**, 451 E. Stop 11 Rd., 317/888-0070, or at the **Indiana State Fairgrounds Event Center Pepsi Coliseum**, 1202 E. 38th St., 317/927-7536.

If you prefer car racing and you just can't wait for the Indy 500, **Stefan Johansson Karting Center**, 3549 Lafayette Rd., 317/297-KART, Web site: www.stafanjohansson.com, offers indoor go-kart racing at its fastest. You can race against your friends and family, or go head-to-head with the clock.

There are more than 80 golf courses within easy driving distance of Indianapolis, so it's impossible to make a call on which one is the best. The course with the most unusual setting is **Brickyard Crossing**, 4400 W. 16th St., Indianapolis, 317/484-6572. It's at the Indianapolis Motor Speedway and gives players a new angle from which to view the track. A new and very highly rated course is the **Fort Golf Resort** at Fort Harrison State Park, 6002 N. Post Rd., Indianapolis, 317/543-9597.

For those who prefer to recreate by watching others compete, the city is home to the NBA's **Indiana Pacers**, 317/263-2100; the NFL's **Indianapolis Colts**, 317/297-7000; the **Indians** of Triple-A baseball, 317/269-3545; and the **Indianapolis Ice** professional hockey team, 317/266-1234.

FOOD

People who live here say **Le Peep Restaurant**, 301 N. Illinois St., 317/237-3447, is the best place in town to get breakfast. It's not bad for lunch either, and

INDIANAPOLIS AREA

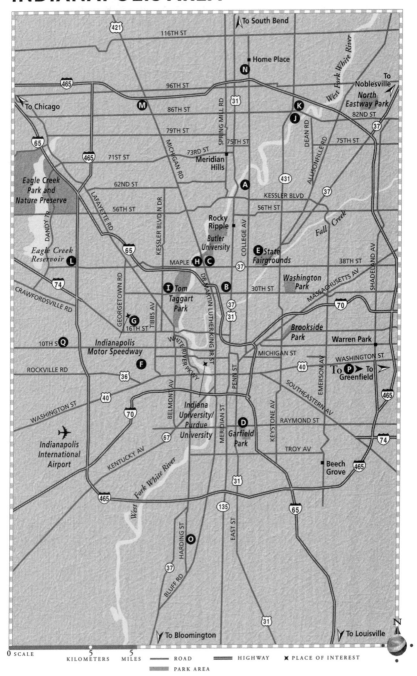

the prices are quite low. Another place for lunch is **Alcatraz Brewing Company**, in Circle Centre, 317/488-1230. In addition to their excellent, moderately-priced wood-fired pizza, you'll want to try the beer they brew themselves. **Bazbeaux Pizza**, 334 Massachusetts Ave., 317/636-7662, also serves first-rate pizzas, and offers a choice of 52 different toppings. For a good sandwich you have to go to a deli, and **Shapiro's Delicatessen Cafeteria**, 808 S. Meridian St., 317/631-4041, is one of the best. Their sandwiches are kosher, big, and affordable. Thanks to Jerry Seinfeld, soup has become a chic lunch choice, and **Soup Masters Cafe**, in Circle Centre, 317/464-0630, offers a great selection each day. They also have delicious salads and sandwiches. If you like turkey you'll be in heaven at **Cooper's Turkey Place**, Circle Centre, 317/635-2874. Even the burgers and hot dogs are made of turkey in this cafeteria-style restaurant.

For dinner, you can't go wrong with Italian. A few of the most authentic Italian restaurants in town are: **Benvenuti**, 1 N. Pennsylvania St., 317/633-4915; **Bertolini's Authentic Trattoria**, Circle Centre, 317/638-1800; and **Iaria's Italian Restaurant**, 317 S. College Ave., 317/638-7706.

For great steaks at decent prices, you'll want to try at least one of these: **Del Frisco's**, 5 E. Market St., 317/687-8888; **Elbow Room**, 605 N. Pennsylvania St., 317/635-3354; the **Majestic Restaurant**, 47 S. Pennsylvania St., 317/636-5418 (the seafood here is fantastic, too); and **St. Elmo Steak House**, 127 S. Illinois St., 317/635-0636.

SIGHTS

- **A** Broad Ripple Village
- **B** Children's Museum of Indianapolis
- **C** Crown Hill Cemetery
- **D** Garfield Park and Conservatory
- **E** Hook's American Drug Store Museum
- **F** Indiana Medical History Museum
- **E** Indiana State Fairgrounds

SIGHTS *(continued)*

- **G** Indianapolis Motor Speedway Hall of Fame Museum
- **H** Indianapolis Museum of Art

FOOD

- **I** Iron Skillet
- **J** Lula's Restaurant & Cocktails
- **K** Peter's A Restaurant and Bar

LODGING

- **L** Country Hearth Inn
- **M** New England Suites Hotel
- **N** Wyndham Garden Hotel

CAMPING

- **E** Indiana State Fairgrounds Recreational Vehicle Campground
- **O** Kamper Korner
- **P** KOA Indianapolis
- **Q** Raceview Family Campground

Note: Items with the same letter are located in the same area.

The **Iron Skillet**, 2489 W. 30th St., 317/923-6353, is a nice place for a quiet dinner. They serve Hoosier food in a comfortable, homey atmosphere. **Peter's A Restaurant and Bar**, 8505 Keystone Crossing Blvd., 317/465-1155, offers an eclectic choice of entrées, including duckling, lamb, and yellowfin tuna. And their wine list here is phenomenal.

A good new restaurant is **Lula's Restaurant & Cocktails**, 8487 Union Chapel Rd., 317/251-5858. It presents a contemporary menu with items such as grilled portabello sandwiches and spicy black-bean ravioli.

For a restaurant with an interesting story, the **Snow Lion Tibetan Restaurant**, 234–236 S. Meridian St., 317/955-1680, is owned and operated by none other than the nephew of the Dalai Lama. It offers both Tibetan and Asian foods, including lots of vegetarian choices—all reasonably priced.

It may be hard to reserve a table at **Palomino Euro Bistro**, Circle Centre, 317/974-0400, but don't give up trying. This is *the* place to eat. From prime rib and garlic chicken to seafood and pizza, you won't find better food anywhere.

LODGING

Some people prefer to stay right in the heart of the city and venture out for their sightseeing. If that's your pleasure, the **Old Northside Bed and Breakfast**, 1340 N. Alabama St., 317/635-9123, is a historic mansion with magnificently decorated rooms that display old-world elegance blended with modern convenience. Not only are there private baths in every room, but they even have whirlpool tubs. There's also an exercise room, an on-call masseuse, and gourmet breakfast. The **Renaissance Tower Historic Inn**, 230 E. Ninth St., 317/261-1652, is another nice option. Each suite here is a studio apartment with a full kitchen. They even have free parking just a few steps from the front door. Rooms at **Stone Soup Inn**, 1304 N. Central Ave., 317/639-9550, have beautiful antique furnishings, fireplaces, and relaxing sitting areas. The **Tranquil Cherub Bed and Breakfast**, 2164 N. Capitol Ave., 317/923-9036, is true to its name. How can you not unwind while sitting on a deck overlooking a lily pond, snuggling in front of a warm fire while you eat breakfast, or rocking quietly on the front porch?

A wonderful downtown hotel is the **Canterbury Hotel**, 123 S. Illinois St., 800/538-8186. It offers concierge service, free continental breakfast, fuzzy bathrobes, and—best of all—it adjoins Circle Centre, so you can go shopping without leaving the building. Another excellent hotel is **University Place Conference Center and Hotel**, 850 W. Michigan St., 317/269-9000. While they are superb at handling large groups, they don't favor them at the expense of the individual traveler. They have an indoor pool and exercise room, too. For a novel and upscale alternative to a chain hotel, try the **Crowne Plaza Union Station**, 123 W. Louisiana St., 800-2-CROWNE, which has an indoor pool, whirlpool, and exercise room. While it's close to all the downtown sights, some of its rooms are sights themselves. Actually, they aren't rooms at all; they're real Pullman cars.

If you're on a budget, the **Methodist Tower Inn**, 1633 N. Capitol Ave., 317/925-9831, has clean, comfortable, nonsmoking rooms at great prices. If you don't want to stay downtown, **Country Hearth Inn**, 3851 Shore Dr., 317/297-1848, has great prices, delicious breakfasts, and—if you stay in the middle of the week—they even have a wine and cheese reception for you. At **Wyndham Garden Hotel**, 251 E. Pennsylvania Pkwy., 317/574-4600, you can pamper yourself in your personal in-room spa tub, or venture out for a swim in their indoor pool.

If planning to stay for more than a day or two, you might want a little more room than most hotels offer. **New England Suites Hotel**, 3871 W. 92nd St., 317/879-1700, has very nicely-appointed two-room suites. They don't have kitchens, but they do have refrigerators and microwaves, plus TVs, VCRs, a library of videos, and you can enjoy a complimentary breakfast.

CAMPING

You won't find as many campsites in Indianapolis as you will in smaller Indiana communities. **Indiana State Fairgrounds Recreational Vehicle Campground**, 1202 E. 38th St., 317/927-7510, is a year-round campground that offers—in season—sites with electricity and water (plus sewer, if you want it) for $12.60 a day. Primitive sites cost $10.50. There is also a shower and bathroom facility, and a playground. At **Kamper Korner**, 1951 W. Edgewood Ave., 317/788-1488, they have a fishing pond, shower and laundry facilities, and a playground. **KOA Indianapolis**, 5896 W. 200 North, Greenfield, 317/894-1397, is about 15 minutes from downtown and offers most of the comforts of home, including a swimming pool. The rates here are $18 for a primitive site and $20 for a full hook-up. **Raceview Family Campground**, 9801 E. County Rd. 300 North, 317/852-5737, is open only when there are events taking place at Indianapolis Motor Speedway or Indianapolis Raceway Park. Rates vary, but expect to spend as much as $13 per person per day.

NIGHTLIFE

Like Chicago, Indianapolis has as much to do at night as some other destinations have in the day. You can enjoy a romantic dinner, laugh till your sides hurt at a comedy club, listen to some of the best music around, and catch all sorts of performances. In season there are many professional sports events happening, too. The following list is far from comprehensive, but we challenge you to sample any two of these in one night and still have the energy to get out of bed before noon the next day.

Go to the **Flashbaxx**, Circle Centre, 317/630-5483, for a big 1970s-style dance party. Be prepared to see people wearing the same stuff you sold in your past five garage sales—platform shoes, polyester, and hip huggers—and be ready to dance all night. **Indianapolis Comedy Connection**, 247 S. Meridian St., 317/631-3536, features many of the area's up-and-coming comic talents. Tim Allen and Rosie O'Donnell are both alums.

Since 1850, **Slippery Noodle Inn**, 372 S. Meridian St., 317/631-6974, has been a hot place to hang out and relax. The oldest bar in Indiana is also known for its great food, drinks, and blues. The guy who owns **Pump's Last Shot**, 6416 Cornell Ave., 317/25-PLUMP, is the one who made the shot that moves grown men to cry, at least when they watch the reenactment of it in the movie *Hoosiers*. This bar is a shrine to Bobby Pump's basketball team, and it serves good food and drinks, too. If the cigar crowd is more your style, you can't help but like **Ybor's Martini Bar**, Circle Centre, 317/951-1621. They serve only the finest liquors and an excellent selection of cigars.

On Friday nights you can catch jazz at **Madame Walker Theatre Center**, 617 Indiana Ave., 317/236-2099. For a great evening under the stars go to the **Deer Creek Music Center**, 12880 E. 146th St., 317/776-3337. Check their schedule for the biggest names in rock, comedy, and much more.

PERFORMING ARTS

If you can talk your traveling partners into exchanging their madras plaid shorts and black socks for a coat and tie one evening, **Ballet Internationale-Indianapolis**, 502-B N. Capitol Ave., 317/637-8879, offers performances of traditional as well as contemporary works. **Indianapolis Opera**, 250 E. 38th St., 317/940-6444, is for serious opera lovers as well as those of us who never studied Italian. While all works are performed in their original language, subtitles are projected above the stage. The **Indianapolis Symphony Orchestra**, 45 Monument Circle, 800/366-8457, performs throughout the year at the historic Hilbert Circle Theatre.

Beef and Boards Dinner Theatre, 9301 N. Michigan Rd., 317/872-9664, has lots of stick-to-your-ribs food and a wide variety of Broadway shows throughout the year. **Indiana Repertory Theatre**, 140 W. Washington St., 317/635-5277, is in a restored 1927 movie theater. The shows here run the range from comedy to drama to musical, but all are entertaining. The **Massachusetts Avenue Arts District** is a mecca of upscale diversion, with a nice selection of art galleries, stores, restaurants, and theaters. Two of the best here are: **American Cabaret Theatre**, 401 E. Michigan St., 317/631-0334, which presents original productions in a wonderful setting; and **Raleigh's Dinner Theatre**, 721 Massachusetts Ave., 800/416-9800, a small dinner theater specializing in musicals. One of the most fun theatrical experiences in town is **Mystery Cafe**, 231 S. College Ave., in the Milano Inn, 317/684-0668. You'll enjoy a gourmet meal while you help solve the evening's mystery. To see some great local talent, visit the **Indianapolis Civic Theatre**, 1200 W. 38th St., 317/924-6770. At **Edyvean Repertory Theatre**, 1000 W. 42nd St., 800/807-7732, the "Jumping Mouse Players" perform pieces that entertain and enlighten. The performers all have developmental disabilities, and that is the main subject of their beautifully done work.

11
BLOOMINGTON

Word is spreading about Bloomington, Indiana. People who live here have known it all along, and alumni of Indiana University have been coming back with kids and station wagons for years because of it. But for most of us, the fact that Bloomington is one of the most beautiful, clean, and safe cities in the Midwest was somehow never mentioned as we discussed our travel plans.

There's a strip of central Indiana, below I-74 and Indianapolis, that has rolling hills similar to those in the southern parts of both Illinois and Indiana. The hills are covered in dense woods, and the natural limestone juts out like buck teeth on a country boy. Now consider Bloomington, plopped down in this natural setting. She has retained the big trees and built her most historic structures from the limestone that seems to grow here. Indiana University is especially molded from the terrain—can you think of another university with a forest in the middle of it?

There are two huge attractions to the area—the outstanding campus and the outdoor recreation provided by the state's largest lake. Indiana University includes the tremendous cultural offerings that separate Bloomington from any of the other small cities of the area, plus the unique restaurants you'd expect from a culturally diverse college town.

Lake Monroe and the Hoosier National Forest rub up against each other just outside Bloomington, creating a bounty of opportunities for outdoor enthusiasts. You'll see pickup trucks towing bass boats, and tourists joining in with their rental boats and fishing gear. Come prepared for camping, hiking, fishing, and tubing—or rent the equipment to do just about anything.

Consider some of the accolades thrown to Bloomington: It's home of one of the five most beautiful university campuses in the country; one of the seven best places to bicycle in the United States; and eighth in the country on a list of places to retire based on personal safety, cost of living, services, climate, and other factors. It seems that a lot of experts have pasted their stamps of approval on Bloomington. You can be assured your vacation here will be rich and fulfilling, whether you're experiencing the great outdoors or the best of cultural attractions.

A PERFECT DAY IN BLOOMINGTON

You could spend an entire day exploring the museums and campus attractions at Indiana University, or you could spend it on the water at Lake Monroe. For a perfect day, do both. Enjoy a gourmet morning meal at your bed-and-breakfast soon after sunrise, then get out early to view the unbelievable documents at the Lilly Library. Spend the early afternoon at the Indiana University Art Museum (one of the best in the world), then eat a late lunch at one of the many oddball restaurants along Kirkwood or Fourth Street. Take off later in the afternoon to set up camp at the Hardin Ridge rustic camping facility, then build a big fire and gaze at the water of Lake Monroe until a chill in the air chases you to your sleeping bag.

INDIANA UNIVERSITY SIGHTSEEING HIGHLIGHTS

★★★★ INDIANA UNIVERSITY ART MUSEUM
In the fine-arts complex on Seventh St., north of Showalter Fountain, Bloomington, 812/855-5445

Indiana University is home to one of the finest art museums in the world. The first thing that strikes you is the building, a modern jaw-dropper designed by the internationally famous architectural firm of I.M. Pei. The modern building has no 90-degree angles, resulting in a structure as unique as the treasures it holds. Inside you'll find original works by masters like Monet and Picasso, but you'll also find an amazing, intelligently displayed collection that represents nearly every culture that's ever produced art—including Indiana's own fine artists and craftspeople.

BLOOMINGTON

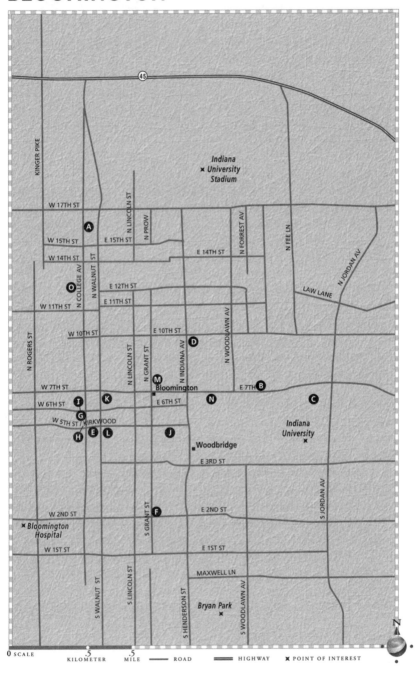

Kinger Pike

W 17TH ST
N Lincoln St
W 15TH ST E 15TH ST N Prow
W 14TH ST N Walnut St
E 14TH ST N Forrest Av N Fee Ln N Jordan Av

Indiana
University
Stadium

A

O N College Av E 12TH ST
W 11TH ST E 11TH ST

Law Lane

W 10TH ST E 10TH ST N Woodlawn Av
N Rogers St N Lincoln St N Grant St N Indiana Av **D**

W 7TH ST **M** Bloomington E 7TH **B**
I **K** E 6TH ST **N** **C**
W 6TH ST
G W 5TH ST / KIRKWOOD
H **E** **L** **J** Indiana
University

Woodbridge
E 3RD ST

S Walnut St S Lincoln St S Grant St S Henderson St S Woodlawn Av S Jordan Av

W 2ND ST **F** E 2ND ST
Bloomington
Hospital
W 1ST ST E 1ST ST

MAXWELL LN

Bryan Park

0 SCALE .5 .5
KILOMETER MILE — ROAD = HIGHWAY ✕ POINT OF INTEREST

N

Details: Wed–Sat 10–5, Sun noon–5; free; wheelchair accessible. (2 hours)

★★★★ LILLY LIBRARY

In the fine-arts complex on Seventh St., south of Showalter Fountain, Bloomington, 812/855-2452

Would you like to see an original Gutenberg New Testament, Robert E. Lee's handwritten surrender to Ulysses S. Grant, George Washington's letter accepting the presidency, or original scripts from the *Star Trek* television series? The only place in the world to see a collection this diverse and precious is at Indiana University's Lilly Library. With more than 6.5 million manuscripts (700 of which were printed before the year 1501), this library has something to fascinate everyone. Amazingly, there are more than 400,000 rare books stored here, and 100,000 pieces of sheet music and compositions.

Don't bring bags, backpacks, or briefcases into the library—they'll be taken away. With a collection of such priceless, irreplaceable items, no chances are taken.

Details: Mon–Fri 9–6, Sat 9–1; free; wheelchair accessible. (2 hours)

SIGHTS
Ⓐ Butler Winery
Ⓑ Indiana University Art Museum
Ⓒ Lilly Library
Ⓓ Mathers Museum
Ⓔ Monroe County Courthouse and Downtown Square
Ⓕ Wylie House

FOOD
Ⓖ Bake House
Ⓗ Irish Lion
Ⓘ Janko's-Little Zagreb
Ⓙ Nick's English Hut
Ⓚ Opie Taylor's
Ⓚ Princess Restaurant
Ⓛ Trojan Horse

LODGING
Ⓜ Grant Street Inn
Ⓝ Indiana Memorial Union
Ⓞ Scholar's Inn Bed and Breakfast

Note: Items with the same letter are located in the same area.

★★★ MATHERS MUSEUM
Corner of Eighth St. and Indiana Ave., at 416 N. Indiana Ave., Bloomington, 812/855-6873

Another great Indiana University museum, this one is dedicated to the study of world cultures. The Mathers Museum was one of the first in the area to offer hands-on exhibits for children, and remains one of the best places in Bloomington to take kids for a combination of education and fun. You'll find some 20,000 objects and 10,000 pictures that try to explain who we are (whether they document sub-Saharan Africa, Latin America, or the United States of America). Be sure to see the Wanamaker Collection of American Indian Photographs.

Details: Tue–Fri 9–4:30, Sat–Sun 1–4:30; free; wheelchair accessible. (1 hour)

★★ WYLIE HOUSE
307 E. Second St., Bloomington, 812/855-6224

The Wylie House was built in 1835 as the home of Indiana University's first president, Andrew Wylie, and his family. Today it's on the National Register of Historic Places and serves as a museum of life in the 19th century. Not only was Wylie one of the first great

INDIANA UNIVERSITY

Indiana Tourism Division

leaders of the institution, he was also a dedicated family man and the father of 12 children. The house has been restored and decorated with period pieces, many of which were in the home when the Wylies lived there. Vegetable varieties that were planted in the early 1800s are grown in the garden, with the seeds for sale to anyone who wants to help preserve the species.

Details: Mar–Nov Tue–Sat 1–4, or at other times by arrangement; free; wheelchair accessible (use the east driveway). (1 hour)

OTHER BLOOMINGTON SIGHTSEEING HIGHLIGHTS

★★★★ TIBETAN CULTURAL CENTER
3655 Snoddy Rd., Bloomington, 812/334-7046

How is Bloomington related to Tibet? In its heart. The Tibetan Cultural Center was established as a means of supporting the people of Tibet, who had been displaced by the Chinese in 1950. It's a prayerful place meant to introduce different cultures; a place where peace is palpable. In July 1996, the Dalai Lama visited to lay the cornerstone for a new temple, and, we assume, to visit his eldest brother who is a professor emeritus at Indiana University. The Cultural Center offers meeting space, regular Sunday-afternoon (1 p.m.) meditation sessions, and informal discussions. The center, set on 90 acres, features beautiful sand art as well as the only Chorten in the United States (it's a monument to the nearly 1 million Tibetans who have died during and since the Chinese takeover).

If you want another taste of Tibetan culture after visiting the center, try one of the two Bloomington restaurants run by the Dalai Lama's relatives: the Snow Lion or the Norbu Cafe.

Details: Wed noon–4, Sat–Sun 10–4; free; wheelchair accessible. (1 hour)

★★★ BLUESPRING CAVERN
1/2 mile off U.S. 50 near intersection with Rte. 37, about 30 minutes south of Bloomington, 812/279-9471

They say that a farmer went out one morning in the 1940s to find his pond had disappeared overnight. It had drained into what is one of Indiana's outstanding show caves, leaving behind a hole that's now used to access Bluespring Cavern. The caverns were formed by underground rivers, but were covered by glacial debris thousands of years ago. Today tours of the caverns are a great lesson in the power of ice and water, and prove that all of the world's beauty is not on the surface. The tours are by boat, so you won't get dirty.

Details: *Daily 9–6; tours leave approximately every 30 minutes, the last at 5 p.m. $9 adults, $5 children ages 3–15. (1½ hours)*

★★★ MONROE COUNTY COURTHOUSE AND DOWNTOWN SQUARE
Square bound by College Ave., Walnut St., and Fifth and Sixth Sts., Bloomington

It's so nice to visit a town this size and find that the downtown square is *vibrant*. The anchor of it all is the 1902 Monroe County Courthouse that's still in use today. It's one of the many historic limestone buildings in town, with a stained-glass dome and a fish weathervane that once stood atop the previous county courthouse. Around the courthouse are a variety of shops and restaurants, and the Fountain Square Mall on the south side of the square houses even more shops. This is a downtown restoration done right, and you'll have a great time exploring it.

Details: *(2 hours)*

★★ OLIVER WINERY/BUTLER WINERY
Butler Winery, 1022 N. College Ave., Bloomington, 812/339-7233

Bloomington is home to two independent wineries. Butler Winery is in an 85-year-old home which serves as a nice place to taste some of Indiana's own. But if you are choosing one winery to visit, go to the Oliver seven miles north of the city. This is the state's oldest and largest winery. The grounds are beautiful, and you're welcome to picnic there or just take a stroll. You'll also get a free tour and a free tasting of their award-winning wines.

Several local restaurants carry wines from these two wineries, so you should be able to try a glass with dinner if you don't have time to visit them.

Details: *Oliver Winery, Rte. 37, about seven miles north of Bloomington; 812/876-5800; both* *wineries are open Mon–Sat 10–6, Sun noon–6; free; wheelchair accessible. (1 1/2 hours)*

SHOPPING

Choose your shopping: antiques, uniques, or a big-mall experience. Bloomington excels at all three with its 90-store mall, its renovated downtown, and its antique mall. Our favorite shopping comes strolling around the downtown square, hitting the unique little stores like **Boca Loca Beads** on Walnut St., 812/333-8767; or **Ted's European Military Surplus** on the next block north, 812/3339723. Around the square are shops offering everything from rare books to pricey sunglasses. Men should check out **J. R. Stallsmith**, 812/332-1953, for excellent menswear and top-notch service. The cook in the family will find something useful in **Goods for Cooks**, 812/339-2200, on the west side of the square in Uptown Plaza.

College Mall, 2896 E. Third St. at the Rte. 46 bypass, 812/339-3054, has the big-name anchor stores and smaller specialty shops you'd expect. It also has an old-time carousel to ride when shopping fatigue sets in.

Finally, even folks who aren't hard-core antique collectors will enjoy a visit to the largest antique mall in southern Indiana, the **Bloomington Antique Mall**, 311 W. Seventh St., 812/332-2290. This 1895 warehouse now accommodates more than 120 exhibitors.

FITNESS AND RECREATION

Bloomington has a blooming ton of recreational opportunities, many of them courtesy of two huge natural resources: the **Hoosier National Forest** and **Lake Monroe**. With the forest surrounding most of the lake, the two jointly provide a tremendous vacation destination, even if you never head into town. Find a nice lakeside camping spot in the excellent **Hardin Ridge U.S. Forest Service Campground**, just off Rte. 446 (follow the signs west on Chapel Hill Rd.), 800/280-2267. For a few more amenities try one of the private campgrounds, many of which include beaches, boat ramps, interpretive centers, playground equipment, and courts and fields for various sports.

Hardin Ridge is a favorite spot for its rustic campsites, a cool cave, and a fire tower with a great view. **Lake Monroe** is the largest inland lake in Indiana. At more than 10,000 acres, there's plenty of room for boating, skiing, sailing, fishing, and anything else you would want to do on the water. Canoeists and anglers will appreciate that the causeway on Route 446 is a dividing line that separates boats moving at cruising speeds from those at idle speeds.

BLOOMINGTON AREA

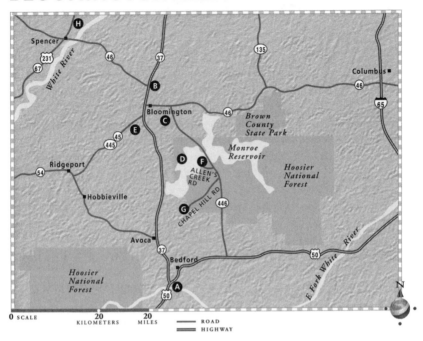

SIGHTS
- **A** Bluespring Cavern
- **B** Oliver Winery/Butler Winery
- **C** Tibetan Cultural Center

LODGING
- **D** Lake Monroe Village
- **E** Winding Woods Bed and Breakfast

CAMPING
- **F** Allen's Creek
- **G** Hardin Ridge U.S. Forest Service Campground
- **H** McCormick's Creek State Park

Another terrific camping and recreation area is **McCormick's Creek State Park**, Rte. 46 two miles east of Spencer. Hike through canyons and ravines, near a beautiful waterfall and a cave where the earth's cool breath summons you to explore. The **Wapehani Bike Park** is a mountain biker's paradise. Located on Weimer Road between Second Street and Tapp Road, its 34 acres of trails are meant solely for use by bikers and hikers. You'll have to don a helmet and sign a waiver before entering; forms can be found at local bike shops or at the Bloomington Parks and Recreation Department.

You can rent everything in Bloomington—boats, personal watercraft, camping and fishing gear, bicycles, and more. A good place to start looking for rentals is the **Indiana Memorial Union** on the IU campus. They provide extensive rentals and trip planning, and have tons of information for your specific needs. Also, the visitors center on North Walnut can give you suggestions on where to rent, ride, hike, or camp.

The best golfing in the area is on the south side of Lake Monroe at the **Eagle Point Golf Resort**, a PGA-championship course that's challenging and beautiful. All of the course's sand bunkers contain white silica sand, and there are two waterfalls. Tennis players will find an excellent indoor facility at the **IU Tennis Center**, also off Rte. 46 near Memorial Stadium and Assembly Hall.

FOOD

Opie Taylor and his dad the sheriff had nothing to do with Bloomington, Indiana, as far as anyone can tell, but the freckle-faced character of the *Andy Griffith Show* is honored with a burger joint one block north of the downtown square. **Opie Taylor's**, 212 N. Walnut, 812/333-7287, has delivered the best burger in Bloomington four years in a row according to one local poll. They're also known for great chili and some pretty cool pictures of little Ronnie Howard from the TV show. Just be prepared for the ugly bathrooms. Also on the square is the **Bake House**, 125 N. College Ave., 812/331-6029, a great place to buy bread and a popular spot to grab a vegetarian lunch or something quick, high quality, and maybe a little unusual. The cafeteria-style service won't appeal to some, but the best soups and pastries in town will make up for that. The **Trojan Horse** is a Bloomington institution on the southeast corner of the square, 100 E. Kirkwood Ave., 812/332-1101. Greek dishes like gyros and *souvlakia* are their mainstays, but locals know they also make some of the best hummus in town.

There are three nice restaurants within a block of the square. The **Princess Restaurant** is relatively new at 206 N. Walnut, 812/336-8821. The restaurant's Mediterranean/Moroccan menu and stained-glass window that fills the entire back wall (both floors!) make for an intriguing evening. Call first because their hours are limited. **Janko's–Little Zagreb**, 223 W. Sixth St., 812/332-0694, is the most talked-about place in town. This is *the* place to go for steak, the garlic rolls are great, and the wine list is among the best in town. When he's home in Bloomington, John Mellencamp occasionally eats here. The **Irish Lion**, 212 W. Kirkwood Ave., 812/336-9076, is pure Irish—from the decor to the delicious soups to the waitstaff. Their coddle cures a hangover, and their Blarney puffballs are a terrific appetizer.

To experience the IU tradition, **Nick's English Hut**, 423 E. Kirkwood Ave., 812/332-4040, is the best place to go. They serve beer by the pound, tasty bar food, and dinner. If you go to this 70-year-old Hoosier hangout, however, just make sure you wear the red and white.

LODGING

With wild support from throughout the state for Indiana University's football and basketball teams, a strong network of hotels is needed to handle the peak periods. Consequently, you'll find a good number of beds provided by the big-name chains. The visitors bureau, 800/800-0037, should be able to help if you plan to visit during one of the busiest weekends. One of the best places to stay if you plan to explore the many sights on campus is **Indiana Memorial Union**, 900 E. Seventh St., 800/209-8145. The rooms are very nicely appointed, and many contain art or antiques from the Union's own extensive collection. There's no place like it in town, and the prices are reasonable.

There are three good bed-and-breakfasts in town. The **Grant Street Inn**, 310 N. Grant St., 800/328-4350, consists of 24 bedrooms and suites created when several homes were joined together. Gas fireplaces in many of the rooms, and hot tubs in the two suites add to the comfort of this very popular inn.

If you like a cabin, but want the pampering only a bed-and-breakfast can provide, try the **Winding Woods Bed and Breakfast**, S. Harmony Rd., 888/832-2246. Wood surrounds you inside, and woods surround you outside. There's a swimming pool, hot tub, and paths across the property's six acres. Have a latte on the porch—this is the best of both worlds!

Finally, **Scholar's Inn Bed and Breakfast** is conveniently located near both campus and downtown at 801 N. College Ave., 800-765-3466. The house, which dates to the 1890s, has been beautifully restored with carefully selected period pieces. Try to get the Caleb Mills Room, a garden suite with French doors, a hand carved fountain, and its own Jacuzzi. Reasonable prices make this a great place to stay.

Cabin and A-frame rentals are available through **Lake Monroe Village**, 8107 S. Fairfax Rd., 812/824-2267. An outdoor pool, playgrounds, and 100 acres to explore on the east side of Lake Monroe should provide plenty of activity for children.

CAMPING

Camping abounds in the Bloomington area, but the good campgrounds here are heavily used. Lake Monroe and the Hoosier National Forest provide many opportunities, including the **Hardin Ridge U.S. Forest Service Campground**, just off Rte. 446 (follow the signs west on Chapel Hill Rd.), 800/280-2267, which accepts reservations, has electric and rustic campsites, a beach, and a concession stand. **Allen's Creek**, 4850 S. State Rd. 446, 812/837-9546, is a state-owned site with no fees but few of the amenities that make family camping easier.

Outside the immediate Bloomington area are a few excellent camping destinations. **McCormick's Creek State Park**, Rte. 46 just east of Spencer, 812/829-2235, accepts reservations and is an excellent park for those who like to explore. There are endless trails and a mile-long canyon that's home to McCormick's Creek. The park includes cabins for rent in addition to heavily wooded campsites.

NIGHTLIFE

You won't have a problem finding quality nightlife in Bloomington since Indiana University provides a constant supply of cultural events. Be sure to check out the schedules for the **Auditorium and University Theater** during your stay. Both are located in the Fine Arts Plaza near Seventh Street and Jordan Avenue. Strong theater and music schools at the university mean good shows at these venues. The Auditorium (undergoing renovations until the fall of 1999), 812/855-1103, books the best entertainers in the nation and is home to both Broadway musicals and a full schedule of other musical and theatrical productions. The University Theater, 812/855-7433, is said to have perfect acoustics and is home to the longest continuing opera program in North America.

Haven't seen a drive-in movie lately? The **Starlite Drive-in Theatre**, 7640 Old State Rte. 37, 812/824-8036, may be a walk into the past for some, but kids are sure to see it as a great new idea. The theater plays the latest movies in a family setting, and offers all the junk food you'd expect at a well-stocked concession stand. It's open seasonally April through September.

12
COLUMBUS AREA

Not many towns of 35,000 people can say that world-famous architect I.M. Pei designed their library. But this community that calls itself "Different by Design" has plenty of brag points like that. In fact, architecturally it's one of the most interesting cities in the nation. Sixteenth-century English diplomat, Sir Henry Wotton, once said of architecture, "Well building hath three conditions: commodity, firmness, and delight."

In Columbus it seems that every building was created not just to house a government office or church or school, but to please the eye and bring joy to all who use it. The list of men who have designed buildings for Columbus includes just about everybody who's anybody in the field, and there are equally impressive credentials behind the sculptures and other artwork of the community. The towers and spires that form the landscape here suggest an appreciation for fine living that is almost extinct in our nation. Where many communities are beginning to look virtually identical, Columbus continues to celebrate its unique blend of ideas and approaches. The museums, parks, and other offerings here are upscale, but casual enough to make a vacationer feel comfortable. A short drive away, Brown County has a very rural flavor, offering entertainment and recreation that make you feel like you're much closer to Nashville, Tennessee, than Indianapolis. A short drive south of Columbus, and you're in rock 'n' roll territory. Seymour is where John Mellencamp grew up.

A PERFECT DAY IN THE COLUMBUS AREA

If you want some help in spotting the design marvels here, start the day with an architectural tour. After lunch downtown, drive to Seymour, where you can look for the locations you've seen in John Mellencamp's videos. Chances are, you'll run into at least one of his relatives, so make sure to have your camera. After dinner at Peter's Bay, catch a show at the Little Nashville Opry in Brown County, then settle in for the night at the Columbus Inn.

SIGHTSEEING HIGHLIGHTS

★★★★ ARCHITECTURAL TOURS OF COLUMBUS
Fifth and Franklin Sts., Columbus, 800/468-6564

After visiting Columbus, you'll have a new realization of that beauty and grace that can result from a little urban planning and foresight. More than 50 years ago a local church funded the construction of a new building that began a new appreciation for architecture. Since then scores of public buildings and schools have been designed by the world's most talented architects.

    Details: *Mar–Nov Mon–Sat 9–5, Sun 10–4; guided tours $9.50 adults, $9 seniors, $5 students, $3 children ages 6–12, ages 5 and under free. (2 hours)*

★★★★ INDIANAPOLIS MUSEUM OF ART COLUMBUS GALLERY
390 The Commons, Columbus, 812/376-2597

Most museums exhibit just a portion of their collection at a time, while the rest is kept in storage hidden from visitors. The people who run the Indianapolis Museum of Art decided to avoid this problem by allowing the city of Columbus to operate a branch of the museum as long as they were willing to help foot the bill. Today the city-operated satellite museum houses some phenomenal exhibits—ones you'd expect to find in a major city without the long lines and higher prices.

    Details: *Tue–Sat 10–5 (until 8 on Fri), Sun noon–4; free. Wheelchair accessible. (1 hour)*

★★★★ J'OLE DAYLE COOKING SCHOOL OF OLSON ACADEMY
10902 N. County Rd. 800 W., one mile west of Houston (how-ston), 812/497-3568

Indiana Tourism Division

So, did you really wanted to go to France on vacation, but you just couldn't afford it? No problem. Just sign up for one of the hands-on courses at renowned chef Joan Olson's school. Tucked away in the Hoosier National Forest, this gastronomic academy fills the ground floor of Joan's beautifully rustic home.

You can take courses ranging from a half day to more than a week. Joan Olson can guide you through the intricacies of preparing everything from French sauces like béarnaise and mousseline to pâtés, tarts, soufflés, and other delicacies. While students enjoy learning to create these—and countless other—gourmet items, the best part of the course is held in the serving room, where the tasting takes place.

Details: *Courses offered spring–early fall; prices range from $50–$200 or more; wheelchair accessible. (1 day)*

★★★ IRWIN HOME AND GARDENS
608 Fifth St., Columbus, 812/376-3331

Most of us can't even imagine living in such a gracious home on such breathtaking grounds, but when you tour the gardens of the former home of banker William G. Irwin it's fun to pretend for a minute or two that it's your place. The formal gardens would make a wonderful kingdom for just about anyone, and visitors really enjoy wandering among the shrubs, statuary, and flowers. The only downside to this place is when it comes time to leave it and return to reality. Oh, and don't try to enter the Irwin house; it's actually someone's home and it's not open to the public.

Details: Sat–Sun 8–4; free. (1 hour)

★★★ T.C. STEELE STATE HISTORIC SITE
4200 S. T.C. Steele Rd., Nashville, 812/988-2785

Just outside Nashville, this sight was once the place where artist T.C. Steele found the natural beauty that inspired many of his paintings. After he died, his widow donated their home—as well as the surrounding buildings and grounds—to the state, so that art and nature lovers would have a place to find similar inspiration. Many of the flowers you'll find in the gardens are the offspring of ones planted by Steele's wife, Selma, years ago. As you walk the trails throughout the property, see how many different flowers, trees, and animals you can identify. But make sure to take notes; there are so many, you'll lose track quickly.

Details: Mid-Mar–mid-Dec Tue–Sat 9–5, Sun 1–5; free, although donations are accepted; wheelchair accessible. (2 hours)

★★★ BARTHOLOMEW COUNTY HISTORICAL SOCIETY
524 Third St., Columbus, 812/372-3541

Decorating buffs will enjoy this sampling of art and furnishing from pioneer and Victorian homes. It's a great place to visit every time you're in Columbus because there's always something new in two of the five galleries. In the pioneer room upstairs, you can even try your hand at old-fashioned chores such as grinding coffee beans. Kids love the children's room with vintage furnishings and antique toys. If you have any ancestors from this area, call ahead and let the staff know—they'll help you do a quick genealogical search in the library.

Details: Tue–Fri 9–4; free, although donations are accepted. (½ hour)

★★ BROWN COUNTY ART GUILD
48 S. Van Buren St., Nashville, 812/988-6185

This gallery features a permanent collection of works by early Brown County artists, as well as exhibits of more contemporary works. Oil is the choice of medium for most of the artists, but you will find some beautiful pottery pieces, too.

Details: Mon–Sat 10–5, Sun 11–5, Jan–Feb open weekends only; free, although donations are accepted. (1 hour)

★★ SOUTHERN INDIANA CENTER FOR THE ARTS
2001 N. Ewing St., Seymour, 812/522-2278

You'll get two sights for one if you come here. Not only will you be in the facility John Mellencamp created to enhance appreciation for the region's architectural, artisan, culinary, literary, and performing arts; but to get there, you'll travel to the community made famous in his song, "Small Town." But don't expect to see the singer around here very often. You can see some of Mellencamp's own paintings, and you will likely find his former art teacher organizing the activities here. Volunteers—or just about anyone else in Seymour—can offer plenty of good stories about John and what he was like when he was growing up here. They're great tour guides and are often willing to help you locate good settings for pictures that will impress your Mellenhead friends.

Details: Tue–Sat noon–5; free, although donations are accepted; first floor wheelchair accessible. (½ hour)

★ COURTHOUSE TOWER TREE
On top of the courthouse tower, which fills the block between Main, Washington, Broadway, and Franklin Sts., Greensburg, 800/210-2832

This is one of the strangest things you'll see anywhere in Indiana—real trees growing out of the courthouse tower roof. Experts at the Smithsonian Institute in Washington, D.C., say the trees are a variety of large-toothed aspen, but no one can figure out for sure how they got there or how they survive. The original trees died many years ago, but new ones have continued to grow in their place, offering a living conversation piece for the entire town. In fact, they've even incorporated a sketch of the tree-festooned tower right into their town's Chamber of Commerce seal.

Details: (15 minutes)

COLUMBUS

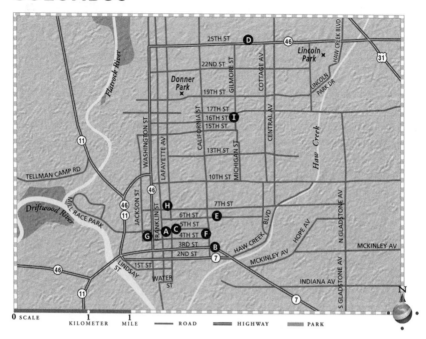

SIGHTS

ⓐ Architectural Tours of Columbus
ⓑ Bartholomew County Historical Society
ⓐ Indianapolis Museum of Art Columbus Gallery
ⓒ Irwin Home and Gardens

FOOD

ⓓ Becker's Drive In
ⓐ Peter's Bay
ⓔ Shorty's
ⓕ The Columbus Bar
ⓖ Zaharakos Confectionery

LODGING

ⓗ Adam Keller House
ⓘ Ruddick-Nugent House
ⓐ The Columbus Inn

Note: Items with the same letter are located in the same area.

EVENTS

One of the biggest and best festivals in the area is the **Chautauqua of the Arts** held in Columbus in mid- to late September. Artists from all over come to participate in this juried art show, and thousands of art lovers come to buy the traditional, contemporary, and folk pieces created for the event.

In late April the **Wildflower Foray** at the T.C. Steele State Historic Site includes nature hikes, tours of some beautiful spring gardens, and plenty of entertainment.

In Bean Blossom the **Bill Monroe Memorial Bean Blossom Bluegrass Festival** gets everyone in a toe-tapping mood each June, with the longest running bluegrass festival in the nation.

In July the **Scottish Festival** celebrates the heritage of many residents with traditional offerings such as sheepdog-herding trials, pipe-band demonstrations, and Highland athletic events.

Each September artists at the **Great Outdoor Art Contest** at the T.C. Steele State Historic Site must be both creative and fast. They set up at seven in the morning and have until two in the afternoon to finish their work before the judging begins.

In October, folks in Vallonia gather for **Fort Vallonia Days**—a celebration of a harder, but simpler way of life. Meanwhile, folks in Columbus celebrate the diversity of our global community with their **Ethnic Expo**, with food, music, dance, and crafts representing a wide array of cultures.

To ring in the Christmas season, **Christmas in Brown County**, in Nashville, includes an art and crafts fair, several holiday performances, and strolling carolers in Victorian costumes. In Columbus they light the way for Santa with more than 1.5 million lights and an electric nighttime Christmas parade as part of their **Columbus Festival of Lights**.

SHOPPING

Antiquers can find plenty of places to spend their time and money in the Columbus area, starting with the **Columbus Antique Mall**, 1235 Jackson St., 812/375-2904. With more than 120 dealers, it's no wonder they have just about anything you could want. Outside the city, Seymour has nearly a dozen antiques shops (call the Jackson County Visitors Center for details, 888/524-1914). **North Vernon** and **Nashville** are also worth visits.

Outlet shoppers have two good options: The **Tanger Outlet Center**, I-65 and Hwy. 50A in Seymour, 800/4-TANGER, Web site: www.tangeroutlet.com, offers Jones New York, Van Heusen, Mikasa, Liz Claiborne, and much more; and **Horizon Outlet Center**, I-65 at U.S. 31, Edinburgh, 800/866-

NASHVILLE

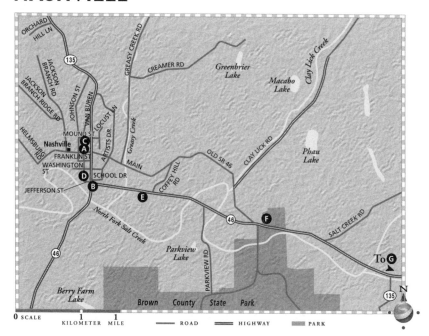

SIGHTS

Ⓐ Brown County Art Guild

FOOD

Ⓑ The Harvest Room
Ⓒ The Ordinary

LODGING

Ⓑ Brown County Inn
Ⓓ Hotel Nashville Resort
Ⓔ The Seasons Lodge & Conference Center

CAMPING

Ⓕ The Last Resort RV Park & Campgrounds
Ⓖ Westward Ho Campground

Note: Items with the same letter are located in the same area.

5900, Web site: www.horizongroup.com, has OshKosh B'Gosh, Spiegel, Dansk, Black & Decker, and Ann Taylor, among others.

For good wines try **Browne County Winery**, Old School Way, Nashville, 812/988-6144; and **Chateau Thomas Winery**, 225 S. Van Buren St., Suite 3, Nashville, 800/761-9463.

FITNESS AND RECREATION

One of the top public golf courses in Indiana—and the nation—is right in Columbus. **Otter Creek Golf Course**, 11522 E. 50 North, 800/579-5484, Web site: www.ocgc.com, offers 27 championship holes. The course includes bent-grass fairways and special deals if you play in the spring or fall.

Atterbury Fish and Wildlife Area in Edinburgh, 812/526-2051, was Camp Atterbury back in World War II. For the last 30 years it's been managed by the Department of Fish and Wildlife, and it's a great place to spot animals or to catch fish. The **Muscatuck National Wildlife Refuge**, 12985 E. U.S. 50, Seymour, 812/522-4352, is designed to help waterfowl find a safe place to eat, sleep, and nest, but it's also home to lots of other animals. If you visit in spring or fall you'll see a crowd of ducks and geese on their way to somewhere else.

For swimming, boating, fishing, and hiking, **Starve Hollow State Recreation Area**, just outside of Vallonia, 812/358-3464, is a great choice. A naturalist, who runs several programs at the Driftwood Interpretive Center, is on duty in the summer. Selmier State Forest, 905 East County Road 350 North, North Vernon, 812/346-2286, and Yellowwood State Forest, 772 South Yellowwood Road, Nashville, 812/988-7945, both are good spots for fishing and hiking. Just off Highway 46 near Nashville, you'll find **Brown County State Park**, 812/988-6406. It's adjacent to the Hoosier National Forest, and has just about every amenity you could imagine in a park—bridle trails, campgrounds, cultural arts programming, fishing, a picnic area and playground, a swimming pool, and tennis courts.

Back in Columbus, even the parks are well-designed. **Mill Race Park** has been selected by recreation professionals as one of the best around. It has great walking and jogging trails, a lake, fantastic playground equipment, and even its own covered bridge and clock tower.

FOOD

Just like the buildings, the restaurants in Columbus have character. Take **Becker's Drive In**, 25th and Union, 812/372-2466. It's only open in the summer, but what true drive-in isn't? And food always tastes better when it's served on a tray that hangs from your car window. **Zaharakos Confectionery**, 329 Washington St., 812/379-9329, will take you back even further in history than Becker's. It's been around since 1900, and they're still serving ice cream the old-fashioned way—hand dipped with fresh toppings. They serve great sandwiches hot off the grill, and they're only open for lunch. **Shorty's**, Sixth and Wilson, is the favorite of local

COLUMBUS AREA

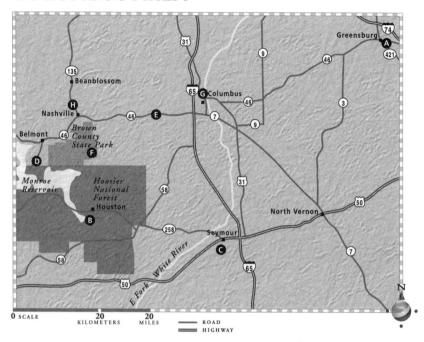

Beanblossom · Greensburg · Nashville · Belmont · Brown County State Park · Monroe Reservoir · Hoosier National Forest · Houston · Columbus · North Vernon · Seymour · E Fork White River

0 SCALE 20 KILOMETERS 20 MILES ROAD HIGHWAY

N

SIGHTS

Ⓐ Courthouse Tower Tree
Ⓑ J'ole Dayle Cooking School of Olson Academy
Ⓒ Southern Indiana Center for the Arts

SIGHTS (continued)

Ⓓ T.C. Steel State Historic Site

LODGING

Ⓔ Country Chalet Columbus

CAMPING

Ⓕ Brown County State Park
Ⓖ Woods-N-Waters
Ⓗ Bill & James Monroe Festival Park & Campground

folks. It's not anything fancy, but the food is good and there's plenty of it—for breakfast or lunch. Another good—and more upscale—lunch spot is **The Columbus Bar** (the "C.B."), 322 Fourth St., 812/372-5252. Try the tenderloin or the fish.

For dinner, **Peter's Bay**, 310 Commons Mall, 812/372-2270, has several steak, chicken, and pasta options on the menu, but the big hits here are the fresh seafood dishes. You can choose from salmon, tuna, swordfish, and more, and they have excellent crab legs and lobster, too. It's a little pricier than many other places, but it's a great way to cap off a visit to this beautiful city.

In Nashville, **The Harvest Room**, in the Brown County Inn, State Rd. 46 and 135 S., 800/772-5249, has a full menu with scrumptious food (pasta, chicken, ribs, steaks, salad bar) at great prices. They also stage live music several nights a week. What really makes this place special, however, is the friendly service. The employees here treat you like a long-lost family member who hasn't eaten in days!

The Ordinary, Van Buren St., 812/988-6166, is named for the term used to identify places where travelers would get together to eat and drink. The name, however, does not do justice to the menu. While you can order things like burgers and steaks, the real treat here is the wild-game feast—turkey and pheasant topped with gravy. The pot roast and roast pork are good, too, and prices are quite reasonable.

LODGING

Lodging options in Columbus include some great hotels, bed and breakfasts, lodges, cabins, inns, and even a resort. The **Columbus Inn**, Fifth and Franklin, 812/378-4298, was once the city hall, and supposedly even hosted a poultry show once in the early 1900s. More than a decade ago it was restored to its original look, and converted to an elegant bed-and-breakfast. It's truly a jewel of the city. The **Ruddick-Nugent House**, 1210 16th St., 812/379-1354, Web site: www.rnugentbnb.hsonline.com, is a bit smaller than the Columbus Inn, but is an elegant place to stay and has fantastic grounds that fill an entire block. The owners will pamper you with a candlelit breakfast and share stories with you about the history of the house and the family who built it.

The **Adam Keller House**, 703 Lafayette Ave., 812/375-2719, is a relatively new bed-and-breakfast. Both of its guest rooms have private baths and antique furnishings. For an exotic—and very private—experience, rent out the **Country Chalet Columbus**, 624 N. Hickory Hills Court, 812/342-7806. You'll become the temporary master of this 1,300-square-foot chalet—and this isn't just any chalet. It has its own two-story waterfall, bridge, and pond—and they're all in the living room! Other features include stained-glass windows and a bathroom with a view of the beautifully maintained grounds. This place is much more than a night's lodging; it's an experience in how the other half lives.

If you prefer something a little more rustic, you'll probably like McGinley's Vacation Cabins, 812/988-7337. Scattered throughout rural Nashville, the cabins each have a name—and personality—of their own. There's even a log cabin that's more than a century old. **Brown County Inn**, State Rd. 46 and 135 S., Nashville, 812/988-2291, is affordable and within walking distance of several local attractions, but its rural flavor makes it a true getaway. **The Seasons Lodge and Conference Center**, State Rd. 46 E., Nashville, 800/365-7327, is also in a beautiful setting, and includes rooms with real fireplaces.

The **Hotel Nashville Resort**, 245 N. Jefferson St., 800/848-6274, is great for vacationers who like to have plenty of space. Their suites include a bedroom, two baths, a living/dining room, and a kitchen (plus whirlpools in some rooms). There's an indoor pool, spa, and sauna, too. It's not cheap, but it is a bargain.

CAMPING

A couple of the great places to play are perfect for camping as well. **Brown County State Park** offers modern sites for $11, more primitive sites with access to showers and restrooms for $7, and primitive sites with no amenities for $5. **Columbus Woods-N-Waters** campground, 8855 S. 300 W., Columbus, 812/342-1619, has sites for both tents and RVs. **The Last Resort RV Park & Campgrounds**, 2248 E. State Rd. 46, Nashville, 812/988-4675 (tent sites $16, RV sites $20), and **Westward Ho Campground**, 4557 E. State Rd. 46, Nashville, 812/988-0008 (tent sites $11, RV sites $17) have pools, too.

Bluegrass fans—and others—like the **Bill & James Monroe Festival Park & Campground**, 5163 State Rd. 135 N., near Nashville, 812/988-0333. A primitive campsite here costs $10, while an RV site goes for $15. Prices are higher during special events.

NIGHTLIFE

If you're in downtown Columbus, stop in at the **Fourth Street Bar**, 433 Fourth St., 812/376-7063, for a cocktail or one of their famous tenderloins. Nightlife in the region often means heading to Brown County for some of the great entertainment in and around Nashville.

The **Little Nashville Opry**, State Rd. 46 W., 812/988-2235, features a few names you might recognize, as well as many local talents, some of whom could be good enough to make it in the other Nashville.

Other country offerings include the **Lloyd Wood Show**, Country Time Theater, at the Ski World complex a few miles outside of Nashville, 812/988-6630, and the **Red Barn Jamboree**, 71 S. Parkview Rd., Nashville, 812/988-

8789. The **Pine Box Musical Theater**, 168 S. Jefferson St., Nashville, 800/685-9624, offers several different musicals each season. If you're wondering about the name, the Pine Box used to be a funeral home.

The **Brown County Playhouse**, 70 South Van Buren St., Nashville, 812/988-2123, has been presenting summer theater for more years than most people can remember, but no one has forgotten what great shows they produce.

If you're trying to find something your kids will enjoy, the **Melchoir Marionette Theatre**, at South Van Buren and Franklin Sts., Nashville, 800/849-4853, presents what we call a puppet show, but a much more upscale and intricately-prepared one than you've probably ever seen.

13
FORT WAYNE

Fort Wayne sits on ground that's always been important, so it's no wonder that Indiana's second-largest city grew here. This is known as the "three rivers" area because the St. Mary's, St. Joseph, and Maumee Rivers come together smack in the middle of the city. In 1794 General Anthony Wayne secured the area for American settlement after years of fighting with Miami Indians who had aligned themselves with the British in the Revolutionary War. The fort built here was named for him.

Today Fort Wayne has a decidedly metropolitan feel. If you're driving in the congested downtown area bring a strong sense of direction—Fort Wayne can be difficult to navigate. But the size and population have their advantages, as Fort Wayne supports several cultural attractions that won't be found in smaller cities. Make sure to see the zoo (perhaps the world's finest children's zoo—really!) and the hottest new Lincoln museum in the country. The city also supports terrific professional sports teams in the International Hockey League (the Komets were champions in the '92–'93 season), the Continental Basketball Association (Fort Wayne Fury, the 1996 American Conference Champions), and Class A baseball (the Minnesota Twins' farm team, the Wizards).

Fort Wayne now bills itself as the "City of Attractions," and as you'll see in the list below, there are several fantastic sights here, especially for families. With so much to see, great accommodations, and more than 400 restaurants, Fort Wayne can be a great vacation destination.

FORT WAYNE

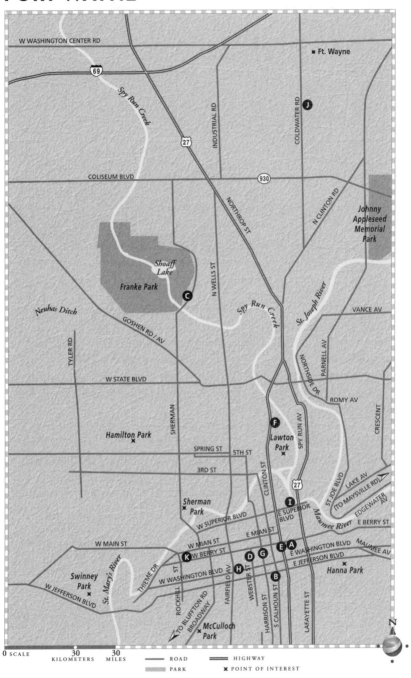

A PERFECT DAY IN FORT WAYNE

For a great start, spend the morning at the Fort Wayne Children's Zoo. You may need a nap afterward, but plan on hitting either Science Central or the Lincoln Museum later in the afternoon. After a nice dinner at any of the high-quality Don Hall's restaurants (each with a different theme), head out to see one of Fort Wayne's professional sports teams in action.

SIGHTSEEING HIGHLIGHTS

★★★★ AUBURN CORD DUESENBURG MUSEUM
1600 S. Wayne St., Auburn, 219/925-1444

Several years ago I went with my grandfather to look at the 115 classic cars and watched his eyes sparkle for nearly two hours as he told the stories these machines ignited in his memory: the first time he saw an automobile, dating my grandmother, and family vacations when my mom was small—it was all in this museum. Listed on the National Register of Historic Places, the old Auburn Automobile Company headquarters has been refurbished into two floors of beautiful art deco showrooms. You'll see the Auburns, Cords, and Duesenburgs made here in Indiana, but also a variety of Detroit hardware, and even some "foreigners" like the Rolls Royce. Now, I can't rent out my grandfather, but there are enthusiastic caretakers at the museum who'll share their own stories about these beauties.

Details: *Daily 9–5; $7 adults, $4.50 students; wheelchair accessible. (1 hour)*

★★★★ FORT WAYNE CHILDREN'S ZOO
3411 Sherman Blvd., Fort Wayne, 219/427-6800

SIGHTS
Ⓐ Allen County—Fort Wayne Historical Museum
Ⓑ Foellinger-Freimann Botanical Conservatory
Ⓒ Fort Wayne Children's Zoo

SIGHTS (continued)
Ⓓ Genealogy Research Department of the Allen County Public Library
Ⓔ Lincoln Museum
Ⓕ Science Central

FOOD
Ⓖ Cindy's Diner
Ⓗ Old #3 Firehouse Museum and Cafe
Ⓘ Old Gas House
Ⓙ The Factory

LODGING
Ⓚ Carole Lombard House

One of the outstanding zoos in the United States, the Children's Zoo alone is reason enough for some folks to travel to Fort Wayne. Choose from the African Veldt (a huge area of free roaming zebras, ostriches, and giraffes, and an African Village), the Australian Adventure (with its river ride and "Australia After Dark" display of nocturnal animals), or the Indonesian Rain Forest (a real rain forest with caged animals, trails near waterfalls, and "Orangutan Valley"). Each special area has bathrooms and a place to get a cold drink.

Details: Apr–mid-Oct daily 9–5; $4.50 adults, $3 seniors and children ages 2–14, under age 2 free; wheelchair accessible. (3 hours)

★★★★ **LINCOLN MUSEUM**
200 E. Berry, Fort Wayne, 219/455-3864
This is the largest museum in the country dedicated to Abraham Lincoln. Its collection is absolutely impressive, from the famous hat he wore (that also carried his letters) to a newly purchased Emancipation Proclamation (one of the few original documents actually signed by Lincoln). The museum's 11 galleries hold many other items that belonged to and were used by Lincoln. In addition, four theaters explain different aspects of Lincoln's career and legacy. Computer programs allow visitors to fight Civil War battles or redecorate the White House (Mary Todd would have loved it!). Spend several minutes at the Lincoln image wall. Photos of Lincoln during the White House years are arranged chronologically, and show the toll that the war and the presidency took on this man.

Details: Tue–Sat 10–5, Sun 1–5; $3 adults, $2 seniors and children ages 5–12, under age 5 free; wheelchair accessible. (1½ hours)

★★★★ **SCIENCE CENTRAL**
1950 N. Clinton St., Fort Wayne, 219/424-2400
If you're traveling with kids, bring them to Science Central. This new museum is totally hands-on, and so fun that even the parents won't want to leave. Bend a rainbow, create an earthquake, ride the world's only indoor high-rail bike 20 feet above the floor, or pick up a starfish from the tidal pool. There's so much to do, and it's all educational.

Details: Tue–Sat 9–5, Sun noon–5; $5 adults, $4.50 seniors, $4 children ages 4–12; wheelchair accessible. (1½ hours)

★★★ ALLEN COUNTY—FORT WAYNE HISTORICAL MUSEUM
302 E. Berry St., Fort Wayne, 219/426-2882

If you believe in the "scared-straight" philosophy of keeping kids in line, visit the jail in the basement of this old city hall. Never again will you worry about Johnny wanting to spend a night in a place like this! Built in 1893, the building and its contents are fascinating. The area's history is traced through artifacts that once belonged to Miami Indian Chief Little Turtle, and through examples of the railroad cars, gasoline pumps, phonographs, and televisions that were designed and built here.

Details: Tue–Fri 9–5, Sat–Sun noon–5; $2 adults, $1 students, ages 5 and under free, $5 families; wheelchair access to the exhibits, but there's no elevator to the displays in the basement. (1 hour)

★★★ FOELLINGER-FREIMANN BOTANICAL CONSERVATORY
1100 S. Calhoun, Fort Wayne, 219/427-6440

This is one of the largest botanical conservatories in the Midwest, and plant lovers will find a terrific variety in natural settings. The conservatory consists of three separate "houses" —the showcase, tropical, and desert. Each is beautifully landscaped with paths and benches, and there's a large waterfall in the tropical house.

You can park free for an hour in the Civic Center parking lot when you visit here, just bring your parking ticket to be stamped.

Kids will like the display of carnivorous plants.

Details: Mon–Sat 10–5, Sun noon–4; $2.75 adults, $2 students grades 6–12, $1.50 preschoolers–5th graders; wheelchair accessible, but there are stairs in some houses that restrict certain areas. (1 hour)

★★ DAN QUAYLE CENTER AND MUSEUM
815 Warren St., Huntington, 219/356-6356

Given our former vice president's record of publicly embarrassing himself, you probably would like to know (as we did) if this place is really cheesy. It's not. As the only museum dedicated to vice presidents of the United States, there's a lot to learn here. Much of the focus is on Quayle as a boy and a candidate, with a nice collection of the gifts he received on trips to other countries. But there are also displays for all of the other U.S. vice presidents, with information on how they were chosen and what became of them.

Details: Tue–Sat 10–4, Sun 1–4; free, although donations are accepted; wheelchair accessible. (1 hour)

★★ GENEALOGY RESEARCH DEPARTMENT OF THE ALLEN COUNTY PUBLIC LIBRARY
900 Webster St., Fort Wayne, 219/424-7241, ext. 3315

Surprisingly, this is one of the major tourist attractions in Fort Wayne. The interest in the study of one's ancestry has been growing rapidly for the past 20 years or so, and this is the largest public database in the United States, adding about 1,000 new resources each month. You might spend a few hours here, but some people spend years looking through census reports, ship manifests, and nearly 40,000 already completed family histories. All kinds of records from the Revolutionary War and Civil War may give you a fascinating story to take home about your own family.

Ask to watch the orientation video first; it will get you started and answer a lot of questions.

Details: Mon–Thu 9–9, Fri–Sat 9–6, Sun 1–6, closed Sun, Memorial Day–Labor Day; free; wheelchair accessible. (2 hours)

EVENTS

Fort Wayne has come together at the **Three Rivers Festival** every July for more than 30 years, and this celebration of community has grown into one of the largest festivals in the state. There is no way to summarize all that goes on here, but every culture of the city is represented, every form of art and music can be enjoyed, and an awesome selection of food can be sampled. There are parades, carnivals, fireworks, sports, races, war reenactments, games, and contests. It's busy and crowded and Fort Wayne's notorious street system is a hassle, but a visit during the Three Rivers Festival is electrifying.

For a tamer experience, try the **Johnny Appleseed Festival** in late September. Yes, there really was a Johnny Appleseed, a man named John Chapman who roamed the United States in the early 1800s planting apple trees. He is buried in Fort Wayne, and the community celebrates the memory of this gentle man. Lots of crafts, food, demonstrations, and reenactments of pioneer life are found in Johnny Appleseed Park.

SHOPPING

Fort Wayne is home to Indiana's largest mall, **Glenbrook Square**, Coldwater Rd. and Coliseum Blvd., 219/483-2119. The mall has four anchor stores and more than 175 specialty shops, virtually guaranteeing that the store or merchandise you want is here. If that's not enough, there are more stores in **Glenbrook Commons** next door. Almost daily entertainment and events within the mall make this seem like a virtual city you may never have to leave.

Karen's Antique Mall, 1510 Fairfield Ave., 219/422-4030, is an expansive antiquing area featuring more than 60 dealers, and is also the home of the Farnsworth TV Museum. It's in the heart of the antiquing section of town, roughly in the area between Fairfield Avenue and Broadway Avenue, and between Williams Street and Washington Boulevard. One neat shop there is **The Woodshack**, 444 W. Baker St., 219/424-2093, which specializes in architectural items saved from old homes. Anyone restoring an older home will appreciate the ornate woodwork and trim that's so hard to find.

About a half hour northwest of Fort Wayne is the little town of Grabill, which is home to a considerable Amish population. It's also home to the **Country Shops of Grabill**, 13756 State St., 219/627-6315. There are two floors and 30,000 square feet filled mostly with antiques, but high-quality furniture reproduction by local craftspeople can also be found. Between the authentic 1800s log cabin that's been brought in, and the fascinating Amish people living nearby, this is a favorite shopping destination in the area.

FITNESS AND RECREATION

While the 12 miles of the **Rivergreenway Recreational Trail** will eventually be expanded to cross the entire county, the section that's already complete is beautiful. Hikers, bikers and runners on the trail enjoy scenic overlooks and a historic fort, and pass through several of the city's beautiful parks.

On the south side, the recreational trail starts in Tillman Park, at Tillman Road and Calhoun Street, and runs to Johnny Appleseed Park, at Coliseum Boulevard and the St. Joseph River. Pick up a map at your hotel, the city's Parks and Recreation Department, or the convention and visitors bureau. You should be able to hop on the trail at a convenient location and plan a hike or ride to the length that suits you.

Fort Wayne is home to several professional sports teams which are enthusiastically supported by the locals. **Fort Wayne's Fury**, the CBA team, and the **Komets** of the IHL, both play in the beautiful **Memorial Coliseum** at Coliseum Drive and the St. Joseph River. The Coliseum is the venue for most of the major concerts that come to town as well, so it's worth finding out

FORT WAYNE AREA

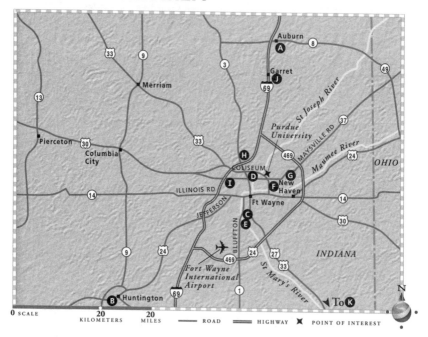

SIGHTS

- **A** Auburn Cord Duesenburg Museum
- **B** Dan Quayle Center and Museum

FOOD

- **C** Casa d'angelo Restaurants

FOOD (continued)

- **D** Elegant Farmer
- **E** Original Drive-In

LODGING

- **A** Auburn Inn
- **F** Coliseum Inn
- **G** Herb Lady's Garden

LODGING (continued)

- **H** The Guesthouse
- **I** Valu-Lodge

CAMPING

- **J** Hickory Grove Lakes Campground
- **K** Indian Springs Campground

Note: Items with the same letter are located in the same area.

---

what's going on there during your stay. Call the ticket office at 219/483-1111. In the warmer months, watch professional baseball at **Memorial Stadium** right next to the Coliseum. The **Wizards** are the Class A affiliate of the Minnesota Twins in the Midwest League. A sunny afternoon spent with Wizards fans can be just as much fun as catching a big-league game!

Ready for something wild and different? Try an afternoon at **Ultrazone**, 1104 W. Coliseum Blvd., 219/482-6719, which bills itself as "the ultimate laser adventure." The indoor arena is all set for you and your friends to "hunt" each other in a war game. Fortunately, when the war's over, you'll still be able to go out and get a beer with your foes.

FOOD

Get ready to let that belt out! Fort Wayne's second nickname is "the city of restaurants" because it has more than 400 from which to choose.

Our first advice on restaurants in Fort Wayne is to look for one of the many Don Hall's restaurants. Don Hall is a local guy who started in the restaurant business with the **Original Drive-In**, 1502 Bluffton Rd., 219/747-7509, but quickly expanded with **The Factory**, 5811 Coldwater Rd., 219/484-8693, and the **Old Gas House**, 305 E. Superior St., 219/426-3411. Now with 15 restaurants, each with it's own unique theme and specialties, the Don Hall spots guarantee quality. Some are casual, some are elegant. All are terrific places to eat. The two **Casa d'angelo Restaurants**, 3402 Fairfield Ave., 219/745-7200, and 4111 Parnell Ave., 219/483-0202, are the local favorites for Italian cuisine.

For home cooking in an upscale atmosphere, the **Elegant Farmer**, 1820 N. Coliseum Blvd., 219/482-1976, is a family-owned treat. For a unique lunch experience downtown, stop by **Old #3 Firehouse Museum and Cafe**, 226 W. Washington Blvd., 219/426-0051. You can look through the firefighting artifacts like horse-drawn pumpers and the earliest motorized fire engines in the museum downstairs, then go upstairs for great soups and sandwiches.

For breakfast anytime, we like **Cindy's Diner**, 830 S. Harrison St., 219/422-1957. This 50s-style diner serves burgers and malts, but we go for the inexpensive breakfasts. One look at this place with its old donut machine and you'll expect Fonzie and Richie to walk in behind you.

LODGING

Once again, it's Don Hall who gets our first endorsement. The man famous for his simply-named restaurants also opened **The Guesthouse** on Fort Wayne's north side, 1313 W. Washington Center Rd. (just east of the I-69/Lima Rd. interchange), 219/489-2524. For luxurious lodging—with amenities like indoor and outdoor pools, sauna, whirlpool, and a free continental breakfast—it's very well priced. The Guesthouse is also the location of one of Don Hall's most elegant restaurants, Mallory's. The **Coliseum Inn**, 1020 N. Coliseum Blvd.,

219/424-0975, is a great place to stay if you plan to attend one of the night games at Memorial Coliseum or Memorial Stadium. Those venues are two miles down the road, and the Lakeside Golf Course is right next door.

If you head to Auburn for the fantastic car museum, consider spending the night in the **Auburn Inn**, 225 Touring Dr., 800/255-2541. This reasonably priced quality hotel has a homey feel, especially when they bring out the cookies and milk at night!

Carole Lombard, one of the greatest actresses of the 1920s and 30s, and wife of Clark Gable, was born in a house on Rockhill Street in Fort Wayne in 1908. She died tragically in a plane crash in 1942, but the house remains and has been restored into a fine bed-and-breakfast. The **Carole Lombard House**, 704 Rockhill St., 219/426-9896, has rooms featuring private baths and VCRs that you can use to watch one of Lombard's comedies.

The **Herb Lady's Garden**, 8214 Maysville Rd., 219/493-8814, is a unique bed-and-breakfast experience. Not only is the restored post–Civil War farm house a museum of antiques and heirlooms, the grounds are fantastic and hostess Louise Rennecker will be happy to spend some time walking you through her extensive gardens.

A good bargain is the **Valu-Lodge**, 3527 W. Colisum Blvd., Fort Wayne, 219/482-4511, with a big outdoor pool and a great buffet that's available at breakfast and dinner.

CAMPING

For campers, there are a couple of options. About 15 minutes north of town is **Indian Springs Campground**, 0981 County Rd. 64, Garrett, 219/357-5194. It's a good place to swim, boat, and fish. In Portland, try **Hickory Grove Lakes Campground**, 7427 S. 300 East, 219/335-2629. It's about a 45-minute drive south of Fort Wayne, and offers a huge array of activities, including horseshoes, basketball, bocce, and even a black-powder range.

NIGHTLIFE

You can take your pick between five city nightclubs, each with great light and sound systems, dance floors, and, occasionally, live bands. **Pierre's**, 5629 St. Joe Rd., in the Marketplace of Canterbury, 219/486-1979, is the only place in town you can go-go dance in a cage, ride a mechanical bull, and sing karaoke all in one night. Feeling a little too old for Pierre's? The **Embassy Theater**, 121 W. Jefferson Blvd., 219/424-6287, will offer you a good time without the gyrations.

Indiana's largest historic theater is the place to catch Broadway shows, performances by Fort Wayne's philharmonic, and an occasional movie. The Fort Wayne Parks and Recreation Department's **Foellinger Outdoor Theater**, 705 E. State Blvd. in Franke Park (near the Children's Zoo), 219/427-6000, is a terrific resource for the people of Fort Wayne, and if you're here in the summer it's a great place to catch a show. Band and choir performances, as well as classic movies on Wednesday nights, are all free.

14
SOUTH BEND AREA

"Traditional" is probably the best word to sum up the South Bend area. Tradition oozes from the campus of the University of Notre Dame, a place so tied to its past that women weren't admitted until 1972. The history of industry can be found here in Copshaholm, the mansion built by the inventor of the revolutionary chilled plow; and in the Studebaker Museum, showcasing the rich history of auto-making in northern Indiana.

Even the city's newest attraction, the College Football Hall of Fame, is all about tradition, done up in a spiffy, computerized, oversized way. It seems fitting that this hall of fame is so close to "the house that Rockne built" and to his grave. The river tradition is alive here, too. South Bend evolved along the St. Joseph River, and the city has always counted on the river to provide recreation as well as transportation. Today there are even more ways to enjoy the water at the East Race Waterway, the nation's first man-made whitewater for rafting or kayaking. Finally, tradition is a way of life for the Amish people in nearby communities like Nappanee, Goshen, and Shipshewana. Visitors marvel at their way of life, and marvel again at the expert craftsmanship of their products.

This is surely one of the most diverse areas in the state of Indiana. Travelers to South Bend will find the ornate beauty of the Catholic Church's greatest educational establishment contrasted against the simple way of life of the Amish. That makes it a great vacation destination. Just make sure to bring along a healthy respect for tradition and you'll enjoy this area.

A PERFECT DAY IN THE SOUTH BEND AREA

First time visitors to South Bend would be remiss if they didn't see the landmarks at Notre Dame, so let's start our perfect day there with a walking tour. Enjoy a leisurely lunch at Honkers, then check the weather. If it's nice, try kayaking or rafting the man-made whitewater at the East Race Waterway. If it's cold or rainy, head off to the College Football Hall of Fame for more fun that you should be allowed to have indoors. Have dinner at Tippecanoe Place (wear your best!), then relax at one of the bed-and-breakfasts just down the road.

SIGHTSEEING HIGHLIGHTS

★★★★ AMISH ACRES
1600 W. Market St., Nappanee, 800/800-4942
This northern Indiana historic homestead supported three generations of an Amish family. You can stay in one of two inns that have the feel of the farm (but with amenities like built-in pools), take a buggy ride, and catch a musical in the round Barn Theater.

Details: Open daily Mar 1–Dec 30, tours run continually 10–5; general admission is free, $6.95 tours, $23.95 Passport package (includes a tour, a documentary film, a buggy ride, and an all-you-can-eat Amish dinner). Call for wheelchair-accessibility information. (4 hours)

★★★★ COLLEGE FOOTBALL HALL OF FAME
111 S. St. Joseph St., South Bend, 800/440-3263
Set in the center of downtown South Bend, this brand-new facility looks like a football stadium. The west side is a large courtyard that's been turned into a football field, complete with Astroturf and a goal post. But the game really comes to life inside. There are films to watch; opportunities to punt, pass, and kick footballs for accuracy; tackling dummies to hit; and tests of strength and balance to see if you could compete. A typical locker room from the 1930s has been recreated next to a modern locker room. The biggest emphasis, though, is on the people who played, coached, and loved the game. Think you know something about college football? Prepare to be humbled.

Details: Jan–May daily 10–5, Jun–Dec daily 10–7; $9 adults, $6 seniors, $4 children ages 6–14; wheelchair accessible. (2 hours)

★★★★ MENNO-HOF
Intersection of U.S. 20 and State Rd. 5 (Box 701),
Shipshewana, 219/768-4117

If you enter campus on Notre Dame Avenue you'll want to turn right to a parking lot which is virtually the only place for visitors to park. There's a brand new visitors center here that has maps of campus and lots of information. You can check out a CD player and take an audio tour of the campus if you prefer to go it alone.

This Amish site is great if you are looking for a completely noncommercialized experience. Menno-Hof is a nonprofit visitors center operated by the Amish and Mennonite communities. You'll learn the history of the faiths, including why they had to flee Europe's persecution. Observing an Amish community will dispel a lot of misunderstanding about what they do and why they do it, and may challenge your thoughts on your own way of life.

Details: *Mon–Sat 10–5 (with seasonal adjustments); free, although donations are accepted; most areas wheelchair accessible. (2 hours)*

★★★★ UNIVERSITY OF NOTRE DAME CAMPUS
For walking tours with real people who know the stories behind the sights, call 219/631-5726

There may be no more famous university skyline than Notre Dame's. With the Basilica of the Sacred Heart's dramatic steeples, and the famous golden dome nearby, no one who walks the campus will ever forget its majesty. And most visitors do walk. It's the easiest way to see the campus landmarks, and if you prefer a guide they're available.

The "must-see" sights on campus include: the **Basilica of the Sacred Heart of Jesus**, which is perhaps more breathtaking inside than out, thanks in part to the recent renovation that restored all the murals. The **Golden Dome** that tops the main administration building is one of the best-known landmarks on any college campus in the world. It will reopen in 1999 after extensive interior renovation. The **Grotto of Our Lady of Lourdes**, sitting between the two lakes on campus (Saint Mary's and Saint Joseph's), is a reproduction of the larger grotto in France. Many visitors light a candle here and say a prayer, and some stay for the Rosary that's said every evening at 6:45.

Also in this area is the **Old College** and its **Log Chapel**, which

SOUTH BEND

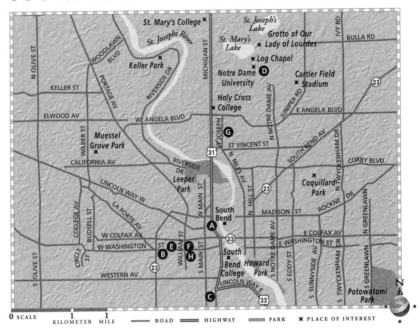

0 SCALE 1 KILOMETER 1 MILE ■■■ ROAD ■■■ HIGHWAY ■■■ PARK ✗ PLACE OF INTEREST

SIGHTS

Ⓐ College Football Hall of Fame
Ⓑ Copshaholm (The Oliver Mansion)
Ⓐ South Bend Regional Museum of Art

SIGHTS (continued)

Ⓒ Studebaker National Museum
Ⓓ University of Notre Dame Campus

FOOD

Ⓔ Tippecanoe Place

LODGING

Ⓕ Book Inn
Ⓖ Marriott
Ⓓ Morris Inn of Notre Dame
Ⓗ Queen Anne Inn

Note: Items with the same letter are located in the same area.

---

offers an interesting look at the roots of the institution. **Touchdown Jesus** is the common name for the mural painted on the side of the Hesburgh Library depicting Jesus Christ surrounded by saints and scholars. Looking north from your seat in the football stadium, you'll swear Jesus is signaling a score for the Irish.

Details: *(2 hours)*

★★★ COPSHAHOLM (THE OLIVER MANSION)
808 W. Washington St., South Bend, 219/235-9664

This is perhaps the most mispronounced name in South Bend. Please don't call it "Cop Shalom," which would be roughly translated to "peace to your police officers" in Hebrew. It's more like "Cop-shaw-home." Formerly the home of the J.D. Oliver family (he invented the chilled plow that changed the way Midwesterners farm), this museum is a rarity because the family left all the contents when they donated it. This is the starting point for learning the history of the area, with both a historic worker's home and a history center on the grounds (the entire complex is called the Northern Indiana Center for History). For children there's also a hands-on history museum that's a lot of fun.

Details: Tue–Sat 10–5, Sun noon–5; fees for Copshaholm alone: $6 adults, $5 seniors, $3 students, preschoolers free; fees for the entire complex: $8 adults, $6.50 seniors, $4 students, preschoolers free; limited wheelchair accessibility. (2 hours)

★★★ HANNAH LINDAHL CHILDREN'S MUSEUM
1402 S. Main St., Mishawaka, 219/254-4540

This is a great place for kids to learn and have fun. There are several "rooms" here with different themes, like the 1800s village with its stores, two-room house, post office, and schoolhouse; or the Japanese house and gardens with a host who explains the culture and performs a tea ceremony. The artifacts and tools are meant to be touched.

Details: Sep–May Tue–Fri 9–4, first and second Sat of each month 10–2, Jun Tue–Thu 10–2; $1 ages 6 and up, 50¢ preschoolers, under age 2 free; wheelchair accessible. (1 hour)

★★★ SOUTH BEND REGIONAL MUSEUM OF ART
120 S. St. Joseph St., 219/235-9102

This museum in the heart of downtown is just across the street from the College Football Hall of Fame (they're connected by a tunnel) and in the same building as the Century (convention) Center. There are four galleries, including an impressive permanent collection, and the work of local and regional artists in temporary exhibits. The artwork spills out of the museum and into the river, too. Through a wall of glass in the commons area between the museum and the convention center you'll see a huge sculpture in the middle of the St. Joseph created especially for South Bend by Mark di Sirvero.

Details: *Tue–Fri 11–5, Sat–Sun noon–5; donations accepted; wheelchair accessible. (1 hour)*

Music events in the evenings can be an especially rewarding time to visit. Also, look for one-of-a-kind gifts like sculptures, pottery, and jewelry in the Museum Shop.

★★★ STUDEBAKER NATIONAL MUSEUM
525 S. Main St., South Bend, 219/235-9714

This museum presents the evolution of American transportation. The display begins with a Conestoga wagon, built in 1835 by the Studebaker brothers' father. Continue past the carriages that carried four U.S. presidents (including Lincoln), then ogle the earliest automobiles. Most cars in this collection are Studebakers, but there are other models as well. There's a separate room dedicated to the company's Avanti line, and several oddities like Studebaker army vehicles, a postal "Zip Van," and the one and only "Predictor," built for the 1956 World's Fair to predict where technology would take the auto industry.

Details: *Mon–Sat 9–5, Sun noon–5; $5 adults, $4 seniors and students ages 12 and over, $2.50 children ages 11 and under; wheelchair accessible. (1 hour)*

★★ RV/MH HALL OF FAME, MUSEUM AND LIBRARY
801 Benham Ave., Elkhart, 219/293-2344

This place is a hoot! Whoever thought to create a museum for recreational vehicles and manufactured homes? It's a quirky and interesting slice of Americana. You will see the tow-along quarters that carried generations to their vacation destinations and wonder how some of these cramped "tin cans" were ever considered an improvement over tent camping! The attached library is worth a look, too, as it houses collections of old publications and photographs.

Details: *Mon–Fri 9–4, weekends by appointment only; free, although donations are accepted; wheelchair accessible. (1 hour)*

SHOPPING

The neighboring towns of South Bend and Mishawaka each have a large mall: **University Park Mall** is in Mishawaka, and **Scottsdale Mall** is at Ireland and

SOUTH BEND AREA

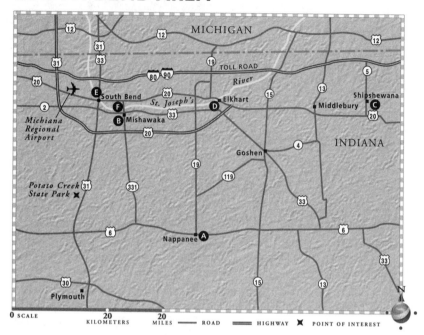

SIGHTS
- Ⓐ Amish Acres
- Ⓑ Hannah Lindahl Children's Museum
- Ⓒ Menno-Hof
- Ⓓ RV/MH Hall of Fame, Museum and Library
- Ⓔ Studebaker National Museum

FOOD
- Ⓔ Carriage House
- Ⓔ Honkers
- Ⓕ Siam Thai Restaurant
- Ⓐ Thresher's Dinner

LODGING
- Ⓑ Beiger Mansion Inn
- Ⓐ Inn at Amish Acres
- Ⓐ Nappanee Inn
- Ⓑ Varsity Clubs of America

Note: Items with the same letter are located in the same area.

Miami Roads in South Bend. University Park gets the nod for true mall-ratting, with anchors like JC Pennies, Hudson's, and Sears, and nearly 100 other specialty shops. University Park also sits in what's referred to as the Grape Road Retail Center, so no matter what you need, it's probably in the area of Grape Road and State Road 23.

For chocoholics the only shopping that matters can be done right at the factory. Tour the **South Bend Chocolate Company**, 3300 W. Sample St., then pick up some of their gooey good stuff here or at their locations in the malls.

The **Antique Avenue Mall**, 52345 U.S. 31/33 North, South Bend, is a collection of some 60 dealers who sell everything from furniture to tiny collectibles. If you really want to get down and dirty, though, head to Shipshewana for the huge **Shipshewana Auction**. This is a combination auction (including livestock) and flea market. You won't believe the assortment of antiques, crafts, tools, produce, and endless other items. Just don't buy a hog unless your bed-and-breakfast hosts are very understanding.

FITNESS AND RECREATION

The coolest thing in town for having fun and exercising has to be the **East Race Waterway**, Niles Ave. and Madison St. This is a training ground for Olympic kayakers and rafters. It was the first man-made whitewater course in the country, and to this day remains one of only a handful. It's run by the Parks and Recreation Department, 219/235-9401. They have rafts and "funyaks" you can use, but if you want to kayak or canoe the rapids, you'll need to bring your own watercraft. They have several strict rules for clothing, height, and experience, so be sure to call before you go.

If you don't need that much excitement, try renting a canoe for a trip on the **St. Joseph River**. Six-mile and twelve-mile routes are available. You'll be shuttled (on weekdays) to a starting point, then left to canoe back to your car. You should call the St. Joseph County Parks, 219/277-4828, for reservations so they can make the shuttle arrangements. Keep in mind that the river runs north here, so the trip starts and ends near the Michigan border.

This is great bicycling country. Moving along via your own power will earn you points with the Amish, the terrain is gently rolling and beautiful, and people who drive cars in the area are already used to sharing the road with slow-moving buggies so you tend to have fewer of those stomach-wrenching encounters with wayward cars. Pick up maps for bike tours at the Elkhart County or South Bend/Mishawaka Convention and Visitors Bureaus, or at one of the local bike shops. There are a half-dozen suggested routes in the 20-mile range.

South Bend is just a half-hour drive from Plymouth, Indiana, home of the **United States Golf Academy**, 800/582-7539. Consider enrolling for three days of school there to earn your "degree," and improve your game.

For a nice day outdoors, consider a ride to **Potato Creek State Park** (drive south on U.S. 31, then continue a few miles west on State Rd. 4), 219/656-8186, where there's a beach area, 11-miles of hiking trails, and plenty of fish to catch. There's a nice campground here as well, and 17 cabins available for rent.

FOOD

The one restaurant where everyone should try to dine in South Bend is **Tippecanoe Place**, 620 W. Washington St., 219/234-9077. Built in 1886 for Clem Studebaker, this 40-room, 20-fireplace mansion has now been reincarnated as the ritziest, most memorable dining experience in town.

The **Carriage House**, 24460 Adams Rd., South Bend, 219/272-9220, is another historic building now home to elegant dinners. The Carriage House is especially known for its excellent wine list. **Siam Thai Restaurant**, 211 N. Main St., South Bend, 219/232-4445, will give your taste buds a ride. If you like Thai food, go here. If you've never tried it, this is a great place to do so. For families, **Honkers** is the most often recommended restaurant, with two locations: 3939 S. Michigan St., South Bend, 219/291-2115, and 211 E. Day Rd., Mishawaka, 219/259-3000.

Visitors to Amish country will have no problem finding delicious food meant to stick to your ribs through a day of chores. We like the **Thresher's Dinner** at Amish Acres, 1600 W. Market St., Nappanee, 800/800-4942, but the truth is many of the smaller restaurants in the heavily Amish/Mennonite towns serve up food that's just as good.

LODGING

The finest hotels are here in South Bend and Mishawaka, offering thousands of comfortable rooms in convenient locations. In fact, the **Marriott** in downtown South Bend, 123 N. St. Joseph St., 219/234-2000, is connected by a walkway to the Century Center and the art museum it houses. With the underground tunnel from the Century Center to the College Football Hall of Fame, you may never have to go outside to see a day's worth of sights!

On the other hand, there's no reason you'd have to stay in a chain hotel, no matter where you want to be. Downtown includes some excellent bed-and-breakfasts. The **Queen Anne Inn**, 420 W. Washington St., South Bend, 219/234-5959, is an 1893 masterpiece that feels instantly comfortable with its period furnishings, original chandeliers, and open sitting areas. Just a few doors down is the **Book Inn**, 508 W. Washington St., 219/288-1990. The rooms here are luxurious, the house a treasure, and it all sits atop a quality used bookstore that should keep you busy for hours looking for "finds." Across the city line, the **Beiger Mansion Inn**, 317 Lincolnway E., Mishawaka, 219/255-6300, is another National Register place with its own craft gallery, plus fine lunches and dinners to go with its breakfasts.

If you've come to town primarily to visit Notre Dame, consider staying at the new **Varsity Clubs of America** hotel, 3800 N. Main St., Mishawaka, 219/277-0500. This is a short drive from campus, and has a good collection of Notre Dame memorabilia on display. The **Morris Inn of Notre Dame**, 219/631-2000, is right on campus.

Finally, the accommodations in the previously mentioned Amish and Mennonite communities are nice. The **Nappanee Inn**, a mile and a half west of the town of Nappanee on U.S. 6, 800/800-4942, is a historic farm with its own theater, restaurant, and lodging. The rooms aren't elegant, but they're comfortable, and they are fitted with the nicest quilts you'll find in a hotel. The **Inn at Amish Acres**, one mile west of Nappanee, 800/800-4942, is nicer than the Nappanee Inn but has the same feeling of simplicity.

NIGHTLIFE

For Broadway shows and symphony concerts call the **Morris Civic Auditorium**, 211 N. Michigan St., South Bend, 219/235-9198, to see what's playing.

Local and regional bands play at **Connor's Lounge** in the Ramada Inn, 52890 U.S. 31/33 N., 219/272-5220; and at **Heartland Night Club**, 222 S. Michigan St., South Bend, 219/234-5200. Heartland tends to get a little more countrified, but they do book some rock bands.

You're in Irish country, so why not try an Irish pub? **Corbly's**, 441 E. LaSalle Ave., South Bend, 219/233- 5326, is a local favorite. Parts of the movie *Rudy* were filmed here.

15
KOKOMO-PERU

Have you ever wondered why there are so many songs about Kokomo? "Kokomo, Indiana" was recorded by a slew of people, including Mel Torme. Both Perry Como and Louis Armstrong recorded "Kokomo (I Love You So)." The Beach Boys' "Kokomo" may be an anthem to Caribbean beaches, (Kokomo, Indiana, is nowhere near any ocean), but the Hoosiers love the song. "Good Morning, Mr. Kokomo," "South of Kokomo," "First Snow in Kokomo"—the list goes on.

It's not a big city, and given its proximity to Indianapolis (45 minutes to the south), Kokomo might have been totally overshadowed. Anderson and Muncie are similar-sized cities nearby, and they don't enjoy the popularity that Kokomo has. So what gives?

The answer may be in the country's love of the automobile, and Kokomo's claim as the home of the first commercially successful car. Natural gas was so common in Kokomo in the late 1800s that it was burned off with a huge fire—visible in Chicago, some said. The city, offering free gas to industries that would locate there, attracted one Elwood Haynes. Haynes worked with metals for most of his life (he invented stainless steel because his wife was tired of polishing the silver) and had an idea for a "horseless carriage." His automobile used gasoline, a byproduct of natural gas processing, and the auto industry was born.

The auto industry is still in Kokomo. Among the largest employers are Chrysler and General Motors' Delco parts facilities. It's easy to see why James

Dean, born just down the road in Fairmount, would have developed a healthy lust for the automobile.

So, Kokomo has its mystique. It was a part of popular culture well before all those songs were written and has much to teach us about the industrial age that grew this nation. You'll find great food, lodging, and shopping, but when you leave Kokomo you'll remember its heritage most.

A PERFECT DAY IN KOKOMO-PERU

Begin your perfect day in Kokomo with a visit to the friendly and knowledge-able visitors center staff, then walk into the adjacent City of Firsts Automotive Heritage Museum to get a dose of local history. Lunch at Pastariffic before heading north to Peru for an afternoon at the International Circus Hall of Fame and Museum. Take a drive in the country to dine at the Country Cook Inn, then head back to Peru for a comfortable—and affordable—night in the Cole House bed-and-breakfast.

SIGHTSEEING HIGHLIGHTS

★★★★ CITY OF FIRSTS AUTOMOTIVE HERITAGE MUSEUM
1500 N. Reed Rd. (U.S. 31), Kokomo, 765/454-9999

There are several auto museums in Indiana, but this is one of the newest, and one of the best. You'll find between 80 and 100 cars here, many of them the very early Haynes and Apperson models that were produced in Kokomo. (Apperson Jack-rabbits were nice looking cars, comical only for the little bunny that was used as a hood ornament.)

A 50s-style diner, 1930s filling station, Elwood Haynes' first home in town, and the Apperson Brother workshop are all being recreated and fit beautifully among the old cars. Best of all, the people who run the place, from the custodian to the curator, are absolutely in love with automobiles and will take the time to pass some of their passion on to you.

The museum is in the same building as the visitors bureau, so it makes a great first stop. The visitors bureau has the latest news on what's happening around town.

Details: *Daily 10–5; $5 per person; wheelchair accessible. (1 hour)*

★★★★ INTERNATIONAL CIRCUS HALL OF FAME AND MUSEUM
3 miles east of Peru off Rte. 124, 765/472-7553

If you don't know the history of Peru's involvement with the circus, it'll come as no small shock that this place is tucked away in the cen-

If you're in the area in the off season, (Oct–Jun), call first and someone will be glad to show you around the grounds and museum.

ter of Indiana. For years, beginning in 1891, these grounds were the winter quarters of the famous Hagenbeck-Wallace Circus. Lions, elephants, and camels occupied its barns, and clowns and lion tamers became Peru residents during the winter months. In 1929, the operation was sold to John Ringling (of the Ringling Brothers), who used the barns until the early 40s. In 1988, the farm was listed on the National Register of Historic Places, and the current circus and museum have moved in since. You can see the circus here (including Emit Kelly's son Pat clowning much like his father did) between May and October. Also, a small museum traces 200 years of circus history with some really interesting memorabilia.

Details: *The turnoff is just east of the bridge over the Mississinewa River, and signs leading the way are easy to spot. Mon–Sat 10–4:30, (activities begin at 10:30), Sun 1–4:30, from late Jun–Labor Day; circus show times are Mon–Sat noon and 3 p.m., Sun 3 p.m.; $6 adults, $5 seniors, $4 children; wheelchair accessible. (3 hours)*

★★★ HOWARD COUNTY HISTORICAL MUSEUM/ SEIBERLING MANSION
1200 W. Sycamore St., Kokomo, 765/452-4314

This house is absolutely magnificent, befitting of its builder, Monroe Seiberling. Seiberling was one of the first industrialists to take advantage of Kokomo's offer of free natural gas and free land to approved factories in 1887, and is the man given most of the credit for Kokomo's transition from an agricultural community to an industrial center. Today the house is a restored museum that speaks to the wealth Seiberling amassed in strawboard and plate-glass manufacturing. Much of the house reflects the life of the Seiberling family, but some rooms provide an education in the county's history.

Details: *Tue–Sun 1–4; $2 adults, children free. (1 1/2 hours)*

KOKOMO

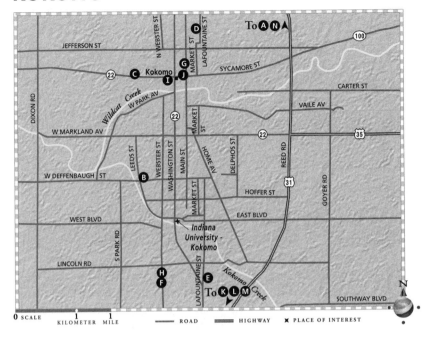

SIGHTS

Ⓐ City of Firsts Automotive Heritage Museum
Ⓑ Highland Park
Ⓒ Howard County Historical Museum/Seiberling Mansion
Ⓓ Kokomo Opalescent Glass Factory

FOOD

Ⓔ Breakfast House
Ⓕ China Clipper
Ⓖ Jamie's Soda Fountain
Ⓗ Pastariffic
Ⓘ Rozzi's Market
Ⓙ Sycamore Grill

LODGING

Ⓚ Courtyard by Marriott
Ⓛ Hampton Inn
Ⓜ Holiday Inn Express
Ⓝ Koko Motel

★★★ **JAMES DEAN GALLERY/FAIRMOUNT HISTORICAL MUSEUM**
425 N. Main St., Fairmount, 765/948-3326
Fairmount Historical Museum: 203 E. Washington St., Fairmount, 765/948-4555
Located just 30 miles west of Kokomo on Route 26, the town of

Fairmount is a required stop for James Dean fans. The James Dean Gallery is a private collection of memorabilia that includes clothing he wore in films, high school yearbooks, screen test films, and hundreds of rare photographs. The more impressive items are in the Fairmount Historical Museum, including his beloved Triumph Trophy motorcycle, his leather jacket, and trophies. The Historical Museum also has a nice collection of Jim Davis memorabilia. The creator of the Garfield comic strip is also a Fairmount native.

Details: *Daily 10–6, $3.75 ages 11 and over. Apr–Oct Mon–Sat 10–5, Sun noon–5, Nov 30–Mar by appt. only; $1 donation requested. (1 ½ hours for both)*

★★★ **KOKOMO OPALESCENT GLASS FACTORY**
1310 S. Market St., Kokomo, 765/457-1829

Kokomo's "Gas Boom" brought a lot of new businesses to town, and this was one of them. In fact, it's the last one operating from that era. Established in 1888, it's still using natural gas to fire huge ovens up to the required 2,600 degrees. The hand-rolled glass (not blown) that's produced is shipped all over the world. Tours require shoes, not sandals, since quite a bit of broken glass covers the factory floor. Also, be prepared for the heat. Most folks tour the plant in spring or fall, but even when it's cool outside you may want to bring a bottle of cold water. It's easy to understand why the oven tenders work in 15-minute shifts. If you can't handle the tour, consider stopping by the gift shop (called the Op Shop) to see the beautiful Kokomo glasswork.

Details: *Call Op Shop to set up tours; wheelchair accessible. (1 hour)*

★★ **GREENTOWN GLASS MUSEUM**
112 N. Meridian, Greentown, 765/628-6206

Ask a glass collector and you'll find out that Greentown glass, produced in Kokomo between 1894 and 1903, is among the hardest to find and most valuable. Though the factory was very small and only in operation for a few years, its "chocolate" and Holly Amber glass products were very popular. The unique glass coloration was the work of glass chemist Jacob Rosenthal, who kept his recipes a closely guarded secret. In fact, no one has been able to come up with an exact replica, so the beautiful pieces you see are highly prized.

Details: *May 15–Oct 31 weekdays 10–noon and 1–4, weekends*

1–4, closed Mon; Mar 1–Dec 31 weekends only 1–4; free; wheelchair accessible. (1 hour)

★★ GRISSOM AIR MUSEUM
6500 Hoosier Blvd., Kokomo, 765/688-2654

Anyone interested in aviation history and military aircraft will get a big kick out of this new museum at Grissom Air Force Base, just north of Kokomo. Kids especially like sitting in the Phantom jet cockpit, and the displays of uniforms, weapons, and survival gear will cause even civilians to linger.

A large collection of aircraft is parked outside, including a recently dedicated F-11F Tiger, a B-17 Flying Fortress, and a B-58 Hustler. One room is dedicated to the exciting accomplishments of aviation pioneer William Kepner, leader of the *National Geographic*–sponsored *Explorer* balloon mission that hoped to reach the stratosphere. They were *really* high when they discovered the rip in the balloon!

Details: *Located on Route 31 between Kokomo and Peru. Tue–Sat 10–4; free; wheelchair accessible. (1 hour)*

★ HIGHLAND PARK
900 W. Defenbaugh St., Kokomo

As city parks go, this one is a gem. The **Elwood Haynes Museum** is here (a great place to learn more about Haynes—1915 S. Webster, 765/456-7500, open Tue–Sun afternoons, free), as is a genuine **covered bridge** from Vermont that was moved to the park in 1958 to save it from destruction. But the two biggest attractions are the **sycamore stump** and **Old Ben**. The stump is huge, with a diameter of 18 feet. It was nearly 600 years old when it stopped growing.

Old Ben is a bull. Actually, he was a bull before he became a steer. Born in 1902 at a whopping 125 pounds, they say Ben had to get on his knees to suckle. He quickly grew to six feet, four inches in height and over 16 feet long—the largest steer on record. At the age of eight he was severely injured when he slipped on ice and had to be shot. The people in town loved him so much they boycotted a shop that tried to sell Ben burgers. His stuffed hide has been displayed for nearly 80 years now. Today, encased in glass, Ben stands next to the stump.

Details: *Free; wheelchair accessible. (1 hour)*

SHOPPING

Kokomo has two small malls. **Kokomo Mall**, 765-457-3211, corner of U.S. 31 and Boulevard St., has 32 stores anchored by JC Penny and Elder-Beerman. Home schoolers, teachers, and just about any parent will want to look around in **Teacher's Delight**, which stocks all kinds of educational items. Even the toys teach.

Markland Mall, 765/457-4457, intersection of U.S. 31 and Markland Ave., is anchored by Sears and Lazarus and includes a **Blondie's Cookies** outlet. If you like cookies, you'll love Blondie's.

The Kokomo Opalescent Glass Factory's gift shop, the **Op Shop**, 1310 S. Market St., 765/457-8136, is a great place to buy gifts and knickknacks that will have special meaning when you get home. The glass factory ships its huge sheets of colored glass around the world, then arranges for the best of their clients to supply manufactured goods to the Op Shop. You'll come away with something unique and reminiscent of Kokomo and the "gas-boom days."

The **Antique District** in Kokomo can be found around the intersection of Markland Avenue and Main Street. Several shops in the 800 and 900 blocks of South Main will keep antique lovers busy for hours. The **Treasure Mart Antique Mall**, 3780 South Reed (US 31), buys whole estates.

Finally, a favorite stop has always been the **L Shop**, 108 N. Main St., Kokomo, 765/452-4006. Its convenient downtown location and its variety of quaint gifts, teas, and china make it very popular for locals and tourists alike.

FITNESS AND RECREATION

Sea Shore Swimming Pool, 802 W. Park Ave., 765/456-7540, is a great place to take the kids on a steamy summer afternoon ($1.50 per person), especially if riding in the car has turned into drudgery. Sea Shore is the Kokomo Park District's pool and water slide. The "inner hub" of the pool is the deep part, and if you can swim to the center of it you can use the diving platform and diving boards. On weekdays the pool is open for adult swimming from 11 in the morning to one in the afternoon; it then opens up for the kids until 6:45 in the evening. The same afternoon hours apply on weekends.

The **Pepper Shak**, 1459 S. 17th St., Kokomo, 765/457-3634, is a volleyball facility that hosts tournaments and league play for the locals. There is dedicated open plays every Friday evening starting at 5:30 ($3 per person). Private court rentals at other times are $15 per hour.

Mississinewa Lake, including both the **Frances Slocum** and the **Miami State Recreation Areas**, is a great place to camp, fish, hike, boat, and get a

KOKOMO-PERU

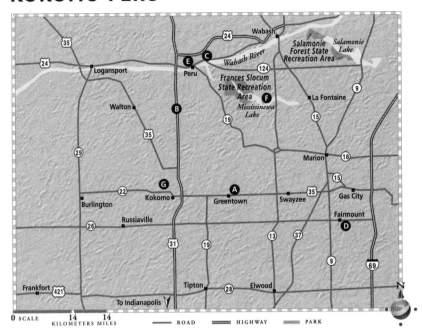

SIGHTS

A Greentown Glass Museum
B Grissom Air Museum
C International Circus Hall of Fame and Museum
D James Dean Gallery/Fairmount Historical Museum

FOOD

A Country Cook Inn
E Treasured Friend Tea Room

LODGING

E Cole House
E Rosewood Mansion Inn Bed and Breakfast

CAMPING

F Frances Slocum
G Jellystone Park Campground
F Miami State Recreational Areas

Note: Items with the same letter are located in the same area.

little history lesson on the area. You'll want to check out the story of Frances Slocum, who as a five-year-old anglo child was taken from her home in Pennsylvania and raised by Indians. She eventually became the wife of a chief. Today there's a state forest named for her (between Peru and the Lake), and the Frances Slocum Cemetery and Memorial sit just off Mississinewa Road. To find these recreation areas and the lake, take Route 124 east out of Peru. In about seven miles you'll see signs that will direct you. The Miami State Recreation Area has the most amenities (including a beach and a Frisbee golf course)—if you're in a camper, go there.

Good golfing can be found at several Kokomo public courses. The **Chippendale Golf Course**, 100 W. 450 South (off State Rd. 26), 765/453-7079, is generally considered to be the best course in the area.

FOOD

Take a drive into the country for dinner, with the **Country Cook Inn**, 10531 E. County Rd. 180 South, near Greentown, 765/628-7676, as your destination. The owners built their restaurant with the north side covered by a grassy hill, using passive solar heating to create high-energy efficiency. The grounds are beautiful and wooded, and inside you'll find meals as simple and wholesome as the setting. There won't be many choices—there are usually two meat selections and a fish alternative—but everything is excellent, and the salad bar is fresh and delicious. Don't miss desserts like peanut-butter pie, or one of the many fresh cobblers and fruit pies. Reservations are required for dinner.

Pastarrific, 3001 S. Webster, Kokomo, 765/455-1312, is a celebration of homemade Italian food. The large menu includes low-fat choices—there should be something here for everyone. The food is well worth the moderate price, and the relaxed setting makes this a very good lunch or dinner selection.

The **Sycamore Grill**, 113 W. Sycamore St., Kokomo, 765/457-2220, was built in an old theater and contains several historic business signs, theater masks, and other interesting items. The entrées are delicious, but the Sycamore Grill is best known for its appetizers. If you're with a group try brewery cheese fondue or steamed east coast mussels, or treat yourself to grilled portabella mushrooms. The beer list, with about 120 varieties, puts most bars to shame.

The **Treasured Friend Tea Room**, 155 W. Main St., Peru, 765/472-3888, is a good place for a sandwich, and their chicken pot pies are great in the winter. The deli at **Rozzi's Market**, 404 W. Sycamore St., Kokomo, 765/459-9218, serves up big, fat sandwiches. The **China Clipper**, 3015 S. Webster, Kokomo, 765/455-3368, is a good, clean, and cheap place to chow Chinese food (try their buffet).

The **Breakfast House**, 3111 S. Lafountain, Kokomo, 765/453-7877, is the town's 24-7 breakfast joint. **Jamie's Soda Fountain**, 307 N. Main St., Kokomo, 765/459-5888, still serves phosphates! (If you're the person in the group explaining what a phosphate is, find someone older to hang out with.)

LODGING

Most of the hotels in the area belong to the big chains. Kokomo has a strip of chain hotels on the south side along U.S. 31, all of which offer nice accommodations. Three are new: the **Holiday Inn Express**, 511 Albany Dr., 765/453-2222, the **Hampton Inn**, 2920 S. Reed Rd., 765/455-2900, and the **Courtyard by Marriott**, 411 Kentucky Dr., 765/453-0800. Our pick is the Courtyard. It's very nice, relatively inexpensive, and the folks who run it are first class.

The **Koko Motel**, 4112 N. Reed Rd. (U.S. 31), Kokomo, 765/452-6715, gets points for the name, but little else. If you're looking for a cheap place to stay, it's the place to go.

Kokomo proper is not big on bed-and-breakfasts, but Peru has a couple of very interesting places. The **Cole House**, 27 E. Third St., Peru, 765/473-7636, was built by Cole Porter's wealthy grandfather, J.O. Cole. The house is now full of period furnishings, parquet wood floors, and chandeliers. Only four rooms are rented, but each has a private bath, and each is priced in the $55 to $65 range. It's a bargain. Also in Peru is the **Rosewood Mansion Inn Bed and Breakfast**, 54 N. Hood St., 765/472-7151. Built in 1872 near the downtown area, it's a little pricier than the other bed-and-breakfasts but it's also more elegant. And it's still a good deal for $70 to $90 per room.

CAMPING

Camping opportunities are limited in the Kokomo area. Your best bet is to secure a spot in the **Frances Slocum** or **Miami State Recreational Areas** on Mississinewa Lake. RVs must use the Miami State Recreation Area, as Frances Slocum offers only primitive campsites. Campers with children may also want to use Miami since it includes amenities like a bathhouse and showers, a beach, and a concession stand.

In Peru, the **Jellystone Park Campground**, County Rd. 200 N., just west of U.S. 31, 765/473-4342, is open year-round. It has a heated pool and tons of fun activities for kids. With a well-stocked camp store, this is a great place for parents who are camping with their children for the first time.

APPENDIX

Consider this appendix your travel tool box. Use it along with the material in the Planning Your Trip chapter to craft the trip you want. Here are the tools you'll find inside:

1. **Planning Map.** Make copies of this map and plot out various trip possibilities. Once you've decided on your route, you can write it on the original map and refer to it as you're traveling.

2. **Mileage Chart.** This chart shows the driving distances (in miles) between various destinations throughout the region. Use it in conjunction with the Planning Map.

3. **Special Interest Tours.** If you'd like to plan a trip around a certain theme—such as nature, sports, or art—one of these tours may work for you.

4. **Calendar of Events.** Here you'll find a month-by-month listing of major area events.

5. **Resources.** This guide lists various regional chambers of commerce and visitors bureaus, state offices, bed-and-breakfast registries, and other useful sources of information.

PLANNING MAP: Illinois/Indiana

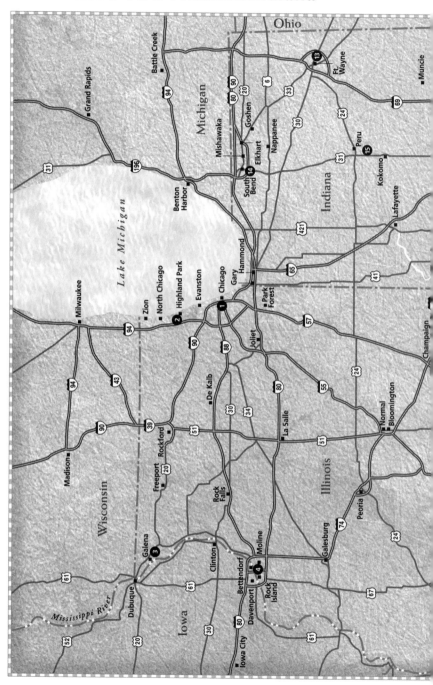

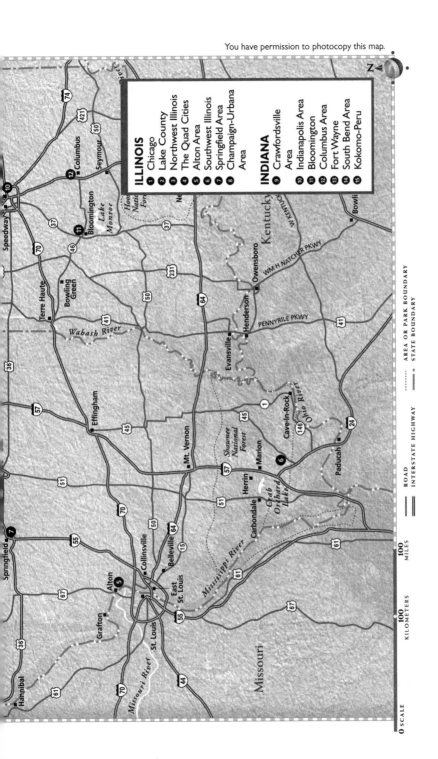

N

ILLINOIS

1. Chicago
2. Lake County
3. Northwest Illinois
4. The Quad Cities
5. Alton Area
6. Southwest Illinois
7. Springfield Area
8. Champaign–Urbana Area

INDIANA

9. Crawfordsville Area
10. Indianapolis Area
11. Bloomington
12. Columbus Area
13. Fort Wayne
14. South Bend Area
15. Kokomo–Peru

ROAD

INTERSTATE HIGHWAY

AREA OR PARK BOUNDARY

STATE BOUNDARY

100 MILES

100 KILOMETERS

0 SCALE

ILLINOIS/INDIANA MILEAGE CHART

	Alton, IL	Bloomington, IN	Champaign/Urbana, IL	Chicago, IL	Columbus, IN	Crawfordsville, IN	Fort Wayne, IN	Galena, IL	Indianapolis, IN	Kokomo, IN	Springfield, IL
Bloomington, IN	229										
Champaign/Urbana, IL	182	169									
Chicago, IL	283	235	135								
Columbus, IN	286	36	167	230							
Crawfordsville, IN	258	96	75	154	94						
Fort Wayne, IN	373	180	244	200	169	171					
Galena, IN	334	401	267	167	396	340	366				
Indianapolis, IN	245	53	124	184	45	51	128	350			
Kokomo, IN	299	112	146	165	101	73	85	331	60		
Springfield, IL	87	254	84	196	252	161	329	247	207	232	
South Bend, IN	351	198	198	92	187	180	113	259	146	90	264

SPECIAL INTEREST TOURS

With the *Illinois/Indiana Travel•Smart* guidebook you can plan a trip of any length—a one-day excursion, a getaway weekend, or a three-week vacation— around any special interest. To get you started, the following pages contain six tours geared toward a variety of interests. For more information, refer to the chapters listed—chapter names are bolded and chapter numbers appear inside black bullets. You can follow a tour in its entirety, or shorten, lengthen, or combine parts of each, depending on your starting and ending points.

Discuss alternative routes and schedules with your travel companions—it's a great way to have fun, even before you leave home. And remember: Don't hesitate to change your itinerary once you're on the road. Careful study and planning ahead of time will help you make informed decisions as you go, but spontaneity is the extra ingredient that will make your trip memorable.

BEST OF REGION

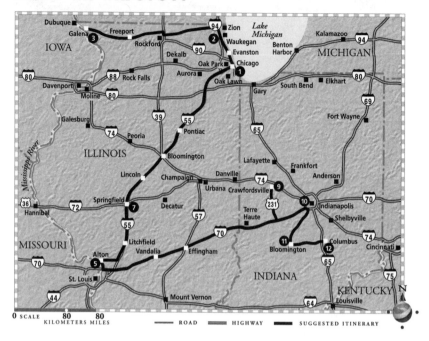

The most beautiful, intriguing, and creatively diverse places in this region are listed below. Because of their varied geography, history, and population, they offer a rich blend of experiences—sometimes offering exercise for the body, other times for the brain, and occasionally just mindless pleasures.

❸ Northwest Illinois (great shopping)
❷ Lake County (theme parks, concerts)
❶ Chicago (skyscrapers, museums, theater, athletics)
❼ Springfield Area (Lincoln sites)
❺ Alton Area (beautiful geography)
❾ Crawfordsville Area (historic sites)
❿ Indianapolis Area (great auto racing, museums)
⓫ Bloomington (extensive museums, outdoor recreation)
⓬ Columbus Area (unbelievable architecture)

Time needed: 2 weeks

NATURE LOVERS' TOUR

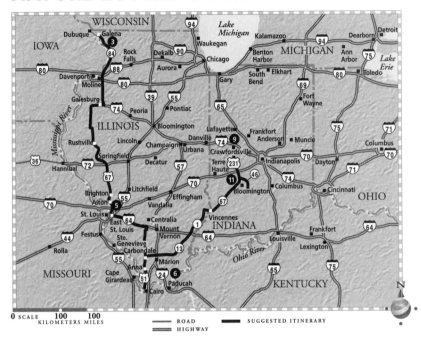

Because this is a rather large region you can enjoy activities as diverse as downhill skiing and spelunking, and just about everything in between. These sites boast magnificent natural playgrounds, including waterfalls, caves, bluffs, forests, cliffs, rivers, and prairies.

⓫ Bloomington (hilly, wooded camping, great watersports, biking)
❾ Crawfordsville Area (canoeing, fall colors, hiking)
❻ Southwest Illinois (outstanding hunting, camping)
❺ Alton Area (river recreation, awesome bluffs)
❸ Northwest Illinois (hiking, biking, skiing)

Time needed: 2 weeks

ARTS AND CULTURE TOUR

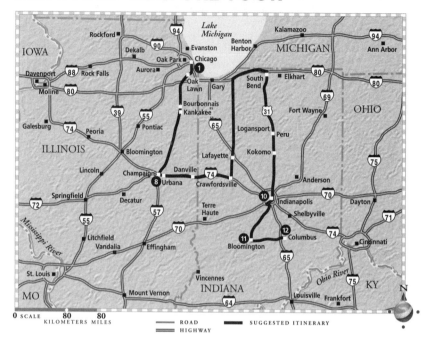

From the world-class symphonies, galleries, and museums of Chicago and Indianapolis to the collegiate sophistication of Champaign-Urbana, South Bend, and Bloomington to the amazing architecture of Columbus, this tour has more class than you can shake a vacation at.

❶ Chicago (Art Institute, Symphony Center, Chicago Theatre, Civic Opera House)

❽ Champaign-Urbana Area (Krannert Art Museum, Krannert Center for the Performing Arts)

❿ Indianapolis Area (Indianapolis Opera, Hilbert Circle Theatre, Indianapolis Museum of Art)

⓫ Bloomington (IU Art Museums, Lilly Library, Tibetan Cultural Center)

⓬ Columbus Area (Little Nashville Opry, architectural tours, Indianapolis Museum of Art Columbus Gallery)

Time needed: I to 2 weeks

FAMILY FUN TOUR

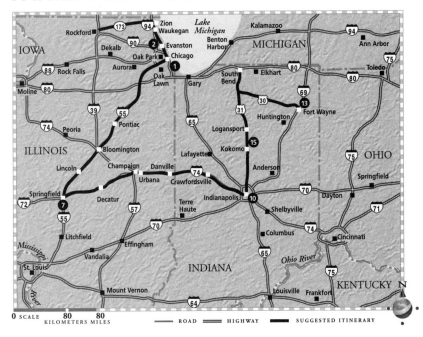

This tour lets you see what it's like to live in an Amish community, watch some of the best professional sports teams in the world, play and learn in the finest museums and historic sites, and ride yourself silly at a state-of-the-art amusement park.

⓭ Fort Wayne (Children's Zoo, Science Central)

⓮ South Bend Area (College Football Hall of Fame, Hannah Lindahl Children's Museum)

⓯ Kokomo-Peru (International Circus Hall of Fame, Highland Park)

⓾ Indianapolis Area (The Children's Museum, Indianapolis Zoo)

❼ Springfield Area (Lincoln sites)

❶ Chicago (John G. Shedd Aquarium/Oceanarium, Adler Planetarium, Museum of Science and Industry)

❷ Lake County (Six Flags, Tempel Farms)

Time needed: 2 weeks

HISTORY TOUR

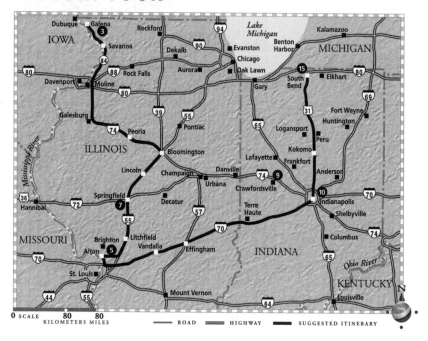

Whether your interest is the Civil War, Native American history, slavery, U.S. presidents, or tracing our collective heritage, this tour will help you find out how we, as a nation, got to be where we are today.

❸ Northwest Illinois (Grant's Home, Native American sites)
❼ Springfield Area (Lincoln sites)
❺ Alton Area (Underground railroad, Elijah P. Lovejoy Monument, Lincoln-Douglas debate, riverboat history)
❾ Crawfordsville Area (Lane Place, Ben Hur Museum)
❿ Indianapolis Area (Eiteljorg Museum of American Indians and Western Art, Benjamin Harrison Home)
⓯ South Bend Area (Notre Dame, automobile sites)

Time needed: 2 to 3 weeks

FALL COLOR TOUR

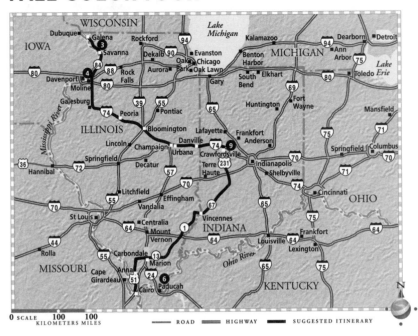

The burst of color that serves as a last hurrah for nature before cold weather sets in makes for a great Illinois/Indiana tour. The brilliant reds, oranges, and yellows of fall are stunning. And—with a little bit of pre-planning—you can also find plenty of great food and fun at the region's many autumnal festivals.

❸ **Northwest Illinois**
❹ **The Quad Cities**
❾ **Crawfordsville Area**
❻ **Southwest Illinois**

Time needed: 1 to 2 weeks

January
Eagle watching, Alton Area

February
Parke County Maple Syrup Festival, Crawfordsville Area

March
Engineering Open House, Agriculture Open House, both in Champaign-Urbana
Saint Patrick's Day Parade, Chicago

April
Cinco de Mayo Festival, Chicago
Mansfield Mushroom Festival, Crawfordsville Area
Wildflower Foray, Columbus Area

May
Buckingham Fountain Lighting Ceremony, Chicago
Galena Triathalon and Duathalon, Galena
Indianapolis 500, Indianapolis
Raggedy Ann and Andy Festival, Champaign-Urbana Area

June
Bill Monroe Memorial Bean Blossom Bluegrass Festival, Columbus Area
Chicago Blues Fest, Chicago Gospel Music Festival, Country Music Festival, and Taste of Chicago, Celebrate on State Street Festival, all in Chicago
Oldsmobile Balloon Classic, Turtle Races, both in Champaign-Urbana Area
Strawberry Festival, Spinners and Weavers Spin In, and Civil War Days, all in Crawfordsville Area
Tour of Historic Homes, Stagecoach Trail Festival, both in Galena

July
4th of July fireworks (7/3), Chicago
Galena Arts Festival, Galena
Hot Dog Festival, Crawfordsville Area
Scottish Festival, Columbus Area
Three Rivers Festival, Fort Wayne

August

Civil War Weekend, Galena

Illinois State Fair, Springfield

Indiana State Fair, AfricaFest, and Brickyard 400, all in Indianapolis

U.S. Hot-Air Balloon National Championship, Urbana Sweetcorn Festival, both in Champaign-Urbana Area

Viva! Chicago Latin Music Festival, Chicago Air and Water Show, both in Chicago

September

Broomcorn Festival, Hoopston Sweetcorn Festival, both in Champaign-Urbana Area

Chautauqua of the Arts, Great Outdoor Art Contest, both in Columbus

Chicago Jazz Festival, German-American Fest, Mexican Independence Day Parade, and Celtic Fest, Chicago

Johnny Appleseed Festival, Fort Wayne

October

Fort Massac Re-enactment Weekends, Southwest Illinois

Fort Vallonia Days, Ethnic Expo, both in Columbus

Halloween events, Chicago

Parke County Covered Bridge Festival, Crawfordsville Area

December

Christmas in Brown County, Columbus Festival of Lights, both in Columbus

Kris Kringle Craft Show, Champaign-Urbana Area

Parke County Covered Bridge Christmas, Crawfordsville Area

Skate on State and Magnificent Mile of Lights Festival, Chicago

RESOURCES

ILLINOIS TOURISM/VISITOR INFORMATION

Illinois Bureau of Tourism, 800/2-CONNECT or 800/406-6418 (TTY),
Web site: www.enjoyillinois.com

Greater Alton/Twin Rivers Convention and Visitors Bureau,
800/258-6645 or 618/465-6676

Carbondale Convention and Tourism Bureau, 800/526-1500 or
618/529-4451

Champaign-Urbana Convention and Visitors Bureau, 800/369-6151
or 217/351-4133

Chicago Convention and Tourism Bureau, 312/567-8500

Chicago Office of Tourism, 312/744-2400

Galena/JoDaviess County Convention and Visitors Bureau, 800/747-
9377 or 815/777-3557, Web site: www.galena.org

Lake County Convention and Visitors Bureau, 800/525-3669 or
847/662-2700

Quad Cities Convention and Visitors Bureau, 800/747-7800 or
309/788-7800

Southernmost Illinois Convention and Visitors Bureau, 800/442-
1488

Springfield Convention and Visitors Bureau, 800/545-7300 or
217/789-2360

INDIANA TOURISM/VISITOR INFORMATION

Indiana Tourism, 800/289-6646, Web site: www.indianatourism.com

Clark/Floyd Counties Convention and Tourism Bureau, 800/552-
3842

Columbus Area Visitors Center, 800/468-6564 or 812/378-2622, Web
site: www.columbus.in.us

Fort Wayne/Allen County Convention and Visitors Bureau, 800/767-
7752 or 219/424-3700, Web site: www.fwcvb.org

Hamilton County Convention and Visitors Bureau, 800/776-8687 or
317/598-4444

Indianapolis City Center, 800/323-4639 or 317/237-5200

Indianapolis Convention and Visitors Bureau, 317/639-4282, Web site:
www.indy.org

Kokomo/Howard County Convention and Visitors Bureau, 800/837-0971 or 765/457-6802

Monroe County Convention and Visitors Bureau, 800/800-0037 or 812/334-8900, Web site: www.visitbloomington.com

Nashville-Brown County Convention and Visitors Bureau, 800/753-3255 or 812/988-7303, Web site: www.browncounty.com

Northern Indiana Amish Country Elkhart County Convention and Visitors Bureau, 800/377-3579

Parke County Convention and Visitors Bureau, 765/569-5226

OTHER USEFUL RESOURCES

AMTRAK, 800/USA-RAIL or 800/523-6590 (TTY)

Bed And Breakfast Clearinghouse, Web site: www.virtualcities.com

Fishing and Hunting Licenses, 217/782-2965

Greyhound, 800/231-2222 or 312/345-3109 (TTY)

Hosteling International, 800/909-4776

Illinois Campground Association, 847/395-6090

Illinois Hotel/Motel Association, 312/236-3473

Illinois Reservation Service/Hotel Accommodations, 800/978-7890 or 800/491-1800

Indiana Driving Tours, Web site: www.indianatourism.com

Indianapolis International Airport, 317/487-7243

O'Hare International Airport, 312/686-2368 or 312/601-8333 (TTY)

Road conditions, Illinois, 312/793-2242

Wheelchair Getaways of Illinois, 800/637-2597 or 847/853-1011

INDEX

MAPS INDEX

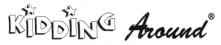

ROBIN & ERIC

ABOUT THE AUTHORS

Robin Neal Kaler and Eric Todd Wilson are former broadcast-journalists who now work together at the University of Illinois' flagship campus in Urbana. Kaler enjoys spending time with her husband, Chris, and their two children, Zoë and Emily. Wilson's free time is devoted to his wife, Gwendoline, and their son, Miles.

This guide is Kaler and Wilson's first, and perhaps only, effort at travel writing, so they made every effort to enjoy the process. They hope that enjoyment is reflected in the stories and information in this book.